ETHAN ALLEN

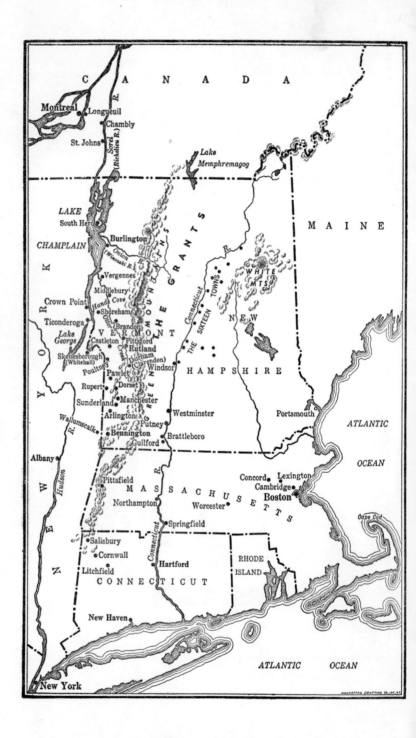

ETHAN ALLEN

BY STEWART H. HOLBROOK

1958

FOUNDED 1891

BINFORDS & MORT, *Publishers,* Portland, Ore.

FOR MY MOTHER

First Illustrated Edition, 1958
L. C. Catalog Card Number: 58-11336

: Printed in the United States of America :

A NOTE ON EDITIONS

The original edition of this book appeared in May 1940 from the old house of Macmillan, New York City. It was greeted in comforting part by what at least the Author was pleased to consider gratifying reviews. In other words, reviews favorable to the book.

It also had the great good fortune to be attacked in a Boston newspaper by Letters-to-the-Editor critics who protested it did violence to a Hero of incomparable luster and impeccable life. The attacks did nothing to impede interest in or sales of the work.

Because of its subject and geography, the book had to face an especially critical audience on the home grounds, and there was no little shooting at the biographer in the commonly genteel pages of the Vermont Historical Quarterly. *From this unseemly brawl I learned that being a native of the Green Mountains did not make me immune, but in fact raised the hackles of academics who may have believed they had a sort of patent on Ethan Allen.*

Both book and Author survived, and for the next seventeen years the work made its modest way through seven modest printings. In addition, it was selected during World War II for the honor of a Special Overseas Edition for the Armed Services of the United States. I still cherish the many letters which came from American soldiers and sailors on all of the numerous fronts.

When in 1957, by virtue of contract, the plates of the original book came into my possession, I was immensely pleased that Mr. Thomas Binford, of the house of Binfords & Mort, should have wanted them in order to bring out the present and first illustrated edition.

STEWART H. HOLBROOK.

Portland, Oregon
May 1, 1958.

Introduction to the General

In Vermont, where I was born and where my people have lived since Colonial times, the name of Ethan Allen is well known, even if few Vermonters know much about the man. In foreign parts (which is to say, anywhere outside the small confines of the Green Mountain State), Allen, if heard of at all, is at best a misty character.

The taking of a fort was responsible for putting Allen into history books and fine marble; and the taking of that fort, regrettably, is about all most Americans know of him. He appears suddenly in school histories as if rising by magic out of the dark backwoods for one magnificent moment. He is seen there at the top of a barrack stairs, waving his great sword and shouting his deathless incredible line. Then, just as suddenly, history swallows him again and he is seen no more.

This is unfortunate, for not in the American scene has there been a livelier, lustier character than the late and profane General Allen. As a tosspot none could match him. His humor was often rude, and boundless always. He was a violent enemy, a staunch friend, and ever a highly original thinker. His command of language, including profanity, was so prodigious that many fine examples have been carefully preserved in old records, which seem still to glow with baleful light, such as brimstone makes.

His judgment—or maybe it was impulse and not judgment at all—was hasty, and usually but not always sound. Not one of the very greatest of Americans, he assuredly was one of the most astounding. Riot and tumult followed naturally in his wake, and New Yorkers compared him to Attila, to the Devil himself, and posted £100 for his capture, alive or the other way.

General George Washington thought him an original, like nothing else that walked. His brilliant work early in the Revolution was really great, and the improbable misfortune that removed him from the active scene was a tragedy for the man and a loss to the Army. No soldier in all the troops suffered more than he, but he was never tamed. Right to the end of his life he was a swashbuckling, hell-roaring, indomitable man—the one and original old ring-tailed peeler.

Before he took Ticonderoga, Ethan Allen lived more lives than most men. Of the fourteen years left to him after that event, he spent two in chains; he wrote a book that scared the daylights out of President Ezra Stiles of Yale College and all other pious men; he chased Yorkers off the New Hampshire Grants, defied Colonial governors and the Continental Congress, kept the British out of his domain, and was the driving force in founding the independent republic of Vermont. I, for one, like to think that something of his spirit and courage still smolders on, not only in Vermont but in all parts of the United States where men stand on their own two hind legs.

I have been shocked in recent years to find that many good Americans had never so much as heard of Ethan Allen; and, worse, that to those who knew of him he was the typical stuffed-shirt hero of schoolbooks, a sort of glittering demigod, immaculate and bloodless—as though some Parson Weems had laid withering hands on his hardy unregenerate soul.

This book is an effort to remedy such a deplorable condition.

STEWART H. HOLBROOK

BOSTON, January 8, 1940

Contents

> *"Sir: I make you a Present of a Major, a Captain and two Lieutenants in the regular Establishment of George the Third."*

CHAPTER I

Classic Moment

———••——

It took an uncommon amount of rum to begin a war in 1775.

On the night of March 13 that year, a mob of doubtful deputies headed by a Tory sheriff imbibed freely at John Norton's Tavern in Westminster, on the New Hampshire Grants, and a few minutes later shed what Vermonters like to say was the first blood of the Revolution.

Then, Paul Revere of Boston, well primed with Medford distillate, rode leisurely through a sunny afternoon to warn the Messrs. Adams and Hancock of British doings. Two days later, filled with the conventional British issue of grog, redcoats marched on Lexington where, there and then in the Buckman Tavern, Minutemen were downing slugs of punch in preparation for the shot that was to be heard round the world.

And now, early in May, a group of backwoodsmen had gathered in the Catamount Tavern in Bennington, on the Grants, and were engaged in the Green Mountain custom of drinking stonewalls, a somewhat incredible concoction composed of rum *diluted* with rock-hard cider.

The Catamount, of course, was already a notorious place. Built near the top of a long sloping hill, its square hulk of two and a half stories rose unpainted above the few shade trees. In the dooryard a pole of pine reared up some twenty feet. And on top of the pole was the tavern's sign—a stuffed catamount, its mouth open in a snarl, facing the New York border with mean grinning teeth.

The big cat did not, like most tavern signs, turn or flap with the breeze. Landlord Stephen Fay had fastened it securely to face nowhere but the west, a symbol of defiance to the hated Yorkers. It was a notable sign, highly regarded by the people of the Grants, although little children feared to pass it at night.

The dim taproom of Landlord Fay's was the official meeting place of a band of hellions known variously as the Bennington Mob and the Green Mountain Boys, which had been formed to defend the disputed claims of settlers who held grants from Governor Benning Wentworth of New Hampshire; but tonight, early in May of '75, there was even graver business afoot: The Colonies were at last at war with England, and talk in the taproom of the Catamount was of Concord and Lexington.

It is well known that alcohol adds to conviviality. What is less often considered is the fact that it also intensifies thought on grim and sober matters. These men in Fay's taproom were talking tonight of what the New Hampshire Grants could do to further the revolt against royal authority, a grim and sober business no matter how you looked at it.

Should the Grants send men to aid the embattled Colonists at Cambridge on Massachusetts Bay? Or should they send their volunteers to Hartford in Connecticut Province, where troops also were gathering?

The talk in the taproom rolled on long after the rest of Bennington had gone to bed. It was very late when one of the men rose to his feet as if to emphasize what he had to say. He was of near gigantic stature, a man to talk to pines, better than a head taller than the sixty-nine-inch fowling piece he had stood in a corner by the fireplace. He was lean and straight. His eyes were bold and roving. Altogether a man of wild appearance.

"By God," he said—and pewter mugs rattled on the tables— "by God, I'd like to take that fort." Then he went upstairs to bed.

The fort Ethan Allen referred to was Ticonderoga, a relic of the French and Indian War that stood on a noble point of the western shore of Lake Champlain. Although troubles with the French in America were over, the British considered Ticonderoga worth holding. It commanded the natural highway between Canada and the Colonies which was formed by Lake Champlain, Lake George, and the Hudson. The fort contained, as Ethan Allen knew, a large amount of ordnance and military supplies. It was held by a British garrison of unknown size.

On the day following the discussion in the Catamount, events shaped themselves rapidly. Riding a winded horse into the tavern yard, Heman Allen arrived from Hartford to inform his tall brother that Colonial authorities in Connecticut desired that the Green Mountain Boys be mobilized for an attack on Fort Ticonderoga. This was the best kind of news to Ethan Allen, who liked to see things going on. Without more talk he sent horsemen galloping out of Bennington to call the Boys from neighboring towns and farms.

Arriving at the Catamount close in the wake of Heman Allen came a delegation from Hartford, lugging with them the "authority" of the Connecticut Committee of Correspondence and, of greater importance, three hundred pounds in cash with which to buy provisions and pay volunteers. Along the way north from Hartford the delegation had recruited some fifty men, many of them old soldiers of the French and Indian troubles. Leading spirits among the newcomers seemed to be Edward Mott, who carried the money, and Colonel James Easton, Captain Noah Phelps, John Brown, and another of Ethan's brothers, Levi Allen.

Taking counsel, and stonewalls, briefly in the Catamount, Ethan as nominal head of almost anything that happened on the Grants, suggested that the entire party go farther north to Castleton, in order to be within striking distance of the objective.

Roads were merely trails through the heavy forest, and muddy trails in May. Brooks grown to rivers had to be forded. And at clearings of farms along the way Ethan Allen paused to sound the call. His call, so men told afterward when they thought it over, was like the deep boom of a war drum, of many drums, that echoed against barn and forest and pounded its way through chinked logs, through cedar roofs, through the toughest homespun, right to a man's heart.

Ethan Allen knew these back-country men from long association, and they rallied. At Arlington plows were left in the furrows, and men got into buckskin to take down their firelocks and join the column. It was the same at Manchester, at Dorset, at Pawlet and Poultney. Grim-faced farm women, tawny as squaws from the smoke in their cabins, hurriedly molded bullets at fireplaces, while boys filled horns with powder. Children cried, dogs barked, horses whinnied, and the mob of marching men grew steadily as it moved northward.

"We're going on a big wolf hunt," shouted Ethan Allen.

Arrived at Castleton, twenty-odd miles from the fort, the free and easy army took first steps toward order and subordination. On May 8th they held a formal council, naming Edward Mott chairman, a sort of secretary of war. Ethan Allen was of course and unanimously elected to head the expedition. Noah Phelps was sent across the lake to try to gain entrance to the fort on some pretext and to take stock of the condition and size of its garrison.

Boats would be needed to transport the troops to the west shore. The committee naturally thought of the huge estate of Colonel Philip Skene, retired British army officer who lived in feudal backwoods splendor at the head of navigation on Lake Champlain. Skene had rowboats, scows, even a schooner. Sam Herrick and thirty men were ordered to proceed at once to Skene's place—known as Skenesborough—take such boats as were needed, and return to a rendezvous in Shoreham, on the east shore. Just to make certain of transportation, Asa Douglas was dispatched to Crown Point, another British post, to steal boats there.

Colonel Allen now sought to call old Green Mountain Boys from the northern towns, many of whom had heard nothing of the sudden developments. Gershom Beach, a blacksmith of Rutland, who must have been a rugged man indeed, was sent on the errand. Striking out from Castleton on foot and ranging like a moose through the woods and rivers, Beach ran, loped, and walked through Rutland, Pittsford, Brandon, Leicester, Salisbury, Middlebury, and Whiting, a-rousing of the Boys. It was a sixty-mile run, and he covered it in less than twenty-four hours—a run to wind an Indian. If Henry Longfellow had lived in Vermont, the Green Mountain State would possess a national character comparable to the Horseman of Boston.*

For a final rallying place before crossing the lake, Colonel Allen had selected Hand's Cove, a timbered and secluded spot

---

* The mighty run of Gershom Beach survives in local folklore and in doggerel which begins:

> You've heard of the exploits of Gershom Beach:
> How he hurried the Green Mountain Boys to reach,
> To call them together to cross o'er the Lake,
> Then march from the shore and Fort Ti to take.

in the town of Shoreham, some two miles by water from the fort. The boats were to meet the troops there.

All night long, as the 9th grew into the 10th, men poured into the thick woods around the cove. Noah Phelps returned from his one-man scouting trip to the fort. He had easily gained entrance by posing as a woodsman who wanted a shave. Barbers, even then, were garrulous, and Phelps came away with the information that fewer than fifty soldiers manned the fort, which he noted was not in the best of condition and had a "capital breach" in the south curtain.

Ethan had posted sentinels along the shore to watch for the two expected parties with the boats. They watched many hours in vain, and things looked bad to Ethan; here he had two hundred men, more or less armed, but almost two miles of deep water lay between the cove and the fort. He was cursing most horribly at the delay when a new complication appeared in the person of a beautifully groomed and mounted man who said he was Colonel Benedict Arnold. He put a heavy accent on the title. Even in the dim light of two o'clock in the morning Colonel Arnold gleamed .with a gorgeous luster. Plumes waved from his hat. Great epaulets sparkled from his shoulders. His uniform was pretty fine. And with him, as a crowning piece of military pomp, was Colonel Arnold's own *valet de chambre*, perhaps the first such ever seen in the wilds of the New Hampshire Grants.

Arnold's arrival was wholly a surprise to the men gathered at the cove, for they didn't know that he had paused the day before at Castleton and had demanded the command from Secretary of War Mott. Mott had refused, saying that Colonel Allen was the official and actual head of the expedition. Arnold had paid no heed but hurried on to the cove. Now he confronted Ethan with an important-looking document which he said was a commission from the Committee of Safety at Cambridge on Massachusetts Bay. He appears to have told

Ethan curtly that the Committee had ordered *him* to take charge of the expedition.

An imperious manner was not the thing to try on Colonel Allen. Exactly what happened next has been lost in one hundred and sixty-five years of controversy, but it is certain that a violent row ensued. Ethan vowed, by God, that he had been elected to lead the attack. Arnold, proud as a peacock and dressed much like one, waved his commission from Cambridge. Somebody, doubtless old Peleg Sunderland, suggested hanging "the fancy barstard," and men shouted that, if they were not to be commanded by their own officers, then the hell with the War, if that was what it was; they would shoulder their arms and go home.

Knowing they had no time to spare, and that a controversy might wreck the expedition, Ethan and his second in command, Easton, told the unruly soldiers that Allen should lead them. Privately, it would appear from the record, Allen gave Arnold permission to march with him at the head of the column.

What worried Ethan more than the subject of command was how he was going to get his troops across the lake. The moon, in its fourth quarter, had set. Dawn was fast on the way, and neither the Herrick party nor Asa Douglas had been heard from.

One of the sentries along the shore gave a shout. Looming up from the misty waters was a small ark, a scow. Poling it in to the beach were two lads, James Wilcox and Joe Tyler, and in the scow was a Negro called Jack, known to be in the employ of Colonel Skene, the Tory of Skenesborough. Jack was driveling from liquor, potted to the eyes.

As the craft was beached the two boys related to Ethan that they had sighted it lying off Bridport, farther down the lake. Hearing from Douglas that Colonel Allen wanted boats, the boys had rowed out to the scow with a jug of rum. With no difficulty at all they got Jack to drinking, then on a pretext induced him to join them on a "wolf hunt" at Hand's Cove.

Ethan lost no time. Asa Douglas was now sighted bringing in a boat he had stolen somewhere. Hurriedly loading the two craft until the gunwales were awash, and leaving Seth Warner, able Green Mountain Boy, in command of the remaining party, Colonel Allen gave the order to push off. In the boats were eighty-three men, including Colonel Easton and John Brown of the Connecticut delegation, and Colonel Arnold. Brisk winds from the north made a choppy sea. Night was fast turning into gray.

The wallowing ships of war landed on the west shore near Willow Point, just out of sight of the fortress. The soldiers debarked. Colonel Allen had them form into three ranks. And now Colonel Arnold stuck in his horn again. He stepped forward and demanded that he command the attack. And now Colonel Allen, his nerves already much frayed, exploded.

"By God, sir," he roared, laying hand to his sword, "I'll have you to understand I am in command here!" Then, turning to Amos Callender, one of his old Green Mountain Boys, Ethan asked, "What shall I do with this damned rascal? Shall I put him under guard?" But Ethan took no further step just then. There wasn't time, if the attack was to be a surprise.

Stepping to front and center of his army, the tall commander delivered a brief army-style pep talk, full of bombastic praise for his gallant troops. He told the Boys that they were the scourge and terror of all arbitrary power. He said that the fortress before them must be taken quickly, once the attack was begun. He called it a desperate attempt which none but the bravest of men would dare undertake at all, and gave the faint-hearted a chance to get out before it was too late. "You that will undertake voluntarily," he said, "will poise your firelocks."

Up went an assortment of rifles, pistols, fowling pieces,

blunderbusses, clubs, hangers, hunting knives. It is doubtful if a greater range of weapons was used in any engagement of the Revolution. Ethan looked the mob over and was content. "Forward march," he ordered. He was at the head of the column, with Arnold beside him, the only figure of military appearance in the lot. Whether or not the Arnold valet was present is not of record.

On past the charcoal oven, past the Pontleroi redoubt, past the well, the army of eighty-three men moved as quietly as its vague discipline permitted. No lights, no sound came from the fort that loomed tall and black and sinister in the morning gray. This was the first time that Colonists had attacked property of the Crown, and many a man must have thought a bit about halters and firing-squads.*

Skirting the east wall, the column came to the south curtain where, as Allen had been informed, a part was in tumbledown ruin. He also knew that according to garrison custom a sentry would be on post at the wicket gate in the fort's main wall, inside the ruined curtain.

Ethan Allen held an opinion that officers should lead their men into action. Without a halt or a word he clambered over the breech, drew his long sword and rushed head on at the sentry, who was dozing. That surprised soldier did what he could. Raising his musket, he aimed at the tall ghost and pulled the trigger. His gun flashed in the pan, misfired. Then he turned and ran like hell through the archway that led to the parade ground, shouting bloody murder. Ethan was close at his heels, and close behind Ethan were his men, coming on the run.

When they entered the fort these men were at best pseudo-soldiers. Now, even though they had not tasted blood, they

* Unknown persons of Rhode Island had in 1772 destroyed the English revenue cutter *Gaspee*. This effort was not, however, in the same category as the formal attack and capture of Ticonderoga.

became as wild as the Indians some of them were accustomed to fighting. Howling, "No quarter!" and imitating the war cries of Mohawks, they tore through the parade ground to batter at the many doors of the barracks. Bedlam had come to Ticonderoga.

One brave but careless redcoat came out of the guardroom to lunge at an invader with his fixed bayonet. Ethan saw the move and fetched the redcoat a terrific swipe over the head with the flat of his sword, felling him to the ground. A heavy comb in the man's hair saved his skull. "Quarter, quarter!" he begged. Ethan poised his sword as if to run the man through, then thought better of it. "Take me to your commander," he bellowed. The fallen man jumped to his feet to lead the way to the foot of a short stairway to the upper portion of the west barracks. "The officers' quarters are there," he said.

With a leap like a catamount, Ethan started up the stairs. "Come out of there, you sons of British bitches," he called in a right clear voice. As he spoke the door opened, revealing an officer wearing coat and waistcoat and a pair of drawers. He carried his breeches over one arm. This apparition was not, as Ethan believed, the fort's commander. It was Lieutenant Jocelyn Feltham, second in command to Captain Delaplace.

The pantsless lieutenant faced enough trouble on the stairs to have made many an officer lose his head. There was the gigantic figure of Allen with a sword not seen every day. Next to Allen was the very military Colonel Arnold. And back of Arnold, crowding the stairs, was a mob of shouting, howling wild men, every one of them displaying arms and most of them crying aloud for British blood.

The lieutenant was as brave as they come. He remained cool. Stalling for time in the hope that his garrison would rally and begin shooting into the invaders, he asked for silence, which was accorded. Then he spoke.

"By what authority have you entered His Majesty's fort?"
he demanded.

It was a proper and logical question for an officer of Ye
Crown to ask of a riotous mob that had disturbed his garrison's
sleep so rudely and so early in the morning. It was not only
a proper question; it paved the way for one of the classic re-
plies of all military history, a sonorous, ear-filling utterance
that drummed its way into history books, into sermons, into
the minds and memories of men for generations to come.

"By what authority have you entered His Majesty's fort?"
demanded Jocelyn Feltham, lieutenant in His Majesty's 26th
Regiment of Foot.

Then Colonel Ethan Allen of the New Hampshire Grants
and the Green Mountain Boys let him have it. "In the name
of the Great Jehovah and the Continental Congress," he answered with some dignity.*

Lieutenant Feltham had probably never heard of the Continental Congress which on that same morning was to meet
for the second time in Philadelphia. Nor had he been accustomed to thinking of the Great Jehovah in a military light.
The whole thing was preposterous. He continued to stall for
time, still hoping that his soldiers would appear belowstairs
and run these hoodlums out of the fort.

"Who are you people," he began, "and who—"

Ethan leaped to the landing beside Feltham. "By God," he
swore, "I shall have possession of this fort and all the effects
of George the Third!" And he waved his great sword over
and around the lieutenant's head. The mob belowstairs set up
a shouting. They leveled their muskets at the one lone and
trouserless redcoat, while Ethan ripped out a series of oaths
so shocking that his own men listened in rapt wonder. "And

* Whether or not Colonel Allen made such an answer is one of Vermont's most cherishd controversies. It will be discussed in its proper place.
The narrative must go on.

if you don't immediately comply," he concluded, "no man, woman or child shall be left alive in this goddam place."

Feltham replied correctly that he was not the commander. Sensing now that the man he wanted to see was in the room behind Feltham, Ethan started to batter in the door. Arnold dissuaded him, and presently Captain Delaplace, fully dressed, came out.

Shoving Feltham into the upper room and placing two sentries, Allen and Arnold took Delaplace below to discuss affairs.

While these events were going forward, the invaders had broken into all the barrack rooms, finding several redcoats still in bed. The garrison's arms were collected and thrown into a room and a guard set. Captain Delaplace was ordered to parade his men without arms, which was done. Ticonderoga was taken, the first British position to fall. A classic Great Moment in American history had passed. But big doings in the fort had only begun.

The attention of the victors, naturally enough, was first directed not to the ordnance captured, but to the vast stores of rum in the fort. The door leading to the private cellar of Captain Delaplace was quickly breached by strong thirsty men wielding musket butts and artillery rammers. It yielded an even ninety gallons of strong excellent stuff. The garrison's issue rum stores were also attacked with vigor.

Daybreak saw the continuous landing of boats bringing Seth Warner and the rearguard from Hand's Cove. Warner demanded the privilege of leading the attack on the near-by and all but obsolete fortress of Crown Point. This was granted him. Taking a hundred men, he pushed off in bateaux for the fifteen-mile trip down the lake.

With things running so smoothly, Colonel Allen, Colonel Easton, and John Brown bellied around the ex-commandant's table in the officers' quarters. They filled mugs to the brim and tossed them down in the manner of two-fisted drinking men. The rank and file went hog-wild. Yelling like crazed devils, they ran everywhere through the fort, breaking into every room, cellar, shed, and cupboard, plundering or scattering whatever they happened on. The twenty-odd women and children must have been frightened out of their wits, but there was then or later no charge of ill treatment in this quarter.

By now more than two hundred Americans swarmed in and around the fort, and they were joined throughout the day by countryfolk from near-by farms, come to see what was up. Soldiers and farmers fell downstairs, tumbled off walls, broke jugs, bottles, windows. Matthew Lyon, the ebullient Irish-Yankee who later became a national character, felt that something special was needed to mark the day. Fetching a bucket of powder from the magazine, he poured it down the gullet of Old Sow, a thirteen-inch mortar—and let her go. It was a blast so mighty, legend has it, that the fort fairly rocked, and five patriots, snoozing dead drunk in Delaplace's cellar, were immediately revived and were able to finish the day on their feet, much to the credit of the Green Mountain Boys.

Colonel Arnold was aghast at the pillage and drunkenness. He attempted to put a stop to it and to force some degree of discipline, but to no avail; and later he reported that Colonel Allen was "a proper man to head his own wild people" but was wholly unfit for military command. Arnold again brought up the matter as to his own "rightful" command of the fort, pointing out that Allen had no commission at all. Hot words passed between the two colonels. The convivial soldiers also took a hand, and again they declared that if Ethan was not their commander, then, by God, they'd up and go home, the whole lot of them—an empty threat so long as the liquor held out.

Edward Mott settled everything. Mott, it will be recalled, had been appointed chairman of the committee of war at the

Castleton meeting when the attack was planned. Mott now sat down and wrote out in his own hand as proper a commission for Ethan as could be desired:

> Whereas, agreeable to the Power and Authority to us by the Colony of Connecticut, we have appointed you to take command of a party of men and reduce and take possession of the garrison of Ticonderoga and its dependencies, and as you are now in possession of the same . . . You are hereby directed to keep the command of said garrison, for use of the American Colonies, till you have further orders from the Colony of Connecticut or from the Continental Congress.

Dusting the ink with a flourish, Mott presented the commission to Colonel Ethan Allen. That made everything "legal"; but Ethan was in any case running the fort, and Colonel Arnold put in some very bad hours. The soldiers hooted him, called him vile names, and he wrote in his memorandum book that at least two of them fired their muskets in a manner to send balls whistling close by him.

Between drinks a heap of writing went on that day. Ethan wrote first to the Committee of Correspondence at Albany, New York, the nearest Revolutionary body, announcing capture of the fort and mentioning that "Col. Arnold enter'd the fortress with me side by side." In this report he showed the strain of circumstances, or of something. He dated it the 11th. Giving this letter and Ticonderoga's flag to John Brown, he ordered him to leave the one at Albany, and to take the other to Philadelphia and present it to the Congress.

Taking another snort of Captain Delaplace's prime stuff, the new commander of Ticonderoga dipped his quill and dashed off a note to tell the "Massachusetts Provential Congress" what was going on up there in the backwoods. He wrote:

> I have to inform You with Pleasure Unfelt Before that on breake of Day of the 10th of may 1775 by the Order of the

General Assembly of the Colony of Connecticut Took the Fortress of Ticonderoga by Storm the soldiary was Composed of about one Hundred Green Mountain Boys and Near Fifty Veteran Soldiars from the Province of Massachusetts Bay the Latter was under the Command of Col. James Easton who behaved with Great Zeal and fortitude. Not only in Council but in the Assault the Soldiary behaved with such resisless fury that they so terrified the Kings Troops that They Durst not Fire on their Assailants and our Soldiary was Agreeably Disappointed the Soldiary behaved with uncommon ranker when they leaped into the fourt . . .

He went on to bestow more praise on Easton, on John Brown, and on his troops of the "uncommon ranker." Arnold was not mentioned in this dispatch, which was given to Easton to take to Cambridge.

Thirty-eight soldiers of the British garrison and twenty-four women and children were now conducted to the boat landing at Lake George in charge of Epaphras Bull and escort, to be taken to Hartford.

A messenger arrived from Sam Herrick's party which had failed to get boats for the crossing. Herrick reported that he had taken possession of the Tory Skene's estate and all persons thereon. The delay of the night previous was not explained.

On the 12th Captain Delaplace and family, Lieutenant Feltham, and Lieutenant Wadam—who had been stationed at the boat landing on Lake George—were sent under guard to Hartford as prisoners of war. Ethan sat down again and wrote a letter, this time to Governor Trumbull of Connecticut. It contained a full head of steam and showed not so much what the Green Mountain Boy had done as what he was planning:

I make you a Present of a Major, a Captain and two Lieutenants in the regular Establishment of George the Third. I hope they may serve as ransom for some of our Friends in Boston. . . . A

party of men under Command of Capt Herrick has took possession of Skenesborough, imprisoned Major Skene, and seized
a Schooner of his. I expect in ten days Time to have it rigged,
manned and armed with 6 or 8 pieces of Canon, which, with the
boats in our Possession, I propose an attack on the armed Sloop
of George the Third which is now cruising on Lake Champlain.
I hope in a Short Time to be authorised to acquaint Your Honour
that Lake Champlain and the fortifications thereon are subjected
to the Colonies. . . . I conclude Capt Warner is by this Time in
Possession of Crown Point. . . .

A bold and cheerful letter from the man who had dared
strike the first blow at the Crown, and who now proposed to
carry the fight to the enemy all the way. Ethan "concluded"
correctly about Crown Point; Warner and his men took that
garrison without a shot. It didn't amount to much, being a
sergeant, eight privates, and ten women and children; but the
fort mounted a number of cannon. Of greater importance was
that a second possession of George the Third had fallen to
the Colonies.

It is little wonder that Colonel Allen and his men were
elated. In two days, and without loss of a man, they had captured two British forts, including important military stores
and cannon needed to blow the redcoats out of Boston.

It should not be forgotten that these were the first offensive
actions of the war. And the importance of the forts and supplies was as nothing to the effect the news of their taking was
shortly to have on the morale of the Colonies. Colonel Allen
had spread the good news as fast as he could, and now, on
May 12, he sat down to write one more letter. It was addressed to the Committee of War at Hartford and was given
into the hands of the prisoner Captain Delaplace.

Sir [it ran], Whereas the Fortress of Ticonderoga has fallen
into the Hands of the Colonies together with the Ordinance
Stores & c and Whereas Capt William Delaplace has in the Fort

ninety Gallons of Rum of his own Property which is greatly
wanted for the Refreshment of the Fatigued Soldiary . . . This
is Therefore to desire the Treasurer of the Colony of Connecticut
to pay Him the Sd Wm Delaplace Eighteen Pounds Eleven Shillings & Nine Pence Lawful money, as the Rum is appropriated
for the use of the Garrison—Your Compliance will oblige the
Garrison and your Humble Servant Ethan Allen Commandt of
Ticondr.*

This is a really great state paper. In it one finds courtesy
and honesty to a fallen enemy; humanity to the "fatigued
soldiary," and a sense of humor in the use of "has" instead of
"had" in reference to the rum stores of Captain Delaplace.
Few state papers have contained so much.

* Captain Delaplace got his money. On June 23, 1775, he signed a receipt
for "18.11.9" which now reposes in the Connecticut State Library.

"*The said Ethan Allen did in a tumultuous and offensive manner with threatening words and angry looks strike the person of George Caldwell to the disturbance of His Majesty's good subjects.*"—Court Records, Salisbury, Connecticut.

10300

At Catamount Tavern, Ethan and the Green Mountain boys prepared their strategy.

CHAPTER II

Backwoods Boy

———•◆•———

Tradition has it that on the 10th day of January in 1737 *
a bitter wind blew down from the north on Litchfield, Connecticut, piling snow into drifts so deep that only the roofs of
the backwoods hamlet could be seen. Wolves howled all that
night in the surrounding timber, town dogs replied in kind,
and Mary Baker Allen gave birth to a son, her first child.

If Joseph, the father, brought out the steelyards to weigh
the boy, it is not of record, but he did his best to give the
infant a proper start in life. He gave him the ancient Hebrew
name Ethan, signifying firmness, staunchness, strength.

Names counted for a good deal in those days, and Joe
Allen was a man who had a fancy for names. He had need
of them. He was at home a good deal, and seven children
followed Ethan in fairly regular order. Although Joe Allen
was highly critical of certain teachings in the Old Testament,
he had a liking for some of its men and women, and with the
advent of a new child, he simply took down his Bible and
contemplated the many biographies therein. He named Ethan

* Old Style calendar: equivalent to January 21, 1738, under the New
Style adopted in 1752.

and the next child, Heman, out of I Kings. Heber and Levi came out of Genesis. Zimri ("a captain of chariots") was from I Kings. Ira stemmed from II Samuel. Of the girls, Lydia's name is found in the New Testament (Acts 16:14), but Lucy seems not to have sprung from holy ground.

That totaled eight children. All but Ethan were born in Cornwall, where the Allens moved soon after the birth of their eldest, when Joseph bought land rights in the new town. Both tradition and the record indicate all the children to have been a lively, intelligent, and rather domineering lot, bold as brass and as tough as the flinty Connecticut hillside they helped to clear and till. In later years, when in a jovial mood, Ethan liked to remark that he knew of but two women who were successfully delivered of seven devils, complete with horns and tails. They were, he said, the Mesdames Mary Magdalene, and Mary Baker Allen.

Cornwall was a brand-new town when the Allens moved there, and the move was typical of the Allens. Joseph's ancestor had come over with the Dorchester company which landed in Massachusetts in 1632. He followed Thomas Hooker, the company's radical parson, on a pilgrimage to the lower Connecticut River valley; and for the next ninety years successive generations of Allens moved often, ever keeping on the frontier of the slowly expanding settlements.

When Ethan first saw it, Cornwall was a collection of log cabins on a level spot beside the Housatonic River. The timber grew right down to the very dooryards, which contained stumps instead of trees. In many of the cabins a broad stump served as a rugged table, not to be tipped over; the floors were of hard-tramped earth unless the bark roofs leaked, and then they were mud.

As in all New England towns of the time, interest centered around the church and in local politics. Joe Allen took a hand in both. He was promptly elected one of the town's select-

men, and at the first meeting was named moderator. Joe went
to church, and so did his family; but he was far from orthodox. He had absorbed many of the beliefs of Jacobus Ar-
minius, the heretic of Leyden, and enjoyed argument with
Calvinists. He must have argued well, too, for he is generally
credited with the apostasy of the Reverend Solomon Palmer,
divine of Cornwall, who one Sunday in 1754 declared publicly
that he could no longer put up with predestination and indiscriminate hell-fire.

Thus Ethan lived his early years in a household dominated
by a heretic—a fact that was to bear fruit later.

Like all backwoods children of the time, the Allens had to
work, and work hard. In his teens Ethan was sent with grist
to the mill at Woodbury, twenty-five miles along a blazed
trail. He fished and hunted and trapped for food for the table
and skins to wear. By the time he was tall enough to swing
the heavy awkward axes then in use, he would duff into a pine
or a maple and fell it quickly wherever he wanted.

Ethan was what today would be termed a precocious child.
He liked to be with his elders, of whom he asked questions
about this and the other world. As soon as he could write,
which was early, he put his boyish thoughts on heavy matters
on paper; and he read the Bible a great deal until he could
lay hands on other books.

He borrowed every book in Cornwall, and seems to have
read them all. When work permitted, he was much given to
contemplation, although he was realistic enough, and ener-
getic. His thirst for knowledge must have impressed his father,
for Joe sent him for schooling to the Reverend Jonathan Lee,
in neighboring Salisbury. He was to be prepared for college.

It is interesting to muse on what Ethan Allen might have
become if he had gone to Yale. He certainly had intelligence
of a high order, a capacity for learning, and a doggedness to
understand everything that had been written or said by the

great thinkers. But he would doubtless have been kicked out of Yale, or out of Harvard, for that matter. His mind was too close to being original.

Ethan had scarcely begun his studies under the Reverend Mr. Lee when Joe Allen died. He returned to Cornwall to help bury his father in the Allen pasture, back of the house, and to take charge as head of the family.

At this he did very well. Not yet of age, he acted as attorney for his mother and sought and obtained a judgment against one Joseph Mather for money owed the late Joe Allen. He took charge of the farm work, traded produce for supplies, and generally acted as the head of the house. It was the French and Indian War that made young Ethan a restless man, not ever again to be thoroughly domesticated.

In the summer of 1757, when he was nineteen, Ethan turned the farm over to his brothers and joined up with a company in the regiment of Colonel Ebenezer Marsh. These troops saw no fighting. They marched to Lake George, arriving too late to aid in the hopeless defense of Fort William Henry, and marched right back to Connecticut. Although he did not re-enlist—this was a professional war, of no interest to farmers—Ethan had now been over the hump, over the mountain, over yonder where the grass is always greener.

Exactly what he did during the four years after his brief army experience is not clear, but he must have done well at something or other, for in October of 1761 he turns up as a bloated capitalist. With fifty pounds of his own money—or credit—he financed purchase of a farm for his cousin, Elihu Allen.

His next venture was in ore. In Salisbury was a large hill containing low-grade iron. Eight men owned and operated it to supply small forges in the vicinity. Somehow Ethan got an idea that a blast furnace to smelt ore would be a good thing. Just about the only industry of the backwoods was making potash. Making potash called for huge iron kettles, and there was a shortage of kettles. By some fine trading, mortgaging, and other financing he secured a right to mine ore in the hill and a right to cut fuel wood on a tract of Tohconnick Mountain timber. Then he went ahead and built the furnace.

The Allen furnace was a pioneer venture and is credited with being the first smelting operation of size in Connecticut. Everybody for miles around was trying to get into the potash business, and young Mr. Allen's furnace had to work overtime to turn out material for making the big kettles. By June of 1762 everything was working fine, with Ironmaster Allen in direct charge on the ground. Money, or probably produce, was rolling in.

It occurred, apparently suddenly, to the new iron baron, that he needed a wife. He got on his horse and rode down to Woodbury, where as a boy he had taken the grist, and married Mary, one of the eleven children of the miller Brownson. The Reverend Daniel Brinsmade received four shillings for his part in the business.

Very little of Mary's personality survives. It is known that she was deeply religious, wholly without humor, and signed her name with a cross. Taking her to Salisbury, where he could be near the furnace, Ethan was soon involved not only in many ore and iron deals but also in a number of real estate transactions. Heman Allen, brother, bought into the furnace. Ethan bought a fine house of one Eliphalet Buell, and ninety-five acres of land. He sold a half-interest in this house and land to Heman. To hold up his end of the deal, Heman mortgaged some plowland. "Paper" was virtually the only medium of exchange, except barter, and a study of the land records of Salisbury indicates that nearly everything in town was well papered with notes and mortgages.

By the house they owned jointly, Heman and Ethan put in a garden which was soon overrun with pigs owned by Sam

Tousley. The Allen boys swore a good bit about the pigs and, as that didn't seem to do any good, they locked the swine up in a pen belonging to Neighbor Sam Keyes. Tousley went to court about it, and the Allens had to pay a fine.

Ethan operated the furnace for about two years and did very well; but his heart wasn't in it. Apparently he had no idea of becoming the greatest ironmaster in the Colony. Brewing ore was too tame altogether. He began thinking about mines, and presently bought into a no-good hole-in-the-ground at Woodbury, and became involved in deals with a Sampson Simpson, a New York merchant who had mining fever. In the meantime he had got himself into a scrape that throws a revealing light on the comparative status of Law and Science in the Colony of Connecticut.

Living near Salisbury and practicing in the village and near-by towns was a remarkable man. He was Thomas Young, an able physician who had calomel in his saddle-bags and a variety of dangerous ideas in his head. With every dose of calomel the doctor casually dispensed some heretical opinion on current theology and politics.

Dr. Young had the best library in northern Connecticut, and he knew his books, which included Tacitus, Aquinas, Plutarch, Isaac Newton, Humphrey Ditton, Charles Blount, and the then modern giants, John Locke and Thomas Hobbes. In a town as small as Salisbury any two unusual minds were bound to find each other. Ethan, with his intense craving for knowledge, must have been attracted to the doctor the moment he met him; and the genial physician must have been happy as well as surprised to find a mind so free and wild among a people who had taken the utterances of Jonathan Edwards as Gospel—or had until the great schism.

It was a time when the name of either George Whitefield or Moses made the sinners quake in their cowhide boots, a period when, if witchcraft was no longer countenanced by the more enlightened clergy, witches and devils and all manner of spirits often assailed folk in the back country. The liberating wind of the Encyclopedists was beginning to make itself felt in France; but in backwoods America most thinking was predicated on the Book and the latest announcements of holy men. Imps with horns sneaked into well houses and soured the cream. Other imps struck cattle dead. And every now and again a bloodthirsty Jehovah hurled a bolt at some house where dice had been played or some pleasant adultery committed.

Dr. Young was amused at such beliefs. He scoffed at preachers and their merchandise. When he felt the need of spiritual consolation he took himself to the Salisbury tavern and had a mug of stout rum punch. So did young Ethan. There and in Young's house the two men spent many evenings, discussing everything from the Virgin Birth to the huge speculations in land then going on in all parts of the Colonies. They read proof on Young's pamphlets attacking the theology of Edwards and Whitefield, and read another treatise the doctor had prepared on the current controversy over jurisdiction of land grants between the governors of New York and New Hampshire. In this pamphlet a phrase occurred which pleased young Ethan immensely: "Liberty and Property, the household gods of Englishmen." The pamphlet had an appendix, titled "Rules of Law, fit to be observed in purchasing land," which, in light of later events, may be said to have influenced Ethan.

Dr. Young and young Allen also discussed medicine and the still novel method of inoculation with smallpox virus, commonly called "ingrafting." Although Cotton Mather, the divine, had long before urged ingrafting as the best method of controlling the dread disease of the Colonies, the practice had met violent resistance at the hands of most theologians; and many physicians of the time, thinking no doubt of his prescription for witches, would have no truck with anything suggested by Mather.* Dr. Zabdiel Boylston of Boston had tried ingrafting on his own son and had been mobbed for his pains. The practice had finally made some headway in Boston and the larger towns, but not in backwoods Connecticut; it was against the law there to give or receive smallpox by inoculation unless consent had been given in writing by the town selectmen—who ordinarily knew less of medicine than they did of predestination.

Both Dr. Young and Ethan Allen enjoyed a little experiment. At Ethan's request the doc opened an Allen vein and dabbed it with pus. Ethan seems not to have suffered from the affair, but news of it naturally got around Salisbury; and presently two of the town's selectmen—the Reverend Jonathan Lee and one Stoddard—made a threat to prosecute Ethan, who lost his temper.

Hauled into local court before Justice Hutchinson, Ethan was charged with breaking the peace and with blasphemy—and no wonder. The complaint reads that Ethan Allen uttered the following:

By Jesus Christ, I wish I may be bound down in Hell with old Beelzabub a thousand years in the lowest pit in Hell and that every little insipid Devil should come along by and ask the reason of Allen's lying there, it should be said because he made a promise here in cool blood that he would have satisfaction of Lee and Stoddard and did not fulfill it.

That is a little complicated, but the stenographic ears of Lee and Stoddard may have been at fault. In its original form the oath and threat were doubtless more direct and were something to contemplate with awe. Ethan had to appear in

---

* In witch trouble old Mather favored the ordeal by water; viz., if your grandmother looks haggard and has a mole (i.e., a witch mark) on her arm, throw her into the water. If she swims, she's a witch and must be hanged; if she sinks, may God have mercy on her soul.

court about it, anyway, and conducted his own defense. The outcome is not known, but no fine is recorded; and he must have won his case, or at least got off with a reprimand.

It wasn't young Allen's last appearance in the local court. In the spring of 1765 the two Allens sold their interest in the iron furnace to George Caldwell for five hundred pounds. How much actual cash changed hands isn't of record; but there must have been some, for Ethan, Heman, and George went on a sizable bender. It was a rousing day and night in Salisbury, and next morning Ethan and George were up before Justice Hutchinson. The charge this time was that "Ethan Allen did in a tumultuous and offensive manner with threatening words and angry looks strip himself even to his naked body and with force and arms without law or right did assault and actually strike the person of George Caldwell of Salisbury in the presence and to the disturbance of His Majesty's good subjects."

Justice Hutchinson thought the disturbance of His Majesty's good subjects worth about ten shillings, and Ethan paid. If His Majesty himself, who was George III, could have known the amount of disturbing this police-court character was to occasion, he might well have had him hanged.

The Caldwell feud, whatever it was, was not yet done. Soon after the first encounter Ethan went to Woodbury to join an expedition to inspect a lead mine at Northampton, Massachusetts Province, in which the New York merchant Sampson Simpson was interested. On the way to the mine Ethan's party met George Caldwell. With Caldwell was one Robert Branthwaite. Ethan, for reasons not now clear, took a poke at Branthwaite. Caldwell interfered, and Ethan hit *him* quite hard over the head with a club. Worse, according to the charge, he did this clubbing in "a violent and angry manner," which is something in the way of an understatement. Branthwaite grabbed the club, and Ethan nailed him again, just as Constable Luke Camp came up and arrested all three men.

Even then it wasn't over. Later on the same day Ethan, "in a threatening manner with his fist lifted up," called Caldwell all sorts of frightful names and "also did with a loud voice say that he would spill the blood of any that opposed him."

No one seems to have been detained very long, for Ethan resumed his way to Northampton after Constable Camp served him notice to appear later in Justice Hutchinson's court.

The lead mine did not pan out well. Ethan acted as "Over sear" and appears to have spent much of his time in the tavern operated by Major Jonathan Clapp. He found Northampton even more pious than Salisbury and gave some thought to the concocting of profane jokes on the local churchmen. He scoffed openly. The Reverend Mr. Judd, pastor, went to the mine on occasion and warned Ethan that he must cease his unspeakable profanities. Ethan paid no heed and the minister had the last word. One day in July of 1767 the selectmen of Northampton held a meeting, then notified Ethan that they would like to have him move out of town, bag and baggage.

That was what could happen to an unorthodox thinker in the Massachusetts of the period; but Ethan was lucky. Fifty years previously his ears would have been cut off, and possibly his neck broken. It is to be regretted that what he said on this occasion (there can be no question that he said something) is lost to history. Loading his wife, one child, and possessions into an oxcart, he returned to comparatively liberal Salisbury, where brother Heman had set up as a general storekeeper. The Allen families doubled up in living quarters over the store.

Ethan must have spent the summer very quietly, for he does not appear in the police court or other records. Doubtless he was doing some thinking about the New Hampshire Grants. Everyone was talking of them. The Grants were well beyond the frontier. Misfits, bankrupts, and restless men of all kinds were moving north into the open spaces along the rivers, and back in the hills, too, where there was only forest. It was said that Benning Wentworth, Governor of New Hampshire, was granting lands in great hunks, as fast as companies could be formed to take it and to pay the Governor a little something for his trouble. There was even quite a town up there in the wilds—Bennington, named for His Excellency —and many of the best citizens of Connecticut were interested in lands thereabout.

Maybe it had been his march through a part of the Grants with the army that prompted him. Possibly Dr. Young's talk of land speculation had an influence. And the difficulties facing a heretic in Connecticut and Massachusetts may have counted. All together, they were reason enough to do some far ranging. Leaving his family at brother Heman's in Salisbury, Ethan struck out alone for the tall timber of the Grants.

He spent the winter on snowshoes in what is now Vermont, cruising through the green-covered hills and mountains, living on venison, sleeping in a bearskin. His brother Ira, who heard him describe his winter in the north, has left a good picture of Ethan as a woodsman, as a man who was at home on the trail. He says that Ethan could and did tire deer by running them until they collapsed of fatigue. When he had to leave a nice hindquarter in the woods for any length of time, he would hang his hat on the meat "to preserve it from the ravens."

One time late in the fall, says Ira, his brother was out in a cold rain and got soaked. Night came on; so did snow. His clothes froze on him. He marked out a path in a circle and walked it throughout the dark hours, to keep from sleep and death by freezing. Before morning came he fell and fell again, but he lasted it out on his feet and afterwards often told that the night had been "among the greatest hazards of his life."

And when Woodsman Ethan set out through miles of unblazed forest for a goal, he never missed it by more than a few rods. Apparently he had that sixth sense of "location" which some but not all woods people acquire at birth. It was told he would never take a roundabout way to get to a point. He preferred the direct route, regardless of rivers and mountains, or even of men.

That first trip alone into the New Hampshire Grants was a cruise that changed his whole life. On it he crossed the mountains, and came down the Connecticut River to Northampton, then home to Salisbury. He had seen the land beyond the Hump, over the Hill, the land of honey and the Rock Candy Mountains, where deer were thicker than chipmunks, where fish were so thick they attacked otter, where wolves devoured all parsons and court magistrates.

"Go your way now, and complain to that damned scoundrel your governor."

CHAPTER III

The Gods of the Hills

Ethan Allen knew well enough that if he moved to the New Hampshire Grants he was entering a howling wilderness, compared to which his native Connecticut was a highly civilized and populous place. It wasn't that white men had never been there, but that they hadn't remained.

As early as 1609 the French explorer Samuel de Champlain had viewed the lake that bears his name and fought, on July 4, a brief battle with Iroquois. This land between the lake and the Connecticut had long been disputed hunting ground, fought over and for by Iroquois and the various Algonquin tribes. With Champlain, the French claimed it by right of discovery, and during the interminable wars between them and the English the Grants formed the highway for battles.

Geography did it. From Quebec and Montreal, the French and their Indian allies found it easy to run up the Sorel River into Lake Champlain. Continuing up the lake and to the head of connecting Lake George, they reached a quick portage to the Hudson. Or, starting in Canada, they could run up the St. Francis to Lake Memphremagog, up the Clyde to Island Pond, and down the Nulhegan to the long Connecticut.

These routes amounted to express highways, and following them, the French and Indians again and again raided English settlements—in New Hampshire, in Massachusetts, in New York.

The French built forts on Lake Champlain—at Isle La Motte, at Ticonderoga, at Chimney Point, while the English erected blockhouses at Dummer and Number Four on the Connecticut River and as far north as the Cohasse Intervales. Thus the two nations, using the deluded red men as allies, fought back and forth across the Grants and up and down their length. This was bloody ground from the first, whence came those scoutings, raids, and massacres which made up the so-called French and Indian War, and the trails were well padded by the feet of hundreds of white captives, who were killed on the spot the moment they failed to keep up with the marching columns.

In this war, at first, the English were driven from every fort and settlement on the Grants. That is, all except Fort Dummer, which managed to hold on in the southeastern corner. Then all the French were driven out. When smoke cleared from the Plains of Abraham, the New Hampshire Grants were British territory.

But this country which had been disputed so long by two different nations was now to be disputed by English governors.

The very troubles they had known had served to keep the Grants a backwoods country. For many years yet it would be referred to as the frontier. In 1768, when Ethan Allen made his first lone trip into the wilderness, the population of the entire territory probably did not exceed four hundred persons. A few of these were old soldiers, tired of the wars and wanting solitude, who struck out into the timber and made a pitch where they would. They did a little clearing, but not much, and lived chiefly on game. Several families lived at Fort Dummer. Other families strung out along the Connecticut River, but mostly on its eastern side. The only place in the Grants that could be termed a village was the settlement at Bennington. All the rest, from Massachusetts to Canada and from the Connecticut to Lake Champlain, was a land of dark forest, a vast silence disturbed only by the howling of wolves and "the mellow cadence of the great owl's solemn note."

The Grants were generally accepted as beginning on the east at the line of the Connecticut River, but how far west they ranged was vague. Vague, too, was the jurisdiction. These conditions had been brought about by the almost incredible lack of knowledge of their American colonies by the English King and his alleged advisers—the same lack of knowledge that was presently to bring on the Revolution itself.

When the King of England appointed royal governors to his American colonies he gave them the right to grant unsettled lands within their jurisdiction. Benning Wentworth was appointed Governor of New Hampshire in 1741. The western boundary of his province, as indicated, had never been very definitely described; it simply ran westward until it met His Majesty's other lands.

New Hampshire had once been a part of Massachusetts, and that province extended west to an imaginary line twenty miles east of the Hudson River. Hence, Governor Wentworth reasoned, New Hampshire must also extend west the same distance. It looked very simple. Wentworth forthwith granted the town of Bennington, which was west of the Connecticut but well within what he thought was his western boundary.

The Province of New York soon raised objections, claiming as its eastern boundary nothing short of the Connecticut. The matter was referred to London and the King. In 1764 the King acknowledged New York's claims, thus placing Wentworth's grant of Bennington—and several more of his grants—in New York.

The matter might well have ended right there except for one thing; and that cannot appear otherwise than as a personal interest in the debated land on the parts of the governors of New York and New Hampshire and their friends. Cadwallader Colden, Acting Governor of New York, had made a few enormous grants for which he charged fees running from £200 to £250 for each township included. Governor Wentworth of New Hampshire charged very small fees—about £20 a township; but in all his deals he stipulated that at least two choice lots be set aside for himself. He was always a very good business man.

On receipt of the King's order placing the Grants within New York, Colden saw fit to assume that Wentworth had never had the right to grant lands in the disputed territory. So, Colden proceeded to regrant certain lands on which settlers with New Hampshire titles were already living and others which, while not settled, were claimed under like titles.

Faced with moving off or paying a second time for their lands, the people in and around Bennington did neither. They sent Sam Robinson, who might have been described as a prominent citizen, to London to tell the King of the injustice they were facing. Robinson did his work well, and in 1767 the King ordered the Governor of New York to cease and desist until the matter could be looked into by the Crown. In 1770 it was still in abeyance.

An intangible also entered the controversy in the form of the great difference of social and economic outlook of the two parties to the dispute. New York had from the first fostered vast manors owned by a few wealthy men, and cultivated, as in the British Isles, by tenant farmers. New Hampshire, as well as all New England, had favored dividing land into comparatively small farms, to be owned by the men who lived on the land and tilled the soil. Had the policies of the two colonies been alike, it is doubtful that the controversy would have lasted very long. But they were not alike, and the very manner in which they differed made a battle not only to be expected but inevitable. The result was to be a long, bitter and violent real-estate war.

Such was the condition in 1768, the year Ethan Allen first visited the Grants and the year when things really started coming to a head. The first signs of the coming storm occurred very soon on the farm claimed, under a Wentworth grant, by James Breakenridge, a determined and mulish man who had been heard to say that he would be damned and double-damned before he would pay again for his farm. Breakenridge was no speculator. Primarily he was a peasant (a word then still in use in New England). He was living on his land. He had cleared timber, built house and barn, and was raising crops.

The Breakenridge place happened to be on an immense tract that had also been granted by New York. Its grantees, all of whom were speculators, and among whom were a Major John Small and a Reverend Mr. Slaughter, secured appointment of a New York land commission to survey and divide their tract. The surveying party was surprised, on arriving at the Breakenridge place, to find it occupied by a much larger group of men than was needed to harvest Farmer Breakenridge's small field of corn. But that was what the men were there for, Breakenridge said, although every last corn-tosser in the crowd carried a long rifle.

Breakenridge told the surveyors to be gone; this was his land, and he needed no surveying of it. John Munro, a New York justice of the peace, stepped up and read the riot act, calling on the mob to disperse. He might have been talking to the trees. The backwoodsmen sat around on stumps, their rifles between their knees, and gave no sign of moving. When the justice was done, Breakenridge again told the surveying party to go away. To this command he added a statement which the Yorkers thought carried a sinister note. "I hope you will not try to take any advantage of us," he said, *"for our people do not understand law."*

The justice and the surveyors looked around the cornfield and counted a score of rifles and men who looked able to use them. They coiled up their lengths of chain and went away.

Next move of New York was to prepare ejectment suits against Breakenridge and many other holders of New Hampshire titles. Several of these men were large proprietors. They lived in and around Salisbury, Connecticut, and after the Breakenridge incident they became alarmed. In March of 1770 they held a meeting in Canaan. Although thousands of acres of land were at stake, they were quite modest in their first step to defend their titles. They agreed to pay fifty cents on each "right" of land into a defense fund, and Charles Burral was appointed receiver-general. Another meeting was held in June. The sum raised is not known, but it must have been small.

Ethan Allen, not long returned from his trip through the Grants, was present at the last meeting. He must have taken a leading part in the discussions, for the proprietors selected him to manage the defense, and gave him the few dollars collected.

Astride a horse Ethan rode to Portsmouth, capital of New Hampshire Province, to confer first with John Wentworth who had succeeded his uncle Benning as Governor. From him Ethan got a copy of the charters of the towns containing the disputed lands. He also did a little business on his own. He purchased one Daniel Warner's right in the town of Poultney and Zenus Person's right in the town of Castleton, paying four pounds for one, six for the other. Both towns were in the tract under dispute. Ethan doubtless figured that one way to have genuine interest in an affair of this kind was to have a material claim. On his way west from Portsmouth he stopped at New Haven to engage Jared Ingersoll, one of Connecticut's leading attorneys, to accompany him to Albany, where the ejectment suits were to be tried. They rode together, discussing strategy on the way.

First case to come up was that of John Small *vs.* Josiah Carpenter. The defendant, Carpenter, sought to offer as testimony a copy of the New Hampshire charter granting the town of Shaftsbury, in which was the land he claimed. Counsel for plaintiff rose to object, saying that no evidence had been given to show that New Hampshire Province *ever* included the town of Shaftsbury within its domain, or that its governor had any right to grant such land.

From the viewpoint of the New York claimants this was a clever move of counsel. The judges sustained the objection—which precluded the defendant from offering any evidence whatever. The trial was over almost before it had begun, and Josiah Carpenter was ordered by the court to get off that parcel of ground.

The outcome of the case could not have been much of a surprise to Ethan Allen and his eminent attorney. They had known that the presiding judge, Robert Livingston, was one of the largest New York grantees of the lands in question, and so were the lieutenant governor of New York, the attorney-general, and many others in office.

On the day after the farcical trial, Ethan had callers at his tavern. They were John Tabor Kempe, attorney-general for New York, and James Duane, lawyer by profession and a well known real-estate operator on the side. They were very suave at first. They were sorry about this title trouble, they said, and felt it was wholly unnecessary. They talked a good deal about "peace and harmony" and wound up by offering Ethan a good hunk of land if he would put in with New

York. They were positive that, if he would espouse the New York cause, all would go well and Ethan would be a wealthy landowner.

Ethan did not hesitate a moment. He turned down the proposal. Now Kempe started to get tough about it. "You should be advised," he said sternly to Ethan, "that the people settled on the Grants will do well to make the best terms possible with the rightful New York landlords. We have might on our side, and you know that might often prevails against right."

"Sir," replied Ethan with a line that has been quoted often for one hundred and seventy years, "the gods of the hills are not the gods of the valleys." It was cryptic, and it had that something about it men remember; but Kempe did not understand.

"What do you mean?" he asked.

"If you will accompany me to the hill in Bennington," said Ethan, "the sense will be made clear."

Bennington was the unofficial capital of the no man's land of the Grants, and Ethan's remark sounded like a threat. ("Our people do not understand law.")

But Kempe and Duane still hoped to get this bold backwoodsman on their side. Kempe ordered a bowl of punch, and the three men sat around and talked some more. Duane offered to pay Ethan's expenses if he would return to Bennington and try to talk the settlers there into recognizing New York's claims and repurchasing their New Hampshire lands from the alleged grantees of New York.

The hill boy was learning the ways of diplomacy. He assented to Duane's offer, accepted a horse from that gentleman, and rode away to Bennington.

Many of the Connecticut holders of land rights had gone up to Bennington, which promised to be the center of things, in order to be near the tracts they might have to fight for.

Ethan arrived at the Catamount Tavern to find a crowd of anxious men waiting to hear his report of the Albany case. His report was a ripsnorter.

He termed the New York courts and officials a junto of land thieves and said there was nothing for the New Hampshire men to do but prepare to defend their lands by force. On the spot a military association was formed of men ready at all times to drop what they might be doing and rally to the defense of New Hampshire settlers. Ethan was elected colonel-commandant. Shortly after the meeting he returned to Albany to leave the borrowed horse with its owner. He told Duane that "everything will soon be adjusted" but apparently did not explain how, and went back to Bennington.

Not all men on the Grants favored New Hampshire jurisdiction. To an actual settler, doing his own clearing and tilling on ground that he called his own, the requirement of a confirmatory title from New York was of no great concern: the cost, for a small farm, was trifling. In the district between the Connecticut River and the Green Mountains, most of the holdings were in just such small parcels—a farm just large enough for one man and his family to work comfortably, was the rule.

This condition did not hold true between the Green Mountains and that indefinite point twenty miles east of the Hudson River. Over there much of the land was in large holdings, claimed by a comparatively small number of men who were interested chiefly in speculation. These speculators were land-poor. Paying for confirmation of such huge tracts would take more money than they had. They preferred to ignore New York and, if necessary, fight.

Thus there was a difference in the manner in which men on the Grants viewed New York; and those favoring New York sent agents secretly to Albany to warn York officials that a "Bennington Mobb" was raising an army to defend its New

Hampshire titles. When he heard of this, Acting Governor Colden was pretty mad. He blew up in a public statement to the effect that he would drive these "rioters" into the Green Mountains.

To indicate what they thought of this threat, the unofficial militia of the Grants, the aforementioned Bennington Mobb, took a title for themselves. Henceforth they were the Green Mountain Boys. The war was on.

The ranks of the Green Mountain Boys contained some pretty tough roosters. Colonel Allen already had the reputation of being a very violent and able young man, full and running over with trouble. His chief field officer, Seth Warner, was considerably quieter; but Seth could be mean, and with a rifle he could shoot an acorn out of a squirrel's teeth.

Colonel-Commandant Allen had a wide acquaintance in Connecticut and on the Grants, and in a little while he had recruited a number of rough-and-tumble fighters. Captains of the Boys, then or soon, included Remember Baker, cousin of Ethan, a wide-ranging woodsman who rather enjoyed violent doings; Robert Cochran, who called himself a Robin Hood and apparently had certain of that outlaw's qualities, and Peleg Sunderland, whose name was spelled in many ways and who was one of the toughest in the hard lot. An old Indian fighter from away back, Peleg had trapped and hunted everywhere on the Grants and knew every stream and mountain. He was the kind of man who liked bear meat for breakfast. Ethan's brother Heman, Gideon Warren, and Wait Hopkins completed the captains' list. All were able men in the woods.

Adjutant of the Boys was another Allen brother, Levi. Called lieutenants were Ira, Ethan's youngest brother (already dabbling in land titles), Ebenezer Allen, a cousin, and John Grand, David Ives, and Jesse Sawyer. The "doctor and surrurgeon" (Ethan's own spelling) was Jonas Fay, son of the Catamount Tavern's keeper.

The first move in what was to be a long war was made by New York. In July of '71 Sheriff Ten Eyck of Albany started a march on the Breakenridge farm, to carry out an eviction, taking nearly three hundred armed men with him. News of the advance came to Bennington by runners of the Green Mountain Boys. The call was sent out from the Catamount, and men in buckskin at work on farms took down their rifles and loped off through the woods in the direction of the Breakenridge place.

When Sheriff Ten Eyck and his army moved into the clearing of the farm, they saw that the house was barricaded and the log walls pierced with efficient-looking loopholes. In the Breakenridge field, within easy gunshot of the house, were forty men with rifles over their arms. The sheriff's party was stopped at the edge of the field by seven armed men, but after a brief parley two of the posse were conducted to a spot near the house where Breakenridge came out to meet them. The resolute old farmer told the sheriff's men that his farm was now under the protection of the town of Bennington, which was prepared to defend it. He waved his hand eloquently toward the forty men in the field, silently chewing tobacco and spitting at stumps. He waved it again, and the sheriff's men noted the heads and rifles of what looked like hundreds of men, peering down at them from behind the top of a near-by ridge. So far as he was concerned, he said, the parley was over.

The two members of the posse returned to the waiting forces of the sheriff. That brave officer gave orders to advance. The posse started but began at once to disintegrate. They dropped away from the march, two or three at a time, then in whole squads. Only the sheriff and about twenty men reached the house. The silent watching men in the field made no move. Obviously they and the half-hidden men on the ridge were awaiting a command.

The sheriff read the writ of ejectment and demanded entrance to the house. Nothing happened. He then shouted that he was going to batter in the door, and at this moment the forty men in the field raised their guns and took a casual bead along the sights. Movements along the ridge indicated that the men there were swinging into action. The sheriff was brave, but no fool. He and the twenty men who had stuck with him retreated and continued back to Albany, where he cursed the kind of deputies he had recruited and informed the Governor of New York that the Grants were in armed revolt against all authority.

Colonel Allen wasn't with the mob at the Breakenridge place. He was out on an offensive campaign. Word had come to him that William Cockburn, a surveyor for New York, was at work running lines in that part of the Grants called Social-borough by New York and which New Hampshire said was part of the towns of Rutland and Pittsford. Two or three days later Surveyor Cockburn was startled at his work by a party of men dressed as Indians even to dark-stained faces. The tallest of these fake savages, who was very tall, did the talking; and it wasn't in Indian but in good rousing Yankee. This tall man vowed that if Cockburn didn't stop running lines and go home where he belonged, then he should have his head cut off—by God. Cockburn immediately started for New York Province.

Ethan washed the stain off his face and returned to Bennington, where there was much to do. Dr. Sam Adams, for one thing, had been talking in a subversive manner. He said that New York had right to the Grants and all they contained. He armed himself and let it be known he planned to shoot dead the first man who troubled him in the least about his opinions. It wouldn't do to let such talk go unchallenged. Ethan dispatched a squad of the Boys to bring the doctor to judgment seat at the Catamount. They took him without a shot and fetched him before the Colonel. After what he called a "trial," Colonel Allen sentenced the doctor to be bound in a chair and hoisted up beside the stuffed cougar that advertised the tavern. It was done, much to the amusement of all hands, and the doctor left suspended for an hour.

Hearing that two New York deputy sheriffs had invaded the Grants and were doubtless up to nothing good, Ethan captured them himself. He locked them in separate rooms on the same side of a farmhouse. During the night he rigged up a straw man which he hung from a limb in sight of both windows, and in the early morning he waked both deputies, one after the other, and told them to look outside. Each was then allowed to escape, thinking the other had been hanged by this tall violent leader of the Grants. Colonel Allen liked a joke now and then, if it suited his purpose.

New York sheriffs and surveyors kept the Boys on the run much of the summer and fall. Legend has it that Ethan alone met a Yorker sheriff and his six men, took them all on at once and left them battered and bleeding on the ground. Another time he picked a surveyor and his chainman off the ground, held them at arm's length and beat them together until they promised to survey no more.

Because he enjoyed doing it, and probably, too, because it made good propaganda, Ethan often gave demonstrations of his immense strength. One of his favorite stunts was to pick up a bushel bag of salt in his teeth and toss it over his shoulder without touching it with his hands. He took to roaring louder than ever, and that was very loud. He shouted that the law of his Green Mountain Boys was backed by "the twigs of the wilderness"—switches of beech—and that death certainly awaited a second offender.

The last engagement of 1771, before winter set in and precluded much surveying or settling, occurred in October. Two Yorkers named Todd and Reid, and Corporal Charles Hutchinson had built houses on land in what New York called

New Perth and New Hampshire designated as Rupert. The New Hampshire claimant to this same land was Robert Cochran, a captain in the Green Mountain Boys, which made it a sad place for Yorkers to settle. So, Ethan, Cochran, Remember Baker, and two or three others went up to look into the matter.

With poor Hutchinson watching, the Boys set fire to his house and watched it burn to the ground, meanwhile passing remarks on the villainy of all Yorkers. When the house had been consumed Ethan told Hutchinson what to do about it. "Go your way now," he said, "and complain to that damned scoundrel your governor." Then he added, "God damn your governor, your laws, your king, council and assembly."

Hutchinson, a pious man, was astounded at such blasphemy. "Colonel Allen," he said, "you curse most horrible!"

"God damn your soul!" Ethan shouted. "Are you going to preach to us?"

The Boys drove the Todds off their place, which apparently had no shelter, and burned the lean-to Reid had erected. "New Perth" was to remain Rupert.

The immediate result of the Hutchinson affair was the outlawing of Ethan, Cochran, Baker and five others who were named in the complaint. When Governor Tryon of New York heard of it, he offered twenty pounds for the arrest of any one of the men cited. To show what he thought of it, Ethan had a copy of Tryon's reward poster put up in a prominent place in the Catamount. Then, on New Year's Day of '72 he held a review of his army, the Green Mountain Boys.

Punch and stonewalls naturally were part of the doings. It wasn't just the place for an outspoken Yorker to be, but somehow that day one Benjamin Buck of Albany happened along. His judgment must have been diluted with rum, for in the Catamount's taproom he said in a loud voice that he believed the York government was in the right in the title dispute and would doubtless get and hold all the Grants.

Before he knew what hit him, Ethan knocked Buck to the floor.

"Why, you damned bastard of old Munro's," he bellowed, referring to the Yorker justice of the peace, "we're going to make a hell of Munro's house and burn him in it—and every son of a bitch that takes his part." Buck went back to Albany and reported the assault.

It was on this same afternoon that Ethan, no doubt fairly well organized, delivered as terrible a pun as could be imagined. Someone read aloud Governor Tryon's name on the reward proclamation. Said Ethan, addressing the governor as if he were present: "So your name is Tryon. Well, try on and be damned to you."

It is one of Ethan Allen's lines Vermont would like to forget.

His next move, however, had real humor in it. He drew up a poster offering a reward of fifteen pounds for the apprehension of James Duane and ten pounds for John Kempe, both New York officials. He termed them "common disturbers" of the public peace and repose of the "honest Peasants of Bennington." Payment of the reward was on condition that Duane and Kempe be delivered at the Catamount Tavern. The poster was signed by Ethan, Remember Baker, and Robert Cochran, all outlaws.

The reward poster was printed at Hartford and given wide distribution on the Grants and elsewhere. Backwoodsmen laughed fit to kill at the idea of two dignified Yorker officials with a price on their heads, but no one got a chance to collect the reward: Duane and Kempe continued to direct their end of the campaign from Albany.

The Governor of New York's offer of reward for capture of Ethan Allen, Remember Baker, Robert Cochran, and five other Green Mountain Boys, however, brought at least one attempt to collect. Baker lived with his family at Arlington. Early in the morning of March 21, 1772, a gang of men led by John Munro, who has been mentioned, broke into the sleeping house.

Surprised and outnumbered but game, Baker reached for a broadax and laid about him. In the battle his hand was so badly cut by a sword that he could no longer hold the ax. Dropping it, he rushed upstairs, tore off some boards, and leaped. The snowdrift in which he landed was deep, and he could not free himself. Meanwhile, Mrs. Baker and her small son had been slightly injured in the affray. Tossing Baker into a sleigh, the party started for New York and the twenty-pound reward, leaving Mrs. Baker naked and bleeding on the floor.

But Arlington had heard the uproar, and soon men on horseback, on foot, and in sleighs were in pursuit. They caught up with the Munro posse at Sancoick, and the kidnapers (or honest supporters of the law—whichever way you look at it) fled, leaving Baker on the snow. Half frozen and weak from loss of blood, he was taken back to his home.

The Baker episode gave Ethan Allen just what he needed, and he was quick to use it. Here was a first-class atrocity story, something to pump the blood faster through the arteries of folks on the Grants, something to raise even the faint-hearted to a fighting pitch. For the *Connecticut Courant*, a paper that always gave a friendly ear to the wrongs of the Grants, Ethan wrote a series of harrowing letters and blistering editorials. Syntax never troubled him in the least, nor his readers, but he knew how to make his point.

Applying the adjective "massacreing" to the Governor of New York, he termed the Governor's councilors "mercenary, monopolizing men, an infamous fraternity of diabolical plotters," and went on to ask: "When New York by the handle of jurisdiction, aim at the property of the inhabitants [of the Grants], and that flagrantly can they expect obedience?" The answer, it seemed, was a thousand times no. Then he brought in the sure-fire effect of the loved ones. "Women sobbing and lamenting," he wrote, "Children crying and Men pierced to the heart with sorrow and indignation at the approaching tyranny of New York."

This was stuff to make men see red. Nor did Ethan forget to paint a picture of the hardships of pioneer life on the Grants. The settlers there were "hard labouring peasants" who were "cultivating a howling wilderness." Likewise, everybody living on the Grants was poor, and naturally, honest. All Yorkers were rich men and crooked as snakes. The issue was thus simplified and made clear to the dullest wit in the remotest hamlet.

To the atrocity stories and other published propaganda, Ethan now added a touch of sheer bravado. The York Governor's offer of twenty pounds for arrest of Ethan still hung in the Catamount Tavern, where it never failed to excite the laughter and scorn of New Hampshire men. One day in the spring of '72 one of Ethan's cronies, over a couple of stone-walls, wagered a bowl of punch that Ethan dared not leave a copy of his own poster, which offered a reward for York officials, in Landlord Benedict's tavern at Albany. Finishing his mug, Ethan called for his horse. He rode to Albany, hitched his horse outside the tavern, and went in. He called for a drink, handed the reward poster to the landlord and requested that it be tacked up in a prominent place. He talked a few minutes with the bar flies, then rode back to Bennington.

It was bravura, pure and simple, also great stuff for the Cause, not at all mitigated by the fact that the common people of York province were then and afterward much in sympathy with the men on the Grants. Ethan Allen was already the greatest figure in the disputed territory. His piece of show-off in the enemy's camp added a full foot to his stature and further degraded the authority of New York.

Shortly after this Ethan was nearly taken—not in New York but right on the home grounds at Bridport. He and Eli Robards, one of the Boys, were staying overnight in the cabin of one Richardson. Right after supper the house was invaded by a squad of regular soldiers, King's troops, from the near-by post of Crown Point. Someone had tipped them off, and they meant to collect the reward.

The soldiers at first pretended they didn't know who Allen was. Ethan set up a bowl of punch, and all hands drank. Ethan regaled them with tales of his hunting days, when he ran deer to earth and cut their throats, of wrestling with bears, of fighting and killing a catamount with a hunting knife. The King's troops were charmed with this lusty giant of the timber. He set up another bowl, and another. His Majesty's men did not realize what a guzzler they drank with. When he had put them safely under the table, Ethan, not even wobbly, and Robards put on their hats and disappeared into the woods.

The Grants was coming to be the liveliest place in all the Colonies. Early in May a spy brought news to Bennington that Governor Tryon himself and a large body of troops were planning to march on Bennington from Albany. Ethan called the Boys. He sent brother Ira to spy at Albany and report back the number of troops to be expected, then prepared an ambush. Ira returned with the news that it was all a false alarm; the soldiers were on their way to Detroit, not Bennington.

Governor Tryon, in fact, was about to try diplomacy instead of the force that seemed to be getting him nowhere. He dispatched a conciliatory letter to the Reverend Jedediah Dewey and other leading inhabitants of Bennington. He asked the townsmen to send any three Bennington men—that is, anybody except Allen, Baker, and Cochran—to New York City

Fort Ticonderoga was taken, the first British post to fall.

to confer on a peaceable settlement of the controversy. Then he went on to "suggest" persons he would like to see on the committee. James Breakenridge, Stephen Fay, and Mr. Dewey, he said, would be highly acceptable.

Leaders on the Grants met at Bennington to consider the letter. They decided they would pick their own committee and named Stephen Fay and his son Jonas, the "doctor and sur-rurgeon." They then drew up a letter expressing a desire for peaceful settlement; yet the tone of the note was firm: it indicated that the settlers felt they should not be made to pay for their farms a second time. They did not intend to pay for confirmatory titles from New York, nor to be driven from their lands by force. The letter closed by speaking politely but vaguely of "submitting to your Excellency's jurisdiction" and asked for his "friendly disposition."

Ethan had been expressly barred from serving on the committee, but he saw a chance for further propaganda. He prepared a long letter which was signed by himself and the two other outlaws—Baker and Cochran. Beginning with an assertion of an intent to yield a "reasonable submission" to the Governor, it went on to say flatly that New York was attempting an unconstitutional exercise of its jurisdiction, that a "set of artful, wicked men are concealing the truth from your Excellency" (by which he paid his respects to Duane and Kempe). He pointed out that the controversy could be settled only by the King, to whom settlers on the Grants had sent a remonstrance, and not by any Province. He let his imagination, which was great, have full play in calling attention to the "fifteen hundred families" who had brought their farms out of a wilderness state into fruitful fields, gardens, and orchards. He closed on a rather stern note, saying that "no tyrannical exertions of the powers of government can deter us from asserting and vindicating our undoubted rights and privileges as Englishmen."

The committee of the two Fays left for the trip to New York.

Presently word came to Bennington via the Green Mountain Boys grapevine that William Cockburn was loose on the Grants again. He was the Yorker surveyor the Boys had driven out of Socialborough the year before. "Well, God damn his malicious, insignificant soul," remarked Ethan Allen, "will he have more of us?"

Peace or no peace, Cockburn should not be permitted to carry on his devilish work on the Grants. Ethan, Baker, Seth Warner, and a party of the Boys hit out for the north.

> *"My authority is this gun. I've run these woods these seven years past and never was catched yet."*

CHAPTER IV

Green Mountain Outlaw

———— ••• ————

A lot of tall timber covered the New Hampshire Grants in 1772. Ethan and his posse knew only that Surveyor Cockburn was up there in the wilderness, somewhere, between the east shore of Lake Champlain and the Green Mountains. Because of a proprietor's natural liking to view with his own eyes, Ethan selected a route that would take the party near the mouth of Otter Creek, where two years before he had purchased five hundred acres from Benning Wentworth, at five cents an acre. Other Connecticut men had purchased surrounding lands from New Hampshire.

In order to hold these lands—to prove up, as it was later called—the proprietors had hired a few families to live on the ground and do a little clearing. These settlers had put up a few cabins and built a sawmill.

Over in New York Province, and at approximately the same time, Colonel John Reid, late commander of His Majesty's 42nd Regiment of Foot, had acquired the same land under a New York title. To hold what he thought was *his* land, Reid had come in with several families and had driven off the settlers of the New Hampshire claimants. Reid also erected a gristmill.

Now, in 1772, came Ethan Allen and his party looking for Surveyor Cockburn, but also ready to do anything else to clear the Grants of Yorkers. They proceeded to drive Colonel Reid's families off the claim. Ethan mildly suggested that if they returned, they should be burned to death in their cabins. He then had the millstones broken in two.

Continuing north the posse finally discovered Cockburn and his gang of surveyors, running lines in the Onion River * country. They captured Cockburn in Bolton, broke his compass and chains, appropriated his supplies, and took him to Castleton a prisoner. Ethan was about to hold a drumhead court when news came from Bennington that the Fays had returned from New York with a message of truce and conciliation on the land controversy. Cockburn was immediately turned loose, with a severe admonition, and Ethan and his party went to Bennington.

The Fays had indeed brought happy tidings. They reported they had been treated with the greatest courtesy in New York, and they brought a letter from Governor Tryon. Landlord Fay, standing on a platform in the Catamount's yard, read it to the largest assembly Bennington had ever seen. It recommended that the claimants under New York titles suspend all civil suits involving these lands until the Crown had made its pleasure known. It stated that all criminal prosecutions against the leaders of the Grants should be suspended during the same period. There should be no more dispossessions, or threats of such. What the Governor proposed, in short, was an armistice.

Most if not all of the assembled "peasants" were jubilant. In any case they voted unanimously to approve the governor's plan. The remainder of the day was spent in firing

* Now the Winooski River.

salutes "by the whole Artillery of Bennington," which consisted of one old mortar, while punch and stonewalls oozed happily down the throats of a notable gathering of drinking men.

The feeling of peace was soon shattered. The tenants of Colonel Reid, ousted by Ethan and his party while the Fays were in New York on their mission, had reported the outrage to Governor Tryon and had garnished the report with numerous "atrocities," alleged or real. That much-harassed gentleman dispatched an angry letter to the Bennington people, terming the ruckus a breach of faith and honor and demanding immediate reinstatement of the evicted settlers.

The Governor's letter put the New Hampshire leaders on a spot. If they gave in and re-established the Yorker Reid's tenants, they would lose faith with their followers, who were ever ready to jump with what appeared to be the strongest wind. If they didn't give in—well, the tone of the Governor's letter was threatening and indicated that force would be used.

Ethan Allen had had considerable practice in the art of writing in recent months. He soon had a reply for the Governor. He stated that the dispossession of Reid's tenants had been made before the truce had been made known in Bennington and ratified. The record indicates this to have been so. Ethan then turned the tables on Tryon by saying that settlers were bound to defend their property, and that acceptance of the truce was conditional on the cessation of any attempts by New York to make further settlements or *surveys* until the King had been heard from—a subtle inference that Cockburn had been caught red-handed in breaking the truce.

As to re-establishing Colonel Reid's tenants, he wrote, that was manifestly impossible, for Reid had "violated all of the laws, restrictions and economy, both of God and Man"—

which was typical Allen bombast, and was good propaganda for home consumption, too.

And there he left the matter, in the Governor's lap.

Although the Governor of New York may not have known it, the leading men of the Green Mountain Boys had become heavily interested in land titles on the New Hampshire Grants. Ethan had purchased those five hundred acres on Otter Creek in 1770. At about the same time, Ira, youngest of the Allens, who had worked hard at dressing and selling deerskins down in Connecticut, and had saved his money, bought several proprietor's rights in Poultney. A year later Ira and an unnamed partner, who was undoubtedly Remember Baker, bought no less than 10,000 acres in Hubbardton, for which they paid a total of sixty-four pounds. These were only the beginnings of the speculations of Green Mountain Boys.

A similar condition prevailed in New York. The individual grantees were only the nominal parties—the front, so to speak —in the recent ejectment suits. The real parties to the controversy were claimants to most of what is now western Vermont and included, as already shown, high officials and even judges before whom the trials were held—men like Kempe, Duane, and Livingston.

Nothing can be clearer, and less surprising, than that the leading spirits on both sides were those who owned, or claimed, the most land. If the tough speculators of New Hampshire couldn't make their titles stick, all was lost; likewise, if New York's wealthier and more influential claimants permitted such titles to hold, then they had lost everything. The issue was clear enough to the vitally interested parties. Whether or not the actual settlers of the land realized the true condition of things will never be known. It didn't matter much, anyway, for settlers counted for little. All depended on who were the more forceful and resourceful leaders.

The boss men of the Green Mountain Boys were rude and

uncultured backwoods "peasants," but they understood clearly what they had to do: truce or no, all Yorkers must be kept off the Grants.

Shortly after Ethan had dispatched his reply to Tryon's letter, Ira Allen, Remember Baker, and three other men were doing some landlooking along the Onion River when they crossed the trail of a new menace. This turned out to be Benjamin Stevens and party, who had surveying chains and a compass in their possession and had brought along a store of supplies large enough to indicate they had a lot of work to do.

This Stevens was a tough and hardy chap, a man to take no threatening talk from anybody, selected by New York proprietors to take the place of Cockburn, who had had enough of trying to run lines on the Grants. In addition to his party, Stevens had engaged a few Indians as bodyguards.

Ira, Baker, and the three other Boys drove off the redskins. They took Stevens and party into camp after a rough-and-tumble fight, during which one of the Yorkers fell or was thrown into a fire and injured. In the progress of the scrap guns were pointed but not fired. The Green Mountain Boys now tied their captives to trees and sat around a good while, drinking the surveyors' rum and debating audibly the efficacy of slow roasting as a way to discourage surveyors from foreign parts. The Yorkers begged hard. They were turned loose and sent on their way with bloodcurdling threats in their ears. The Boys appropriated their supplies, including "5 gal of Jamaca Sperits," and got potted as so many owls.

From Bennington, Ethan continued to send sizzling articles for publication in the *Connecticut Courant* of Hartford, calling York officials all the names the *Courant*'s editor would allow in print, and bidding the honest men of the Grants to be of stout heart.

And now Ira Allen, very young but already the slickest trader in the backwoods, proposed a business scheme. He and

Baker, as related, had done much landlooking along the Onion River and had been charmed at what they found there —broad, rich intervales without a tree, fit for farming at once; much level ground; and where the Onion flowed into Lake Champlain, a fine harbor. Ira proposed to his cousin Baker and brothers that they form a company to secure these lands —the best on the Grants, he said—and go into the land business.

When it was first broached, Ethan was against it. He owned perhaps a thousand acres already, and that seemed enough. Besides, he was being vastly entertained by his battle of wits and force with the Province of New York. Ira argued well. He got Ethan to make a trip with him through the lands in question and talked his idea incessantly. It would be a family company. They would first get hold of these lands—which could be done cheaply; then they would survey, divide, advertise, and sell such of the property as they did not wish to hold, for farms.

Ethan was never by inclination a business man, and Ira must have painted a rosy future, for the tall brother finally gave in. Sometime during the winter of 1772–1773, Ethan, Heman, Zimri, and Ira, all brothers, and Remember Baker, first cousin, organized what was first called Ethan Allen & Company but seems to have been referred to always as the Onion River Company.

It was planned to build a road to the property, as soon as it had been acquired, then to erect sawmills, gristmills, a store, and possibly a fort. Ira knew surveying. He would run the lines. When all was ready—or almost ready—they could begin advertising farms for sale.

First thing to do was to get possession of the lands, especially the choice lands bordering the lake, held by Edward Burling of White Plains, New York. They would have to see him.

In New York, just then, Ethan Allen was worth twenty

pounds to anyone who would take him to a sheriff. (The truce had been considered broken by the Cockburn, Reid, and Stevens incidents.) So was Remember Baker. Twenty pounds would be a fortune to almost any informer. So, Ethan and Remember rigged themselves up for the trip as British army officers. Heman Allen went along, too, but not in company with the others. He often made trips to New York in his business as trader and had no fear of constables. Ira decided he would go as a British officer, too.

The three disguised men put up at a tavern in White Plains. Heman got into touch with Burling, arranged a secret meeting, and the Company purchased all of Burling's holdings. Little money could have changed hands, for the Company had little, but land deals in those days were pretty much on the cuff.

When the business was done and they were ready to strike out for home, Ethan could not resist letting the damned Yorkers know he, the outlaw, had been among them. Said he to a peddler who was about to leave the tavern for New York City: "You might inform your governor that Ethan Allen has enjoyed a pleasant few days in his goddamned province."

All Yorkers in the taproom were astounded that the noted outlaw was among them, but before the Law could be assembled, the officials of Ethan Allen & Company were riding into the Connecticut hills.

There was more land buying to be done before the Company had what it wanted. On the route home to the Grants the real estaters stopped with Benjamin Ferry, a Quaker preacher, who was astonished at the weapons his visitors were carrying. "And what does thee do with those things?" he asked. They replied they were not for use among friends but to "protect our persons and property against the unjust claims of the land jobbers of New York," which was one way of scattering propaganda. They purchased certain of the old Quaker's rights in the town of Shelburne, and more lands from one Elijah Doty.

Ethan and Baker now rode on to Salisbury, while Ira went to Judeah. He wanted to rid himself of some poor lands he had acquired—on a note, of course—from Samuel Averill, who lived in Judeah, and at the same time get possession of some Onion River rights owned by Averill. Mr. Averill wasn't at home but was expected late that night. Slick Ira laid his plans. He talked much of Onion River lands to Mrs. Averill, telling the old lady that he was preparing to build a road through the lands, and that he had come to collect Averill's just share of the cost, which would be great, due to the rough terrain and heavy timber.

While he talked, Ira noted the interior of the Averill house and saw it was not plastered. What happened next is best told in Ira's own account:

"Of course," he related, "it would not be hard to hear from one room to another. I therefore wished to get to bed before Mr. Averill got home; as I expected some dialogue would arise between Mr. and Mrs. Averill concerning me. To effect this I grew sleepy—it was noticed by Mrs. Averill—I was soon sleepy again—Mrs. Averill kindly invited me to go to bed."

To bed Ira went, and there he lay, as awake and alert as a nighthawk. At about two o'clock old Averill, who must have been something of a rounder, came home, and he and his wife, thinking Ira fast asleep, discussed what to do about the lands. "I learned all the secrets," Ira says, "and went quietly to sleep."

In the morning, of course, Ira was in no hurry to deal with Mr. Averill. He played his cards and waited, meanwhile stressing how much it was going to cost to build the road into the Onion River country. Sure enough, late in the afternoon old Averill came to his milk; he not only gave Ira back his note but for the "priviledge" of being allowed to do so, gave Ira a premium of ten rights to lands in Middlesex—right where Ira wanted land to round out the Company's holdings. "Thus," gloated he, "I got ten rights of land without paying one shilling."

Ethan Allen & Company, commonly known as the Onion River Company, was getting under way.

While Ira was in Judeah playing sleepy and getting land, Ethan and Baker were selling lots on Onion River to Salisbury citizens. They sold several hundred acres that winter to Thomas Chittenden who, significantly enough, was to play a big part in the row with New York. Jonathan Spafford and Abijah Pratt also bought farm lands from the Company. The customers agreed to start clearing their lands within a year and to employ three men constantly at the business, except in winter.

Now, in advertisements in the *Connecticut Courant*, Ethan Allen & Company announced they owned 45,000 acres of Onion River land which contained broad treeless intervales—an obvious inducement to settlers. Using imagination a bit, this pioneer "development" company went on to say: "Little or no timber is growing thereon, except a few scattering buttonwood, elm and butternut trees. The land rises from the intervale, in graceful oval hills, and spreads into swails of choice mowing ground. There is no tract of land of so great quantity Between New York and the Government of Canada, that in a state of Nature can justly be denominated equally Good.* A number of men are already gone to cut a Road to the premises from the Otter Creek which is about twenty miles, and a Settlement will forthwith be carried into execution. . . . N.B. Said purchase and settlement is Insured on a

---

* An additional reason for buying these lands, which appeared in some of the advertisements, was that the Onion River abounded "with a diversity of sorts of excellent Fish particularly the Salmon."

title derived from under the Great Seal of the Province of New Hampshire."

That was telling New York.

If the "junto of land thieves" in Albany had really known the men they were dealing with, they might well have given up the struggle just as soon as the Onion River Company announced it had 45,000 acres of land *insured by a New Hampshire title.* The use of that "insured" in the advertisements could have nothing but a sinister connotation to anyone acquainted with Ethan Allen and his mob. And the Onion River Company soon demonstrated exactly what it meant by insured.

In the spring (1773) Ira, Baker, and a gang of men started building a road—that is, blazing a trail—from New Haven Falls on Otter Creek into the Onion River country. They had just begun the job when they got a surprise; Colonel Reid's Scotch settlers were back again on the ground Ethan had driven them from the year before. The broken stones of the gristmill had been hooped, and the mill repaired. New cabins had been built. The place looked dangerously settled. Ira sent a runner to inform Ethan, who was making his headquarters in Bennington "to manage political affairs &c" for the Onion River Company. The business of Reid's returned settlers must have come under the "&c" clause, for Ethan buckled on his sword and started north, collecting a crowd of husky young farmers on the way. Here was an insult not only to the Grants but to the Onion River Company.

"We're going on a big wolf hunt," shouted Ethan Allen.

If the men and women of the little settlement at New Haven Falls were sensitive to sounds from the woods, they must have thought, one evening soon, that hoot owls were breeding fast in the neighborhood. Hoots might have been heard to the north of them, to the south, to the east. These were the signals of the Green Mountain Boys, moving in on three sides. They burst suddenly into the several clearings, a hundred of them. Ethan called the squatters around him and told them to get their household effects out of the cabins at once if they wanted to save them. One settler, Angus McBean, said he intended to hold his house and property as they were.

"God damn your soul," Ethan told him, "if you attempt such a thing I'll tie you to this stump and skin you alive. And if I lay hands on your Colonel Reid I'm going to cut off his head." This promise was made with "evil countenance and angry gestures."

The Green Mountain Boys proceeded to burn every cabin flat. They pulled down the gristmill, and this time broke the stones into small particles and heaved them into the creek. Ethan then sent the squatters (if that is what they were) on their way with a brief but positive warning. "My authority is this gun," he said, pointing to his long rifle, "and we are a lawless mob. I've run these woods these seven years past and never was catched yet, and by God, if any of you hereafter attempt to build houses here, the Green Mountain Boys will burn them up, and whip you into the bargain." *

With the poor squatters on their way to report the outrage at Albany, Ethan and his men set to work. The Onion River Company was to fortify its domain. Felling timber right and left, and using the remnants of the gristmill, they put up a blockhouse fort. A small party was left here to be on guard should Colonel Reid and his Yorkers return.

Going on to Onion River, Ethan, after consulting with Ira and Baker, decided that forts would be a fine thing for the Company. Selecting a suitable spot near Onion River Falls,

* In his Autobiography, Ira Allen makes a typical understatement in his report on what happened to the squatters at New Haven Falls. Says he: "In the course of this Summer, Col. Ethan Allen and about one hundred Green Mountain Boys came to New Haven Falls and erected a block fort, *disconcerting* [my italics—S. H. H.] a party of Scotchmen brought out from Scotland by Col. Reed to settle there."

they went to work on another. This fort was twenty by thirty-two feet, the smallest timbers used being eight inches thick. In the second story were thirty-two portholes. The roof was so constructed that it could be thrown off entire, in case it should be fired by attackers. The second story jutted four inches over the lower, to permit firing down close to the walls. Every door was double. Heavy wood blocks were made to fit the windows. And beneath the ground floor of the fort was a fine boiling spring that looked as if it would be never-failing. "In this situation," as Ira remarked, "we were a Terror to the New York claimants &c."

Indeed they were, and the only forts in all the New Hampshire Grants were those of the Onion River Company, dealer in fine lands.

Hearing presently that a York surveyor, a new one named Gale, was at large on the Onion River domain, Ira, Baker, and a crew set out to find him. They cruised through Waterbury, Middlesex, Kingland, and across the mountains to Bradford and Haverhill on the Connecticut River, seeing signs of the Yorker's nefarious work but never catching up with his party. Stocking up at Haverhill with provisions and "sperits," the Onion River boys chased back over the mountains again, hot on Gale's track. That gentleman wanted no Twigs of the Wilderness on his back. Apprised of the posse looking for him he drove his last stake in Montpelier township and fled to New York, never to return to the Grants.

In the meantime Ethan was having his hands full with "politics &c." The town called Durham by Yorkers and Clarendon by people of the Grants had been settled largely by Yorkers who insisted, in spite of their dangerous geographical location, that they were subjects of the Province of New York. This wouldn't do at all. Ethan sat down and wrote the Durhamites what he was pleased to call a "Friendly Appistle." He said that the Green Mountain Boys would be glad to assist the Durham settlers in buying New Hampshire titles to their property.

Some of the Durhamites did purchase new titles, of New Hampshire. Others, in the majority, refused. And now Ethan gave them more rigorous treatment. He made a personal call at Durham and informed residents there that if they did not at once recognize the validity of New Hampshire, his Boys on their next visit would "reduce every house to ashes and leave every inhabitant a corpse."

This resounding statement is typical of Ethan Allen's tactics, then and later. He would rather frighten recalcitrants into submission than use actual violence. But the majority of Durhamites refused to be scared. Benjamin Spencer, a Durham judge with a New York commission, and the Reverend Benjamin Hough, Anabaptist minister, were leaders in Durham, and they were determined men. They sent word that they were staying where they were—under New York jurisdiction.

On the 20th of November, 1773, at about eleven o'clock at night, the front door of Judge Spencer's home was battered in by men using a big pine log for a ram. Colonel Allen followed the ram into the Spencer kitchen and immediately set up a shouting for "that damned old offender Spencer." Spencer got out of bed. Ordered to dress, he seemed to be taking a good deal of time. Colonel Allen whaled him lightly once over his rear to accelerate things, then took him out of the house. Spencer was held prisoner overnight in the near-by home of Thomas Green.

Next morning Judge Spencer was given a "trial." Ethan, as usual, was in the judgment seat, aided in his deliberations by such noted judges as Remember Baker and Seth Warner. Spencer was of course found guilty of "cudling with the Land Jobbers of New York." Baker and bystanders demanded that the culprit be given the Twigs of the Wilderness, the Beech Seal. Judge Allen thought this would be a bit harsh. He considered, he said, that Spencer's house was a nuisance and should be burned.

Spencer pleaded that this would put great hardship on his wife and children, who were tearfully present. Judge Allen could deal with men and be severe, but today his heart was touched by Mrs. Spencer and the children. He softened, and decreed that the Spencer roof should be removed, then replaced, and the case considered settled, provided that Spencer declare that henceforth it was a New Hampshire and not a Yorker house. Spencer agreed, and the sentence was carefully carried out, leaving the house intact. Bystanders declared Judge Allen had shown great moderation, as well as ingenuity of thought.

The Durham-Clarendon affair was the last campaign before winter. The proprietors of the Onion River Company spent the cold months in Bennington and Connecticut, selling lots and farms and tracts of land in their domain, which now had a "road" and was protected from "enemical persons" by two staunch forts. They also did some buying, getting rights in the town of Charlotte, just south on Onion River.

During the winter, too, the Governor of New York heard of the raid on Durham. He came out with an edict that was a dictator's crack-down. A gathering of three or more persons on the Grants, it said, would henceforth be prohibited and punishable by death. Officers exercising commissions of New York Province were absolved from any penalty for killing or injuring persons in the execution of the law. Moreover, the Governor now put up a "premium" of one hundred pounds each for the arrest of Ethan Allen and Remember Baker, and fifty pounds each for Seth Warner, Robert Cochran, Peleg Sunderland, Sylvanus Brown, James Breakenridge, and John Smith.

This savage statute frightened no one into compliance.

Meetings were soon held to discuss it in Manchester and Arlington. Ethan addressed the gatherings and declared the New York statute to be a "bloody law." He called for action to resist any attempt to enforce it. Then he wrote a letter to Governor Tryon which was signed by the eight proscribed men. In it he said that the makers of this Bloody Law were not only malign, but also "insatiable, avaricious, overbearing, inhuman, barbarous, and blood-guilty," which would indicate that Colonel Allen needed no thesaurus. He condemned the "legerdemain, bribery and deceptions of one sort or other" that had been used by "these designing schemers and land jockeys." And then he defied them all in classic fashion.

"Draco, the Athenian law-giver," he wrote, "caused a number of laws (in many respects analogous to those we have been speaking of) to be written in blood. But our modern Dracos determine to have theirs verified in blood. They well know we shall, more than three, nay, more than three times three hundred, assemble together, if need be, to maintain our common cause, till his Majesty determines who shall be and remain the owners of the land in contest."

Spirited as this was, Ethan was not content. He wrote a number of letters on the subject which the *Courant* was pleased to publish. He also composed his soon-to-be-famous pamphlet, "A Brief Narrative of the Proceedings of the Government of New-York." When the manuscript was ready, he set out ahorseback to Hartford to have it printed.

In the Connecticut city an attempt was made to win the New York "premium" of one hundred pounds for Ethan's arrest. One Robert McCormick and posse had laid plans to take him by force and rush him into New York in a sleigh already hired for the purpose. Someone tipped Ethan off. He walked up to McCormick on the street, accused him of the plot, and showed him a neat pair of pistols, remarking that he had been long sought by New York but that you "had to

catch a man before you could get the bounty on his head."
McCormick seems to have taken the hint.

Before long the *Courant*'s press was turning out the pamphlets. Ethan's treatise could hardly have been called conciliatory. "Inflammatory" would have been a better word, and the author must have smiled happily over the proofs as the galleys of common sense mixed with bombast and mouth-filling phrases unfolded before his eyes.

If violence plus ink could save the New Hampshire Grants and the Onion River Company, they were as good as in the bag.

> *"I wish to God America would at this critical juncture exert herself agreeable to the indignity offered her."*

CHAPTER V

Storm Breaks over Champlain

The full title of Ethan's pamphlet, in keeping with literary custom of the day, required an entire page, but with this out of the way he got right down to business. He said flatly that the New York statute—the Bloody Law—was unconstitutional and was an emblem of the inhuman disposition of the damnable Yorkers.

The pamphlet was unusual in that it admitted certain of the charges made against Green Mountain Boys by New York, but stated that these so-called lawless acts had become necessary because New York Province had put the lives and property of the people of the Grants in jeopardy and they had no recourse to law.

One section of the treatise was addressed with canny psychology not to New York officials but to the common people of that province, "our Friends and Neighbors who inhabit the lands adjacent to the New Hampshire Grants." Here Ethan held out the open hand. He touched on the mutual intercourse and trade that had made for a universal acquaintance and friendship between the two districts. So had the ties of marriage and blood relationship. He pointed out that all the trouble was over land titles, that the Grants could not expect justice from courts operated by land jobbers.

With acute understanding he divorced the common people of both regions from the magistrates, the sheriffs, constables, and other catchpoles of New York who, by strong inference, were the natural enemies of all honest men. In short, he made a rousing good case for sympathy between the countryfolk and backwoodsmen, as opposed to city slickers, on both sides of Lake Champlain.

But Author Allen showed no weakening, no desire for peace at any price. Just to make sure everyone understood exactly how the Green Mountain Boys felt about it, he displayed the mailed fist. One can actually feel the author's quickened heart action as he suddenly swings from the hand of friendship for the common people of New York to a rousing challenge to their officials. Now he vows that any Yorker attempting to lay hand on the Green Mountain outlaws will be "inflicted with *immediate death*" (which he had the printer set in italics). He goes on to say that the Grants can muster as good a regiment of marksmen and scalpers as America can produce and invites, by name, the eminent land jobbers of New York to come and view the "dexterity of our regiment."

In closing, the pamphlet proclaims undying loyalty to His Majesty's government which, as is pointed out again, is the only proper authority to settle the land dispute. Then, the invitation to fight it out by arms is extended once more. Come on, says Ethan Allen, and "take possession of our vineyards—come on, we are ready for a game of scalping; for our martial spirits glow with bitter indignation, and consumate fury, to blast their infernal projections."

This was fine swashbuckling prose, just the thing to make strong men pound their pewter mugs on taproom tables and start to cleaning the old smoothbores. And as a final piece of tinder Ethan got Thomas Rowley of Shoreham, on the Grants, to contribute a strophe. Rowley was a Green Mountain Boy and has been called "the pioneer minstrel of Vermont." He was active in most of the "riatous proceedings" of the mob and often made up narrative verses on the spot, telling of the noble deeds and great sufferings of his fellows. For Ethan's seething pamphlet Bard Rowley lifted his voice and sang of ancient Rome:

> When Caesar reignèd King of Rome
> St. Paul was sent to hear his doom;
> But Roman laws, in a criminal case,
> Must have the accuser face to face,
> Or Caesar gives a flat denial—
> But here's a law made now of late,
> Which destines man to awful fate,
> And hangs and damns without a trial.

Possibly that was not poetry, but it was simple and easy to remember and quote—the kind of stuff good propaganda is made of. So were Ethan's bombastic, sizzling phrases, couched in a combination of lurid rhetoric and homespun language.

Loading a bundle of this dynamite into a sleigh, Ethan sent his brother Levi off to Portsmouth to sell or give away the pamphlets as he could. Taking another bundle himself, Ethan headed west. On January 18, 1775, he sold a copy to Mr. Bull of Lenox, Massachusetts Colony, and left three copies with a Mr. Dibble of the same place. At Lanesboro he gave three more to a Mr. Smith. Landlord Waterman bought one; so did one Clesson. On the 20th he left twenty copies with Eben Leonard, five with Martin Powel.

He even invaded York Province, where he was still worth one hundred pounds to any bold informer, and a Mr. Dole of Albany was glad to accept four copies. Going to Bennington, he distributed them to the many Boys he found in the Catamount taproom. In Manchester he discovered a keen demand; Elijah Dewey took a dozen; and here a messenger caught up with him: Colonel Allen was wanted at once in Sunderland.

The occasion at Sunderland was the "trial" of the Reverend Benjamin Hough, the doughty Anabaptist preacher of Clarendon (Durham), where York settlers had stood on their own rights and the roof of Ben Spencer's house had been removed and replaced by the Boys.

The Spencer incident had not frightened the Reverend Mr. Hough. He had continued to serve as justice of the peace under a New York commission and had busied himself at working up opposition to the Green Mountain Boys. He had gone to Albany to report the Spencer trouble, which seems to have lost none of its atrociousness by the telling. Further, Hough had said in the hearing of Ethan's spies that he was prepared to shoot anyone who attempted to arrest him.

Captain Peleg Sunderland of the Boys had taken the preacher without a shot and now held him in the village of Sunderland for trial. Colonel Allen ceased temporarily the laying of his powder train of pamphlets and went to preside. This was considered an important trial: the parson was a man of great influence, and he must be found guilty by a full court. Seth Warner, Sunderland, Cochran, James Mead, Gideon Warren, and Jesse Sawyer served as judges with Chief Justice Allen. The crowd was large, so a show of pomp was made. The prisoner was brought in, guarded by men with drawn swords, and the farce began.

Hough spoke his piece with dignity, asking if he had ever been accused of injustice in his office as a (York) magistrate. Judge Allen replied that that had nothing to do with the

business before the court. The question was simple: Had
Hough accepted a commission from New York? He had.

Hough was naturally found guilty as hell. His back was
stripped. He was tied to a tree, and four men, spelling one
another, laid on two hundred lashes with whips made of
cord. It was the severest physical punishment inflicted by the
Green Mountain Boys. Hough's back was torn and bleeding.
A Dr. Washburn patched him up, and the judges gave him
a paper saying he had "received full punishment for his
crimes committed heretofore against his country." Then he
was put in charge of Captain Peleg Sunderland for escort into
New York Province.

Hough went directly to New York City, where he exhibited his wounds and petitioned for troops to protect loyal
Yorkers who were so unfortunate as to live on the Grants
and tried to live under New York laws. The York Council
hemmed and hawed. Hough told the Council to their faces
that he had heard Ethan Allen say that York officials were
a pack of damned cowards who dared not stand up for their
own people. Even this did not rouse the wary Yorkers. The
Council deliberated, then said they found it inexpedient just
then to spare troops for the Grants. But the Councilmen
were sympathetic: they gave the Reverend Mr. Hough permission to beg financial aid of the people of New York.

Men on the west side of the Grants met in Manchester to
discuss what they should do if New York took retaliatory
steps in the Hough affair. The meeting turned into a sort of
formal convention, the first held on the Grants, and of course
was dominated by the personality of Ethan Allen. He recited
the wrongs of the settlers, and when he had the meeting of
forty-six men at the right pitch he proposed a written compact to bind those present to defend their "liberty and property, the household gods of Englishmen." He drew up such

a compact which, among other things, called for officers of the Green Mountain Boys to see that every member of the company was equipped with "a good firelock, one pound of powder, ball or buck shot, answerable, and a good tomahawk."

These were ominous doings, high treason of the worst sort, but forty-six tough and bronzed men signed the compact, which was sent to Hartford for printing.

Author Allen went from the meeting to the job of distributing more pamphlets. He ranged down through Massachusetts, into Connecticut, and back north again. In Pittsfield he talked a long time with John Brown, an up-and-coming young lawyer who had become active in the so-called Liberty party and was working with the semisecret Committee of Correspondence which was fanning the revolt of all the Colonies against the Crown.

This brief meeting of Brown and Allen was to have stupendous results. Brown confided that he had been commissioned by the Boston Committee to take a letter to undercover agents in Canada, the idea being to find out how the Canadians felt about cutting loose from England. Brown did not know the wild country he must pass through on the trip, and he asked Ethan for a guide. That old woodsman fixed him up with two of the hardiest rangers on the Grants—Peleg Sunderland, the old Indian fighter, and Winthrop Hoit, another able Green Mountain Boy.

Before Brown and his guides left, Ethan explained that the condition on the Grants was complicated; the people there were more interested in shaking off New York than they were in shaking off George Ye Third. It would seem, too, that he discussed with Brown the great advantage to the Colonies, in case a revolt broke out, of taking the British fort at Ticonderoga. He must also have intimated to Brown that the Green Mountain Boys were likely lads to clear the Fort and Lake Champlain, too, of the British *—and incidentally, of any Yorkers who happened to be around.

Brown left on his mission to Canada. Ethan distributed more pamphlets, and on March 1 he wrote a letter to a friend, Oliver Wolcott, showing what was uppermost in his mind; he proposed nothing less than the carving of a new and independent state out of the New Hampshire Grants. It was a bold thing to propose, even in a private letter, and was the first intimation of Vermont in the making, even though Ethan then suggested no name for the new state.

Now troubles that had been brewing quietly in the eastern part of the Grants flared into a riot that made the doings of the Green Mountain Boys seem tame. At Westminster on the Connecticut River, men had met to read the resolutions of the Continental Congress sent from Philadelphia. They knew of the Boston Port Bill, the tax on tea, and other unpopular acts of His Majesty's government. They declared themselves in opposition to Parliament, and formed a Committee of Correspondence, which was the usual Revolutionary step first taken.

Westminster was the only town in all the Grants dignified, or cursed, with a King's court. A regular session of this court was about to be held. Times were hard in 1775; debtors had little with which to pay, and the shadow of the advancing sheriff and his ruinous sales could be seen by many a settler in the twenty-odd towns which did their business in Westminster.

The regular sitting of the court was scheduled for March 14, and as that day approached a group of settlers went to Judge Thomas Chandler to ask that the session be post-

---

* Brown wrote to the Boston Committee a fortnight later: ". . . the Fort at Tyconderoga must be seized as soon as possible should hostilities be committed by the Kings Troops. The people of the N. Hampshire Grants have ingaged to do this Business, and in my opinion are the most proper Persons for this Jobb."

poned. The judge replied that the one murder case on the docket should be the only one brought up, that he would postpone the civil trials. The settlers did not trust his word. They feared that, because of the state of tension then prevailing, the sheriff might bring armed forces, and the court would go ahead and hold the numerous bankrupt and other civil cases. Just to make sure, the anti-court party laid plans to take possession of the courthouse just before time for the court to convene.

News of the plan leaked. Sheriff William Paterson raised a crowd of twenty-five men in near-by Brattleboro. Armed with clubs, this doubtful posse set out for Westminster on the 13th, enlisting more pro-court men on the march. At least fourteen of these new recruits were armed with muskets.

Reaching the courthouse at sunset on the 13th, Sheriff Paterson found about one hundred men of the anti-court party already in possession. They refused to come out of the building at his command. He read the riot act. "I'll give you just fifteen minutes to get the hell out of there," he said, "and if you are not out, then by God, I'll blow a lane through you."

Men of the Grants refused to take that kind of talk, even from a sheriff, and the men of the Westminster towns in particular had little use for law in any of its vile forms. From inside the building Charles Davenport, a carpenter, gave the proper reply. "It will take us just fifteen minutes," he shouted, "to send you and your party to hell."

The reply was none too brilliant, but it gave the sheriff pause. He and his party withdrew to John Norton's tavern, where they drank heavily of punch while they discussed strategy.

Early in the evening Judge Chandler went to the courthouse, where the defenders complained to him that the sheriff had brought arms, contrary to the promise of the judge. To this Chandler replied that the arms had been brought without his approval. He said that the sheriff's party should be disarmed, and he promised the men in the courthouse that they might remain there until morning, without molestation. He would see that the sheriff made no attempt to evict them.

Leaving a small guard within the building—just in case—the rest of the anti-courters returned to their homes. All might have gone well had it not been for the strong punch of John Norton. At about eleven o'clock, after imbibing over a period of four hours, the drunken deputies set out in small parties to attack the courthouse from all sides. It was to be a surprise.

But "a waning moon, tipping their bayonets as they marched," had warned a sentry. He roused the sleeping men, who appear to have been armed only with clubs.

The sheriff staggered up the steps. The sentry pushed him away. Again he lurched to the platform. This time he was not only pushed but clubbed good and plenty. He stepped back and commanded his men. "Fire," he said. "God damn you, fire!"

A volley roared out, and William French, young man of Brattleboro, went down in the courthouse with a ball through his head and four other wounds.* Daniel Houghton fell, to die later from loss of blood. Ten other defenders of the

---

* French was buried across the road from the courthouse, and his grave soon became a shrine of Revolutionary patriotism. Says the marker: "In Memory of WILLIAM FRENCH, Son of Mr Nathaniel French, Who was Shot at Westminster March ye 13th, 1775, by the hands of Cruel Ministerial Tools of Georg ye 3rd, in the Corthouse at 11 a Clock at Night in the 22nd year of his Age." Below this inscription are a few lines, possibly by Bard Thomas Rowley:

> Here William French his Body lies
> For Murder his Blood for Vengance cries
> King Georg the Third his Tory crew
> tha with a bawl his head Shot threw.
> For Liberty and his Country's Good
> He lost his Life his Dearest blood.

building were wounded. All casualties were on one side.

News traveled fast and in all directions that night. Next day at least two hundred men, mostly anti-courters, arrived from New Hampshire Province, and Captain Robert Cochran marched into town at the head of a hundred Green Mountain Boys from the western side of the Grants.

And where was Colonel Allen during this excitement and bloodletting? He was somewhere in Connecticut or Massachusetts, conducting a word-of-mouth campaign against New York and all it contained, and distributing his pamphlets. On March 15 he went to a meeting, apparently the first, of the Onion River Company's board of directors in Sheffield, Connecticut. Heman, Zimri, and Ira Allen and Remember Baker were present, a full board.

Although the bookkeeping was rather vague, the directors figured that the Company had sold 16,793 acres of land, and still held rights to 60,289 acres. The costs of printing Ethan's violent pamphlet were, significantly enough, charged to the Onion River Company. Fort Ticonderoga must have been discussed at the meeting, for directly afterward Heman Allen went to Hartford and told the Committee of Correspondence there that it could be seized by Green Mountain Boys.

After the Onion River Company's meeting, Ethan ranged over into York Province again, distributing pamphlets in Spencertown. No effort was made to take him and claim the reward. Hearing now of the bloody doings at Westminster and of a convention to be called there to discuss the "massacre," he hurriedly crossed the mountains. Although he was from the west side of the Grants and could have no vote in the Westminster doings, he was put on a committee to draft a remonstrance against New York courts; and his hand is to be seen in the document which, among other things, asks that the Grants "be taken out of so oppresive a jurisdiction, and

Reverend Hough was escorted into New York Province.

either annexed to some other government or erected and incorporated into a new one."

Vermont wasn't in the bag yet, but it was taking shape.

Before the Westminster convention was over, word arrived that the King's troops had marched on Lexington and
Concord and had killed honest farmers. Ethan Allen jumped
on his horse and rode like the wind to Landlord Fay's in Bennington. The taking of Ticonderoga followed.

There, for a brief moment, American History paused long
enough to catch the picture of a tall man on the barrack
stairs, waving a sword and shouting one lurid sentence fit to
echo from schoolbooks and Fourth of July orations with the
best that America has to offer. Then, the mists close round
the tall man, and he is seen no more on the great pages of
history. This is regrettable. Colonel Ethan Allen was just beginning his career.

News of the capture of the British forts at Ticonderoga
and Crown Point sent a thrill through all the Colonies. It was
the first attack on the Crown. Moreover Ticonderoga, with
its long and bloody history of battle, was by far the most
noted fortress in the Colonies. Its fall proved something many
good patriots had doubted; namely, that Americans could
match arms with their rulers.

Many historians have attempted to belittle the taking of
Ticonderoga as a military engagement. They point out that
the fort was manned by fewer than fifty soldiers, that it was
in no condition to stand much of an assault. They conven-
iently forget that the place was garrisoned by *trained* troops,
that it contained efficient cannon and plenty of ammunition.
They overlook the fact—which was well known—that in
1758 the French General Montcalm with a skeleton force
easily held Ticonderoga against Abercrombie and fifteen

thousand British regulars, routing them four ways from the middle, with terrible losses. Old Ti had the reputation of being impregnable. In May of 1775, moreover, it was a bold man who would touch property of the Crown.

The Crown's property at Ticonderoga totaled fourteen mortars, two howitzers, and forty-three cannon of bores up to 5½ inches. Their total weight was 119,000 pounds. There was an unrecorded amount of powder in the magazine, ten tons of musket and cannon balls, and "three cartloads of flints." The warehouse was filled with material for building boats. In December following, General Henry Knox, the artilleryman, on Washington's orders reached Ticonderoga to remove the cannon and stores to Boston. By the 6th everything had been moved by scows to the head of Lake George. There the General stopped while his troops, able men with axes, whacked forty-two sleds out of green timber, hired or stole eighty-one yoke of oxen, and began the trek overland to Cambridge in the dead of a fierce winter. On January 24 the General arrived at Washington's camp with his "noble train of artillery." It was a military feat of the first class, this sledding of fifty-nine cannon a distance of two hundred miles through deep timber and snows—a feat worthy of more room than most histories have accorded it.

General Washington promptly set up the Ticonderoga cannon on Dorchester Heights and blew the British out of Boston.

Whether those cannon and that fort were taken in the name of the Great Jehovah and the Continental Congress is a matter of some importance in Vermont one hundred and sixty-five years after the event. The expression attributed to Colonel Allen did not appear in print until nearly four years later, when Ethan himself wrote his narrative of the affair. Lieutenant Feltham, the trouserless officer who met Ethan on the stairs, did not mention the resounding expression in his report made shortly after his capture. This is not surprising, for Feltham, even had he heard it, would not have known what the Continental Congress was. And in any case such an obviously fancy remark would have had no place in a sober military report. British army officers were rigidly conventional. The "Great Jehovah" was not in their decalogue of war.

Many years after the event Israel Harris, who died in 1836 aged ninety, and had been with Ethan at the surrender, said that the only mention he heard of Jehovah at the time was in eight or ten horribly blasphemous and unprintable oaths that rolled from Colonel Allen's lips and fairly stunned all within earshot.

On the other hand, most of the men who had been present were still living in 1779, when Ethan's account of the affair appeared, and old soldiers are notoriously argumentative about the minor points of battles in which they have taken part. None seems to have disputed the Colonel's own tale.

The expression, too, has the quality of Ethan at his very best, and is comparable to his "The Gods of the hills" and certain lesser known but equally lurid lines. It is to be regretted that wars in those days had to be fought without newsreels and stenographers; but there can be no doubt that Ethan Allen independently planned the fort's capture and carried it out successfully in his own way, regardless of the backing of Jehovah and Congress.

It is doubtful that anyone else than Colonel Allen could have taken Ticonderoga with the undrilled and poorly equipped forces at his command. They were nothing less or more than a mob of hunters, trappers, farmers, and itinerant woodsmen who had no regard for formal discipline. The only man to lead them was he who could roar louder, drink more, jump higher, and spit farther than any man on the claim—a man whom horned devils could not frighten.

Ethan Allen qualified in all these matters, and in more besides; his daring did not stop short of recklessness. With the two forts subjugated, he began laying plans to invade Canada and capture the city of Montreal.

Lake Champlain is ninety miles long. Ticonderoga, now sobering up late in May of 1775, was at the south end. At the far northern end, on the Sorel River, was the post of St. Johns, held by a garrison of British regulars and re-enforced by an armed sloop of war. Colonel Allen, Colonel Arnold, and Captain Warner held a council of war, and Arnold was commissioned to sail north in a schooner the Green Mountain Boys had captured at Skenesborough, surprise and capture the sloop, then take the garrison. Colonel Allen was to support the venture with a hundred men in bateaux.

Arnold provisioned the schooner, named her *Liberty*, loaded her with armed men, and sailed down the lake. Ethan's flotilla of bateaux left a day later, sailing when they could and rowing all the time; but strong head winds delayed them, and they were not in time for the action. Arnold had taken the sloop without a shot and was sailing back up the lake with his prize in tow. He hove to, and Colonel Allen went aboard. Arnold told him he had the St. Johns garrison of one sergeant and twelve men below in irons.

First thing the two commanders did was to drink "several loyal Congress healths." Then—it must have come to him mighty suddenly—Ethan declared that he and his party would continue on to St. Johns and hold it against any possible re-enforcements from Canada. Arnold tried to talk him out of the plan, saying that St. Johns was of no importance so long as Americans controlled the lake.

Colonel Allen would not listen, but sailed on for the deserted British outpost. He had hardly arrived when he learned that two hundred of the King's regular troops were approaching from Montreal. Knowing that his crowd of ninety farmers and hunters, equipped mostly with hunting arms, would be no match for such an army, he crossed the Sorel River and pitched camp on the shore. All was quiet through the night, but morning brought action enough. Setting up six fieldpieces on their side of the river, the British awakened the Green Mountain Boys with a salvo of grape that sent them sailing up the lake as fast as wind and oars would take them. It was a complete rout, the first the Boys had ever known, even though Ethan tried to make light of it in a private letter to Captain Noah Lee in which he remarked that "we were met with a Cannonading of Grape Shot the Musick was both Terrible and Delightfull."

The attempt on St. Johns was cockeyed from beginning to end, and the blame must rest on Colonel Allen. It was glory hunting of the worst sort.

Back at Fort Ti, Ethan, Arnold, and their council of war met to consider a plan to fortify the small Isle aux Noix, in Lake Champlain some ten miles south of St. Johns. Before any decision had been reached a messenger arrived from the Continental Congress at Philadelphia with what was perhaps as startling an order as a commander in the field ever received. Congress ordered the immediate removal of cannon and stores from Ticonderoga to the south end of Lake George. Startling enough, in Colonel Allen's eyes, but not nearly so startling as the reason for removal.

The Continental Congress seemed to be hedging on the war. It wanted the cannon removed so that they "might be safely returned to His Majesty" when—not *if*—the "former Harmony" between Great Britain and the colonies, "so ardently wished for by the latter," rendered it consistent with the "law of self-preservation."

The feelings of Colonel Ethan Allen can be imagined—the leader whose men had taken this fort, these cannon, and who had believed that a war was on. Was this so-called Congress a meeting of Americans, or was it a collection of British catchpoles, scared lest they offend the "cruel ministerial tools of Georg ye 3rd"?

Colonel Allen blew up like a siege mortar. "The dilly-dally bastards!" tradition has it he exclaimed when he read the order. "By God, we're giving nothing back to the British except blow for blow." He fumed sulphurously awhile, then sat down and wrote a long letter to Congress, tempering his language but pointing out clearly that the colonies should at once prosecute the war "more vigorous," and proposing that an army of two or three thousand men be sent to capture Montreal. He let his scorn of fence-straddling show in one sentence. "It is bad policy," he wrote, "to fear the resentment of an enemy." Congress doubtless had wiser men than Ethan Allen, but none so resolutely bold and ready to risk his head.

The commandant sealed his letter and sent it. He remarked over a bowl of punch that he would be god-damned a thousand times before he would move a cannon out of Fort Ti for return to the Crown. He let the guns remain where they were. Not even under orders would he be party to a half-war.

Congress did not reply to his letter, and so he tried again. This time he attempted to rouse the Congress to his own pitch of enthusiasm, and he also made a specific proposal.

"I wish to God," he wrote, "America would at this critical juncture exert herself agreeable to the indignity offered her by a tyrannical ministry. She might rise on eagles wings, and mount up to glory, freedom and immortal honor, if she did but know and exert her strength. Fame is now hovering over her head. A vast continent must now sink to slavery and poverty, bondage and horror, or rise to unconquerable freedom, immense wealth, inexpressible felicity, and immortal fame. I will lay my life on it, that with fifteen hundred men, and a proper artillery, I will take Montreal."

What Colonel Allen wanted was a war with more action in it, and that is exactly the kind of war he was shortly to get.

> *"I perceived that this would be a day of trouble, if not of rebuke."*

CHAPTER VI

Jehovah Holds Montreal

While Arnold sailed up and down the lake in his new navy, Colonel Allen and other officers at Ticonderoga became restless at the inaction of a Congress which seemed bent on doing nothing that might offend the King whom they already had repudiated. Ethan wrote a letter to the French-Canadians in Canada asking for neutrality, if they were not prepared to fight on the side of the Colonies. "Pray let old England and the Colonies fight it out," he said, "and the Canadians stand by and see what the arm of flesh can do."

Benedict Arnold also did some writing. Not proved to be his, but attributed to him by historians, is a letter signed "Veritas" which soon appeared in Connecticut papers. Veritas asserted that Arnold was the real leader of the Ticonderoga expedition, and that Colonel Easton, Allen's second in command, did not enter the fort at the time of the capture, but skulked in the rear.

Colonel Allen took no part in the controversy. The fort was taken, and now it was time to carry on the war "more vigorous." Talking it over with Easton, Warner, and others at Ticonderoga, he thought the thing to do was to put a bee under the tail of Congress. A regiment of Green Mountain Boys, well equipped, could capture or drive the British out of Canada, he thought. But it must be done speedily.

The backwoods Colonel could not wait for routine action of a Congress that seemed not to know what it wanted, anyway. With Seth Warner he set out for Philadelphia by way of Bennington.

Legend has it that the two men arrived in Bennington on a Sunday, when the Reverend Jedediah Dewey was to preach a sermon of thanksgiving for the capture of Ticonderoga. It must have taken something like that to get Ethan into a church at all. The Reverend Mr. Dewey, like most preachers of the time, was noted for his interminable prayers. On this occasion he got into an uncommonly long one, praising God over and over again for His bounty in the matter of Fort Ti.

Colonel Allen, who undoubtedly had stopped at the Catamount for a nip to help him through the long session, interrupted the prayer. "Parson Dewey," he growled, "aren't you going to tell the Lord about me being there, too?" The old preacher looked up. "Ethan Allen," he bellowed, "thou great infidel, be quiet!"

The "great infidel" and Seth Warner went on to Philadelphia, where they appeared before Congress on June 23. Ethan stated his proposal to raise a regiment of Green Mountain Boys for service with the Continental army, and retired from the floor.

Congress must have caught at least a little of the boundless enthusiasm of the tall man from the Grants. It authorized pay for those who had taken part in the Ticonderoga expedition, just as though they had been regularly enlisted. It authorized organization of a regiment from the Grants to serve under officers chosen by its members. This provision was suggested by John Hancock, who must have been told (possibly by Ethan Allen himself) that Green Mountain Boys would not serve except under officers of their own choice. Congress made it clear, however, that this new regiment must serve under, or at least be a part of, the New York Provincial militia. The various resolutions were then forwarded to the New York Congress, as that province's legislature was known.

Not liking the provision which brigaded them with their old enemies the Yorkers, but seeing they could hope for nothing better, Allen and Warner went to New York and on July 4, after some debate, were admitted to the legislative floor. Here were two outlaws, with rewards still officially on their heads, in the halls of the authority they had defied for five years. It was a dramatic moment when the two backwoodsmen—Warner six feet tall, Allen a giant in comparison —marched down the aisle under the curious gaze of their enemies and took their seats near the Speaker's desk.

Colonel Allen was wearing his best manners, but there was nothing of the lackey about him. He stood up like a pine tree, presented to the Speaker a list of the officers proposed for the regiment, and sat down. The legislature voted to raise the regiment as authorized by Congress.

This surprisingly cordial reception stirred Ethan Allen's generous spirit. Two weeks later he wrote the New York legislature a letter in which he reflected on the unhappy state of affairs in the past and contemplated with joy the friendship and union which had now taken place. This new condition, he said, would bring "a united resistance to ministerial vengeance and slavery." He vowed that he and Warner and the Green Mountain Boys would "retaliate this favor by wholly hazarding their lives, if needs be, in the common cause of America." He closed on a most happy note, saying that when the common cause had been won he would be ready to "settle all former disputes and grievances on honorable terms."

With everything settled, Allen and Warner started back

for the Grants. At Bennington they met one Bennett, just back from Canada, who was to have an influence on Ethan's next expedition. Ethan believed and had been preaching that both the whites and the Indians in Canada would join the Colonies in their revolt against the Crown, or would at least be neutral. Now Bennett, fresh from the ground, strengthened him in this opinion by saying that all the Canadians needed was some encouragement—the capture of Montreal, for instance.

Allen and Warner went on to Ticonderoga, recruiting for the new regiment along the way. A meeting of the various town committees was called for July 26 in Cephas Kent's tavern, at Dorset on the Grants, to elect officers up to the rank of lieutenant colonel. The colonel, New York had ruled, was to be named by General Philip Schuyler, who was to command all the New York militia.

The result of the Dorset military election must have been a surprise to everyone. Seth Warner was named lieutenant colonel by a vote of 41 to 5; and Samuel Safford, major, by 28 to 17. Heman Allen was made a captain; Ira Allen, a lieutenant. The name of Ethan Allen was not mentioned in the balloting.

It was a terrible blow to the man who had led the Boys in raid after raid on the Yorkers, who had led the attack on Fort Ti, who had been the one great fiery spirit around whom the men of the Grants had rallied these five years.

Yet, there were several good reasons why he was not named to head the new regiment. For one thing the voting was done, not by active Green Mountain Boys, but by some fifty of the older and more sober leading citizens of the several towns. Many of these were pious men who had often been shocked by Ethan Allen the scoffer. He most certainly was a heretic if not an infidel to farmers who couldn't have told a deist from a shorthorn. It was a case such as has often set the orthodox herd to trampling. Again, the solid old men of the towns, considering Allen unrestrained in his enthusiasms (which assuredly he was), passed him over in favor of the able, but cautious and uninspired Warner.

General Schuyler, thinking it a foregone conclusion that Ethan would be named lieutenant colonel, had already directed his paymaster to make out a warrant to that effect; but he was relieved. He wrote to John Hancock that he had dreaded Ethan's "impatience at subordination."

The effect of the election on recruiting for the new regiment was bad. Many who had enlisted under the impression that Colonel Allen was to lead them, now sought to refuse to serve. Others who had planned to enlist now preferred to join regiments in Connecticut and New York. A cabal was formed of men who said they would serve only under Colonel Allen. A lesser man would have then and there made the raising of the regiment an impossibility, but Ethan did not commit sabotage. No skulking in his tent. He and his brothers rallied to aid Warner and his officers in recruiting. If Seth Warner had been as generous a man as Ethan, he might have insisted that Ethan be given some place in the regiment. But he did not. Even the beloved old name of Green Mountain Boys was dropped, and the new force appeared in the rolls of the New York militia as "Colonel Seth Warner's Regiment in the Servis of the United Colonies." *

Early in September, General Schuyler gathered his troops and began an advance on Canada. Ethan had met the General and persuaded him to take him along. He was given no com-

---

* Apparently Ethan Allen's only written comment on the election was in a letter to his friend Governor Trumbull of Connecticut: "Notwithstanding my zeal and success in my Countrys Cause the old Farmers on the Grants who do not incline to go to war . . . have wholly omited me. . . . I find myself in favour of the Officers of the army and the young Green Mountain Boys how the old men came to reject me I cannot conceive inasmuch as I saved them from the incroachments of New York."

mission, and was sent ahead of the army as a scout and propagandist. Schuyler believed with Ethan that if the French-Canadians and Indians were told that the Americans were fighting only the English and had no designs on the liberty or religion of the settlers, they would at least remain neutral, and might even help the Americans.

Scout Allen and John Brown, the Pittsfield lawyer who had been so active in the Ticonderoga expedition, took interpreters and went into the woods of Quebec Province. They advanced down the Sorel River to Chambly, telling Indians and Frenchmen alike of the all-powerful army that was coming to lay the English low. No one else had anything to fear. Americans were very brave, but kindly. They loved Indians and Frenchmen. English were enemies of all good men.

Scout Allen and his party had every reason to feel happy at their reception. The Indians reported that they really disliked the English but were kept in bondage by the free rum put out at the British garrisons. The Frenchmen were outspoken in their hatred of the redcoats. Returning up the river, the scouts found the American army encamped before the town of St. Johns, with a new general, Richard Montgomery, in command. Schuyler was ill and had returned to Albany.

The British garrison at St. Johns had dug in for a siege, and Ethan, whose small force had once been routed by this same garrison, hoped to have a hand in taking this enemy outpost. But General Montgomery had other ideas. He sent Ethan back into Quebec on another scouting trip. With him went a Captain Duggan, who seems to have been far from a resolute man, six Canadians, and a squad or two of Connecticut militia.

Preaching politics, as he called it, Scout Allen and his party went down the Sorel again. His propaganda must have been effective, for the Frenchmen flocked to join him. In four days he had raised two hundred and fifty Canadians, all armed with some sort of weapons. In fact, Ethan thought he had quite an army already and began to consider his service of supply. He appointed one Jan Minner, a farmer, to be commissary and ordered provisions, among which were bread, pork, beef, and six hogsheads of rum—which was sufficient rum, even if the liberal scale of Ticonderoga be used, to take at least three forts.

Going on to the settlement of Longueil, directly across the St. Lawrence from Montreal, he set up his headquarters. He had no commission, not even an official place in the American army, but he was feeling fine and dandy. He sat down and wrote to General Montgomery: "As I march, they gather fast. . . . You may rely on it that I shall join you in about three days, with five hundred Canadian volunteers. I could raise one or two thousand in a week's time. . . . I swear by the Lord I can raise three times the number of our Army in Canada, provided you continue the siege."

Ethan's plan was to leave a guard at Longueil and proceed with the rest of his volunteers to St. Johns, to aid with the siege.

Ten miles up the St. Lawrence was another body of scouting troops headed by Lieutenant Colonel Seth Warner and Major John Brown. They got into communication with Ethan and said they were planning an attack on Montreal. This could mean nothing in the life of the uncommissioned Allen; he had nothing to say about the disposition of troops and was on scouting and recruiting duty only. So, with about eighty men he started back to report to his general at St. Johns.

Before they had marched more than two miles they were met by Major Brown, who said he was coming to meet Ethan on a very important matter. Repairing to a farmhouse, Brown proposed that Ethan join with him to take Montreal. Ethan and his men should return to Longueil, Brown said, get canoes, and cross to the Montreal side of the St. Lawrence. At the same time, Brown and two hundred men would cross the river at Laprairie, which is above Montreal, and the two forces would attack the city simultaneously.

Although he couldn't have known it, this meeting with Brown was an evil moment in the life of Ethan Allen, probably the most disastrous meeting in his career. He liked Brown's idea. It was somewhat grandiose, to be sure, but if it worked it would make a great noise: the capital of all British Canada falling to the Colonies, and with the help of Ethan Allen. It was magnificent to contemplate. It offered that action he had felt the prosecution of the war to lack. And it ought to be rattling good fun. Scout Allen had no commission, no authority, but—well, here was the kind of thing he liked. Major Brown certainly had authority. Ethan hesitated not a moment. "Here's for Montreal, or a turf jacket," he said.

Marching his men back to Longueil as fast as they could go, he secured several canoes. As night fell, the wind rose, and the broad St. Lawrence became rough with dangerously high waves. But not high nor dangerous enough to stop Scout Allen, now turned into a combat officer with a city to take. Making three trips during the night he landed his rag-and-bobtail army safe and undiscovered on the Montreal side. They numbered one hundred and ten men, of whom ninety were Canadians, seduced for the moment by Ethan's promise of fifteenpence a day, plus a share in the plunder of Montreal.

Ethan set guards to stop all persons who were passing toward the city and thus prevent news of his approach being carried to the British garrison in the town. He also posted sentries to guard against a surprise attack and especially to listen for Major Brown's expected signal that his troops were ready for the attack. The signal agreed upon was "three loud huzzas."

The sun rose and mounted two hours high, with Ethan champing his bit and cursing most ably. No huzzas, loud or otherwise, were heard. He was out on a very long limb. Even with his unbounded enthusiasm it seemed idiotic to attempt to take the city of Montreal and its garrison with a troop of a hundred men, most of them *habitant* farmers with no battle experience.

Even the guards he had set on the road were incompetent. They had allowed a native they had stopped to escape into the town and he had gone to General Carleton, British commander, with the news that rebel Americans were advancing. The informer must have been given to exaggeration, for the General was thoroughly alarmed and began preparations to abandon the town. But a spy brought word that the rebel forces were a mere handful of farmers and backwoodsmen, and amounted to nothing. Taking courage, General Carleton collected a body of five hundred men, some of them King's troops and including several Indians, and sallied forth to meet the invaders.

Ethan himself and perhaps a third of his men could easily have recrossed the river in time to escape the vastly superior forces coming out to battle; but he knew he would not have time to move all his men, and Ethan Allen was no commander, commissioned or otherwise, to leave his troops in the lurch. "I therefore concluded," he says, "to maintain the ground if possible, and all to fare alike."

No Major Brown appeared. Rolling out a string of profanity against men who did not keep their word, Ethan picked out the strongest position he could find and prepared to give battle. When he saw the comparatively immense force advancing, he knew that this "would be a day of trouble, if not of rebuke"; but he rallied his men, telling them with incredible assurance that all they had to do was to fight bravely for a little while, that re-enforcements were on the way.

The engagement began about two in the afternoon, the British firing as they advanced. Ethan's men, or some of them, returned the fire from behind woodpiles, stumps, and from a ditch. Ethan himself ranged all along his front, cursing, praising, shouting defiance. He thought that things were pretty hot but going as well as could be expected, and that they could hold out until nightfall, then withdraw. Calling Captain Duggan, he ordered him and a detachment of fifty Frenchmen to try a flanking movement on the right of the enemy. Both Duggan and his men started—and kept going. They were never seen again.

With half his force deserted, Ethan called Richard Young, one of the volunteers, gave him ten men, and told him to flank on the left. Young and his gang made as if to do so, then completely disappeared.

The enemy's fire became thicker and closer. Bullets tore past Ethan's head, but he was not hit. The ground was coming to be covered with his men, some wounded, a few badly so. He now started a retreat but found himself wholly surrounded. A British officer closed in on him, firing a pistol shot that went close. Ethan fired back, and missed. He shouted to the officer that if he were assured of fair treatment for himself and his men he would surrender. The officer agreed. Another officer coming up just then "confirmed the treaty."

The Battle of Montreal was over—or almost. Right after he had surrendered, Ethan ordered the men left to him to ground their arms. They numbered thirty-one effectives, seven wounded. "I never," Ethan said afterward, "saw so much shooting result in so little damage." The British suffered as little.

As soon as the rebels were disarmed, an Indian of the

British forces leaped at one of the prisoners, William Stewart, and felled him with a blow of his tomahawk, cutting his head open. The savage would have finished him there, had not an officer intervened.

Nor was Ethan any safer. Just as he handed his sword to an officer, another redskin, a huge man half naked and daubed all over with war paint, came running at him with "malice death, murder and the wrath of devils and damned spirits" on his countenance. This monster was on no friendly errand, but his intended victim was ready. "In this condition," says Ethan, "I twitched the officer between me and the savage; but he flew round with great fury, trying to single me out and shoot me without killing the officer; but by this time I was near as nimble as he, keeping the officer in such a position that his danger was my defense; but in less than half a minute, I was attacked by just such another imp of hell; Then I made the officer fly around with incredible velocity, for a few seconds at a time, when I perceived a Canadian taking my part against the savages; and in an instant an Irishman came to my assistence with a fixed bayonet, and drove away the fiends, swearing by Jasus he would kill them. This tragic scene composed my mind."

With his mind so soothingly composed, Ethan was prepared to talk with his captors. One of the British officers remarked that he was happy to see Colonel Allen, to which Ethan, who hadn't lost his humor, replied that he would much rather have seen the British at General Montgomery's camp.

Now began the march of the captives into the city. His captors were most courteous. They strolled along together, discussing war, and one of the officers laughed because he had lost an eyebrow in the battle of Montreal. All went well and seemly until the captives were taken before General Robert Prescott of the British garrison.

The General, who was of the apoplectic type, looked very stern at Ethan. "Are you the Colonel Allen who took Ticonderoga?" he asked.

"I am that very man," replied the prisoner.

The General went into an immediate rage, shaking his cane at Ethan and calling him vile names. This was no way to treat an honorable prisoner of war. Ethan stepped up to the fuming officer and doubled up his great fist, which he shook under the surprised General's nose.

"By God, sir," he said, "you will do well not to cane me, for I am not accustomed to it."

At this point a staff officer, Captain McCloud, put a hand on the General's arm and cautioned him. That officer now turned his attention to thirteen of the captured men who had been identified as Canadians and therefore were the worst sort of rebels. He ordered a sergeant and men to come forward with fixed bayonets and to kill the rebel Canadians.

This was contrary to treaty. "It cut me to the heart to see them in so hard a case," says Ethan, "in consequence of their having been true to me." They were wringing their hands and saying their prayers. It was too much.

Stepping between them and the waiting executioners, Ethan faced the General. Then he bared his breast in good melodramatic style, and demanded that he be killed but not the Canadians. "I am the sole cause of their taking up arms," he pleaded.

For what seemed a very long moment the General considered the matter. "I will not execute you now," he said, including Ethan in his gaze, "but you shall grace a halter at Tyburn, God damn you."

Ethan Allen was to have a long stretch in prison. Jehovah had been on the wrong side this time, but that desertion did not trouble the prisoner nearly so much as what had become of Major John Brown, the lad who had got him into his present fix.

It is a question that has never been satisfactorily answered. Warner and Brown had planned the attack. Brown had proposed it to Ethan. Brown and Warner had more men than Ethan. They had better men—in fact, they could not have had worse soldiers than the majority of Ethan's sad gang. But Brown did not cross the river at all. Worse, he sent no word to Ethan that he had failed to do so. It was shoddy treatment.*

It has been claimed for Brown—or for Warner and Brown—that the river was too rough for them to cross that night. Ethan Allen and his crowd made it, in small canoes and before daylight, a bare ten miles below. It has even been intimated that Warner, at least, in his new position as a lieutenant colonel, feared the competition of the brilliant leadership of Allen. But this hardly sounds like Warner and is an unfair assumption to make on no evidence.

Perhaps a partial explanation is to be found in two letters written by General Montgomery to General Schuyler, during the ensuing campaign in Canada. "Pray send me Yorkers," he wrote on October 9, "they don't melt away as fast as their eastern neighbours." By which he referred to men of the Grants. And a bit later: "The rascally Green Mountain Boys have left me in the lurch after promising to go to Quebec." These "Green Mountain Boys" were none other than "Colonel Seth Warner's Regiment in the Servis of the United Colonies."

Possibly Warner and Brown discovered in time that the quality of this body of troops was not very good. Recruiting

---

* Ethan Allen never fought battles in retrospect. His *Narrative* of his captivity does not contain a line that can be construed as reproach for either Brown or Warner, the men responsible for removing him from the Revolutionary scene. Few men, violent or otherwise, have been so generous in like cases.

for it, once Ethan Allen was out, had been difficult. Many of the veteran Green Mountain Boys had enlisted elsewhere, leaving Warner to take what he could get. It is likely that Warner and Brown, even if they never admitted it, felt they could not take Montreal with the poor sort of cannon fodder at their command. The like hadn't stopped Ethan Allen, the scout with no commission. But then, there have been few men in America, then or since, who were fired by the spark that burned so strong in the man who had taken Fort Ti with a crowd of hill-billies. Ethan Allens sprout less than once in a century.

After he had been properly goddamned by General Prescott and promised a halter as soon as he got to England, guards led Ethan away to a schooner-of-war, the *Gaspee*. Here he was taken to the lowest part of the hold, given a chest to sit on, and put into irons.

On the evidence of the record, there can be no doubt that orders were given to break the spirit of this tall rebel, and the first effort made in the campaign was to be seen in the irons. The handcuffs were of the sort ordinarily used at the time, but the leg irons were something special. They weighed forty pounds, so the guard told his prisoner, and were attached to a bar of iron eight feet long. "Very substantial," Ethan remarked of them. He was trussed in such a manner that he could lie down on the chest only on the flat of his back. It was a tough position for an active giant.

To make doubly sure, an armed sentry stood on guard.

"Damn him," said the guard in awe, "does he eat iron?"

CHAPTER VII

Georg Ye Third Entertains

———•◦•———

The old warrior's spirit was going to take a deal of breaking. On the morning after he had been weighted with irons and promised a halter, he called like a lord for ink and quill and addressed a letter to General Prescott. He reminded that officer of Colonel Allen's generous treatment of British taken at Ticonderoga, and contrasted it with the mean condition he found himself in at the hands of the British of Montreal. He demanded that it cease.

Hearing nothing from Prescott, he wrote a letter to General Carleton, but still received no reply. For the next six weeks he remained in the heavy irons, sitting on the chest in the darkest hold of the ship. During this period he was subjected —possibly on orders from higher up—to all sorts of abuse by many but not all of his captors. He replied to all insults with a steady stream of profanity so gorgeous that the guards, who were British regulars and therefore able men at cursing, were often stunned into silence.

Everything possible was being done to break the prisoner's spirit, but even solitary confinement, forty-pound leg irons, and insulting language failed to do it. From the stinking murk of his dungeon, the old eagle of the Grants sent forth growls and rumblings to tell of a spirit chained but still burning with hot defiance.

The ship's surgeon, a Dr. Dace, took particular delight in badgering the shackled man, telling him he had long been ripe for hanging. One day Ethan went into a fury at the doctor. Raising his handcuffs to his mouth, he set his strong teeth around the head of a large nail that was driven through the mortise of the handcuff bar. He twisted it this way and that, in a frenzy, and pulled the spike out with his teeth. Spitting nails and throwing off his wrist shackles with a mighty effort, he stood erect in an effort to strike the surgeon. But the leg irons held him fast and the heckler escaped. It was a stunt, however, that frightened the doctor, who never again troubled the prisoner; and it also greatly impressed the guards, one of whom expressed himself. "Damn him," he said in awe, "does he eat iron?"

After six weeks, things took a turn for the better. Ethan and other captives were placed on another vessel and taken down the river to Quebec. This ship was commanded by a Captain Littlejohn, who appears to have taken an immediate liking to the tall Yankee. Ethan's cruel irons were removed, and he was quartered with the ship's officers, eating at their mess and generally having the run of the place. "No brave man shall be treated like a rascal on board my ship," quoth the good captain.

Captain Littlejohn appears to have been a sea dog in the best tradition. At Quebec he went ashore to "pay his respects" to certain ladies of the town and while there got into an argument with a lieutenant from a man-of-war. The outcome was a challenge to a duel, to be fought on the Plains of Abraham, which was a fine level spot for a duel. The time was set for next morning.

That evening Captain Littlejohn returned to his vessel and confided to Ethan about the coming affair of honor. That gallant prisoner, wishing to show his gratitude for decent treatment, offered himself as a second and was accepted. He promised that, no matter what happened, he would return to the ship; and it was agreed that he should go ashore in military disguise. In the morning, however, high army and navy officers interposed and the controversy—doubtless over some loose hussy—was settled without resort to arms.

Ethan's nine or ten days of fine living were over. He was transferred to the *Adamant*, in charge of men who took pains to tell him that he was as good as a dead man, that they were taking him to England only for the purpose of a public hanging. On top of this greeting the captors shoved thirty-three prisoners, taken with Ethan, into an oak pen about twenty feet square, and ordered the guard to put Colonel Allen with them.

The colonel protested this inhumanity to his men and to himself, and was told that capital offenders had no right to talk of humanity. An officer of the guard spat in Ethan's face and told him to get moving. With a howl like an animal, the prisoner sprang at the officer, felling him to the floor with one blow of his manacled hands. The officer leaped up and ran for the cabin, his prisoner at his heels. The guards now took a hand. With fixed bayonets at his back, Ethan was forced into the crowded dungeon.

For more than a month the thirty-four men existed in this hellhole. There was nothing in the way of bunks or bedding. Two tubs served the needs of nature. No water for washing was permitted, and only a small portion for drinking. The place was filthy enough within twenty-four hours, and it was a horror for the remainder of the voyage. The prisoners were given plenty of coarse food and, of even greater importance, as Ethan reported, "a gill of rum per day, which was of the utmost service to us and probably was the means of saving several of our lives."

The interminable voyage ended at Falmouth, England, from which the prisoners were taken to Pendennis Castle, overlooking the Channel about a mile from town. People came from miles around to see this first batch of American prisoners of war. They hung from windows and ranged the roof tops. The streets were so jammed that King's officers had to draw their swords in order to force a passage.

The parade through the village was like a circus day, with the prisoners serving as a menagerie. The English were astounded at the size of the Yankee colonel who had taken Fort Ticonderoga. He looked more like a gigantic savage than a military man, for he had changed into Canadian backwoods clothes when he began his scouting trips into Quebec. A cap of bright red woolen was on his head. He wore a double-breasted jacket of fawnskin, probably fringed, and breeches of sagathy. His hair, uncut for months, tumbled down over his shoulders, and his beard was like that of a warrior of old. An Indian chief in all his regalia could not have created more noise in Falmouth.

As soon as he arrived at his new prison, Ethan asked permission to write a letter. This he addressed for purposes of his own to nobody but the Illustrious Continental Congress of the United Colonies. He well knew, of course, it would never reach that body, but it might serve him well all the same. In it he recounted his ill treatment by his captors, putting it on very thick indeed, but suggested that this evil had been instigated by the horrendous General Prescott of Montreal. He desired that Congress should desist from retaliation on British prisoners until he saw how he was to be treated now that he was in England.

If his present jailers, he said, should not treat him and other prisoners in the decent manner they deserved—in which case he would so advise the Congress—Congress might then go ahead and make life a hell for all English soldiers who fell into the hands of Americans. He hoped, he said, that such retaliation would not be in proportion "to the smallness of my character, but in proportion to the importance of the cause for which I have suffered."

It was a letter shrewdly arranged to give his English captors pause—not only as to hanging him and his men, but also in reference to their treatment at Pendennis Castle. Ethan knew it would never be read by his illustrious congress, but he was quite sure it would be read by important Englishmen; and it was: it went direct to Lord North, prime minister.

Ethan's letter may not have been the sole reason he was not hanged promptly, as he most certainly deserved to be, but it pointed out the many possibilities of retaliation. Not then known to Ethan, but known to the British boss men in England, was the fact that the revolting Americans now held several important Englishmen as prisoners, among them the same General Prescott who had first threatened Ethan with execution at Montreal.

The British cabinet, in fact, was wondering what to do with this cocky captive colonel. Unknown to him, the cabinet met to discuss his case. Solicitor General Wedderburn proposed that they try to buy Ethan with a full pardon and a promise of a command of a regiment of rangers to clear the New Hampshire Grants, not of the Yorkers but of the Yankees themselves; plus assurance that after the general revolt had been put down, Colonel Allen should retain titles to his lands under the triumphant Crown.

What action the cabinet took on this suggestion, if any, is not known; but the treatment accorded Colonel Allen by Lieutenant Hamilton, commandant of Pendennis Castle, showed immediate improvement. Lieutenant Hamilton sent a fine breakfast every morning from his own table to the colonel, and every night an excellent dinner, with a bottle of wine to wash it down.

Yet, so far as Ethan knew, the halter still hung over his head. He resolved, in order to keep up his own spirits and those of his fellow prisoners, to put on more brass than ever. He felt that a "Good example of American fortitude" was called for, and he was the man to produce it.

The story that this gigantic Ethan Allen, this white savage in a buckskin jacket, liked to chew nails and other iron had somehow spread through Cornwall. People came in droves every day to the Castle, and Ethan was taken out of his cell and allowed to walk in the Castle yard, where the curious all but mobbed him—asking him questions, feeling his strange clothes, and remarking, as at a zoo, on his immense size.

The prisoner thoroughly enjoyed it. Asked by a Cornishman what his occupation in life had been, Ethan replied that he had studied divinity in his younger days but was now a conjurer. The man replied that he seemed to have conjured himself into prison. Ethan replied that this was true and had been due to a matter of miscalculation, such as any magician might make in a moment of aberration. He took pains to remind his caller, though, that he had at least conjured the British out of Ticonderoga.

Every day was circus day at Pendennis Castle. Pious visitors told Ethan he was sure to be hanged and asked if he was prepared for the other world. To which he replied that although he knew nothing of the world of spirits, he expected nevertheless, when he should arrive at such a place, to be "as well treated as other gentlemen of my merit."

Whenever he had a good-sized audience—which was often —he talked of little but the necessity of freedom for the American colonies. He recited the wrongs of taxing a people who had nothing to say about their government, and he piled

There can be no doubt that orders were given to break the spirit of this tall rebel.

horror on horror in the manner of good propagandists. In politics he continued to be a resolute rebel.

When two clergymen called one day, he discussed philosophy and Christianity and demonstrated that he understood and could fashion a syllogism, of which he had ever been inordinately fond. One charmed visitor ordered a bowl of punch for Ethan, who refused to take it from the hands of the visitor's servant but was happy to accept it from the gentleman himself. With fine showmanship he lifted the big bowl to his lips and drank it all in one stupendous draught.

"By God," exclaimed hard-drinking Cornishmen, "there's a man!"

Colonel Allen's reputation soon became fabulous in the district. It was told and believed that he actually chewed iron to work up an appetite for breakfast, and that he drank a full gallon of rum daily. Not a day passed but open-mouthed Cornish folk came to see the tall wonder at the Castle.*

This happy state of things lasted only about two weeks. Then, Ethan and several other prisoners were ordered on board the frigate *Solebay*, part of a fleet which presently put in at the harbor of Cork, Ireland. Captain Symonds of the *Solebay* was a disciplinarian. He had the prisoners paraded on deck, and read to them a special order of rules to govern their conduct, with appropriate penalties.

In what part of the ship the common prisoners were kept is not clear, but Captain Symonds tucked Ethan away in a hole on the cable tier, below. Here he made friends with one Gillegan, a petty officer with a kindly heart who allowed Ethan to share his small quarters on the entire trip to America.

Two memorable incidents happened while the *Solebay* lay at Cork: a mighty storm came up and frightened hardy old

* The vision of Ethan Allen a prisoner in Pendennis Castle caught the fancy of young Herman Melville, who has an effective scene in his *Israel Potter*, published in 1855.

salts into saying their prayers; and a delegation of Cork men, hearing that Colonel Allen, victor of Ticonderoga, was on board, came out to the vessel. Captain Symonds was absent, and these generous Irishmen were permitted to board the ship and to present Ethan and the other Americans with an astounding quantity of things. To each of thirty-four common prisoners went "a suit of clothes from head to foot, including a surtout, and two shirts; and two pounds of tea and six pounds of sugar." Colonel Allen received "superfine broadcloth sufficient for two jackets, and two pairs of breeches, eight fine Holland shirts and socks ready made, with a number of pairs of worsted hose, two pairs of shoes, two beaver hats, one of which was richly laced with gold . . . a gratuity of wines of the best sort; old spirits, Geneva; loaf and brown sugar, coffee, tea and chocolate, with a large round of pickled beef, and a number of fat turkies." And, just in case he got a chance to use it, the Irish supplied him—hopefully, no doubt—with a dagger.*

It is little wonder that Colonel Allen was staggered. "I was not only supplied with the necessaries and conveniences of life," he remarks quaintly, "but with the grandeur and superfluities of it."

When Captain Symonds returned to his ship he was furious that the Irishmen, "damned rebels, too," had been allowed on board. He permitted Ethan to retain his new clothing, but confiscated all of the provisions and liquors. "The taking of my liquors was abominable," says Ethan. However, the captain didn't get them all, for the thirsty colonel managed to hide a two-gallon jug of old spirits and some wine. He also kept the dagger, which was unsuspected.

Before the *Solebay* left Cork, another delegation of Irishmen attempted to call on Ethan. They rowed out to the ship

* This dagger is to be seen in the Ethan Allen Collection at Fort Ticonderoga Museum.

and were hailed by Captain Symonds himself. When he learned they were bringing sea stores to the American prisoner, he damned them very heartily and ordered them away. The spokesman for the Irish then asked that Colonel Allen be permitted to visit the city of Cork and that they would be responsible for his safe return. Captain Symonds told them to begone.

Setting out from Cork on the 12th of February, 1776, the *Solebay* and other ships of the fleet ran into such a storm that they put in at Madeira. Ethan remained on the *Solebay*, but certain of the other prisoners were removed to other ships. Ethan observed that the great storm must have put the fear of God into his captors' hearts, for the prisoners on his ship were better treated for some days afterward.

A brief stop was made at Madeira, then the fleet set sail for America. It carried troops for an expedition commanded by Lord Cornwallis, who happened to make his crossing on the *Solebay*. "His Lordship was a large noble looking man," says Ethan, "and he took the most ground to stand on of any man I ever saw." His Lordship was also very haughty, but that did not stop Ethan from attempting to walk the quarterdeck. Seeing the tall Yankee in this hallowed place, Cornwallis became angry. "Mr. Allen," he said, "do you know that the quarterdeck is the place for gentlemen?"

"Yes, by God, I do," the Colonel responded, "and that's the reason I'm here."

The fleet arrived at Cape Fear, North Carolina, and part of it was sent to make an attempt on Charleston. Ethan and other prisoners were loaded into the frigate *Mercury* and taken to Halifax in Canada, where they lay in the harbor. Ethan felt nearer home now. He was ill much of the time, but his spirit was strong. He managed to write and send off undetected a number of letters that eventually reached the Connecticut Legislature, telling of his plight. The Connecticut leaders, among whom at this time was Levi Allen, began efforts to effect an exchange for Colonel Allen.

Scurvy had long since broken out on the *Mercury*. Both sailors and prisoners were affected. The sailors were now taken ashore to Halifax every day, and their legs covered with earth in a trench, as a curative measure. The prisoners were kept on ship and given no medical attention whatever. One of them managed to buy two quarts of strawberries from Indians who came out to the fleet, and was "almost cured of the scurvy."

A doctor's mate secretly gave Ethan a "large vial of smart drops" which proved to be good for the disease, but it wasn't enough for all. Ethan now began writing letters again—to the commander of the ship, who presently told his men not to trouble him with any more such missives. Somehow or other, Ethan got a letter off to the royal governor of Halifax, Arbuthnot, in which he related the terrible condition of the common prisoners. The governor was a humane man. He had the sick men moved ashore at once and quartered in the city jail, where a doctor treated them. The food improved, and vegetables were added to the fare.

In mid-October all the American prisoners except two, who were too weak to be moved, were put on a man-of-war and started south. A Captain Smith was in command. He greeted Colonel Allen as an equal and had him to dinner at his table. This treatment so affected the sick old warhorse that he was unable to speak immediately to express his surprise and gratitude. However, he soon had opportunity to show the latter.

Among the prisoners on board was a new man, one Captain Burk who was said to have been captured while commanding an American armed vessel. This Burk seems to have been a bold man and an adventurer. He had somehow learned that the ship was carrying thirty-five thousand pounds sterling, and that certain of the crew had in mind a mutiny.

Aided by the loosed prisoners, the crew would take over, kill the captain, put the officers in irons, and sail the prize ship into an American port.

Burk put the plan up to Ethan. Certainly it was an adventure which ordinarily would have delighted him. But he reflected on the courtesy and generosity shown him by the captain. Ethan actually talked against such a move. He told Burk and the other plotters that if the attempt were made, he would fight with the captain; but that if the conspiracy were dropped, he would say nothing of it. It never came off.

What was to be Ethan Allen's last voyage landed him in New York City late in October of 1776. That town was still in the hands of the British. Ethan and three other American officers were admitted to parole, and were not to leave the city. The common prisoners were herded into a church and there kept in a horribly filthy condition.

In ill health himself, so haggard that the few men he knew in town failed to recognize him, and without funds, Ethan somehow managed to live and enjoy life. By the time he had got his land legs he was up to his old tricks—writing letters to the British commander calling attention to the awful "mortality ranging among the prisoned Americans." He was not speaking for himself, he wrote, but for the men herded into churches and houses nigh to suffocation, and dying of disease and starvation.

He was also getting cocky again. Whenever news, or even a rumor, of an American victory got into New York he and other paroled officers held a binge in its honor. And presently Ethan had a caller, a man of such high importance in the British army that Colonel Allen was amazed. This officer, Ethan says, made him a proposition. He should go to England first. There he would be "clothed equal to an introduction to the King," which would follow, and then given a commission to embark with General John Burgoyne for the Colonies and aid that jolly soldier in the "reduction of the country which would infallibly be conquered." Ethan was promised good pay for this work and not "in paper rags but hard guineas," and when the war was over he should have a large tract of land "wither in the New-Hampshire Grants or in Connecticut, it would make no odds, as the country would be forfeited to the Crown."

When he had heard the officer out, Ethan replied that the Devil himself had once made such an offer of land when the damned rascal did not own one foot of land on earth. As for himself, Ethan Allen, he wanted no part of it. The officer called him a bigot, "whereupon I returned to my lodgings."

During the period of British occupation of New York City, James Rivington was editor of the *Gazette*, a noted Tory paper. Rivington knew how to write for his side, and he poured it on in the *Gazette*'s columns. Colonel Allen, even though he enjoyed his partial liberty on sufferance, took pains to disagree loudly and violently with the *Gazette*'s editorial policy. In taverns he liked to say that one of these days he was going to knock the hell out of Editor Rivington. And one day he set out to do so.

Rivington himself has told the story of their meeting. He was sitting in his office at the corner of Pearl and Wall streets. He had just dined and was about to go to work on a bottle of fine old Madeira when he heard a cheer in the street below. Going to the window he saw an immense figure in a cocked hat and tarnished regimentals, with an enormous sword, followed by a crowd of boys who cheered and cheered. The watching editor noted that the tall man seemed insensible to the cheering boys and was obviously bent on some errand. Something told Rivington that this man was Ethan Allen, coming to carry out his threat.

Just then Rivington's clerk came into the room pale as a

ghost, wringing his hands. "Oh, master," he stammered, as Rivington himself told it, "he is come. He came in and asked if you lived here and if you were at home. I told him I would go and see. And now, master, what is to be done?"

Rivington looked at the bottle of fine old wine on the table. It had hardly been touched. "Show him up," he told the clerk. Then "there was a fearful moment of suspense," the editor recalled. "I heard him on the stairs, his long sword clanking at every step. And in he walked."

"Sir," demanded the tall man in the tarnished regimentals, "is your name James Rivington?"

"It is, sir, and no man could be more happy than I am to see Colonel Ethan Allen."

"Sir, I have come—"

"Not another word, my dear Colonel, until you have taken a seat and a glass of old Madeira."

"But, sir, I don't think it proper—"

"Not another word, Colonel. Taste this wine. I have had it in glass for ten years. Old wine, you know, unless it is originally sound, never improves by age."

Colonel Allen took the proffered glass. He swallowed the wine and smacked his lips, shaking his head approvingly. "Sir," he began again, "I come to—"

"Not another word until you have taken another glass, and then, my dear Colonel, we will talk of old affairs, and I have some droll events to detail."

They thereupon finished two bottles of the rare vintage and, says Rivington, parted as good friends as "if we never had cause to be otherwise."

In January of 1777 Colonel Allen was permitted to remove from New York City to the western end of Long Island. Here he was soon in very comfortable quarters, made possible by two pounds sent him by his old friend Jonas Fay of

Bennington, and thirty-five pounds from his brother, Levi Allen. Colonel Selah Hart forwarded him eight pounds due for his services in the Continental army.

Now came a letter from Heman Allen saying that Ethan's only son had died of smallpox. Although he had never seen much of his family since the day he went to the Grants in 1768, Ethan had never failed of support. He wrote Heman, "I fear some quack doctor has murdered my son to improve the art of innoculation," and added that if he found this to be so he would kill the doctor.

On Long Island he enjoyed about seven months of comparative comfort and freedom; but somehow during this time he must have broken the rules of his parole. He denied this, calling his arrest a matter of "artful, mean and pitiful pretences." Whatever the reason, one day in August he was taken to the provost jail in the city and locked in a room that was under guard.

Even here he seems to have had unusual liberties. Locked up in the same jail was a Captain Travis of Virginia. The two men were kindred spirits, both liking to philosophize, drink rum, and argue. Sometimes their arguments were carried to the point of violence. John Pintard, who was present, told of much drinking in the provost jail. He said that at one time Colonel Allen and Captain Travis began a discussion as to the relative merits of the Green Mountain Boys of the Grants and the Buckskins of Virginia. It was quite an argument. In the ensuing battle, Travis all but gouged out one of the Colonel's eyes, and Ethan pushed the Captain's nose out of place. Guards were called to stop the uproar, and were ordered to parade the combatants. The clothes of both men were torn to shreds.

A fellow prisoner who got to know Ethan well at this time found him a remarkable man in more ways than one. In his *Memoirs of a Life Chiefly Passed in Pennsylvania* (published in 1811), Alexander Graydon thus recalled him:

"His figure was that of a robust, large-framed man, worn down by confinement and hard fare—a suit of blue clothes, with a gold laced hat that had been presented him by the gentlemen of Cork enabled him to make a very passable appearance for a rebel colonel. I have seldom met a man possessing, in my opinion, a stronger mind, or whose mode of expression was more vehement and oratorical. His style was a singular compound of local barbarisms, scriptural phrases, and oriental wildness; and though unclassic and sometimes ungrammatical, it was highly animated and forcible. Notwithstanding that Allen might have something of the insubordinate lawless frontier in his composition, he appeared to me to be a man of generosity and honor."

It is probably a fair picture of the man.

Ethan remained in the provost jail until early in May of 1778, or about eight months. He was restless and wrote friends that paroled officers like himself were "mere ciphers exempted from both danger and honor." He felt futile, for he knew the Revolution was rolling forward in glorious fashion. News of the Battle of Bennington must have made him glad as well as sad that he was not there to help old John Stark to drive the "damned Heshland" troops off the New Hampshire Grants. By the time an exchange was arranged for Colonel Allen, Burgoyne had surrendered to Gates and Louis XVI had signed a treaty with the thirteen united states. Benedict Arnold had been made a general in the Continental army, even though Colonel John Brown, the man who had failed Ethan at Montreal, was saying publicly of Arnold, "Money is this man's God, and to get enough of it he would sacrifice his country." And Ethan's old friend and cousin, Remember Baker, had been killed on a scouting trip against the British.

On the 3rd of May, 1778, a guard came to the provost jail to remove Colonel Allen to British headquarters on Staten Island.

"*There is an original something in him that commands attention.*"—GENERAL GEORGE WASHINGTON in a letter to Congress.

CHAPTER VIII

Return of a Hero

In command at British headquarters on Staten Island was General Henry Campbell, apparently a genial as well as a diplomatic soul who thought that American prisoners up for exchange should leave the British lines in as good spirits as possible. For two days he dined and wined Colonel Allen in royal style, admitting him to his own table and discussing everything under the sun.

Ethan found this very diverting, but it failed to remove the evil memories of more than two years. He told the General to his face that he, Colonel Allen, would be happy to give the British credit for two days' good usage.

On the third day came Mr. Boudinot, American Commissary of Prisoners, bringing Colonel Archibald Campbell for exchange. Colonel Allen and Colonel Campbell saluted each other, and each made the natural remark that he had never been happier to see any gentleman than the other. Ethan was landed at Elizabeth, New Jersey, and was thrilled—"liberty ground," he called it—and in company with Colonel Elisha Sheldon and Josiah Bartlett, New Hampshire Congressman, went to Valley Forge.

General George Washington, a very busy man at the time, went to some pains to greet the still haggard giant. He introduced Ethan to all his staff and talked long with him. Washington sensed that vital spark, possibly of real genius, that burned inside the tattered regimentals. He wrote to Congress soon after Ethan's visit: "His fortitude and firmness seem to have placed him out of the reach of misfortune. There is an original something in him that commands attention." The General observed that Colonel Allen appeared very desirous of continuing his military service, even though he did not expect a high rank. Washington intimated that Congress should make a place for him in the army.

Ethan wrote the Congress in appreciation of his exchange and offered his services. He fancied, he said, that the army had less need for officers than private soldiers and reported that he would "gladly attend the British with a Bayonet." Not many crowned heroes have made such an offer. In his letter to Congress he also inserted a dirty dig at the way the British treated prisoners. "Their Officers," he wrote, "affected to Treat me Very Politely the Last Two Days I was with them (a poor amends)." He thought their "ill Success last Campayn and our Alliance with France has Turned their Haughty Tone of Conquest to that of Love." It didn't fool him for a minute. He figured, he said, that the British army in America was about done for.

General Horatio Gates, the hero of Saratoga, was at Valley Forge when Ethan arrived. He had been active in securing Ethan's exchange. As he was then traveling to the Northern Department, which he commanded, he asked the hero of Ticonderoga to accompany him. They rode as far as Fishkill together, and Ethan found the General a fine companion, interested in both real estate and philosophy. "A noble man," Ethan remarked.

Going first to Salisbury, Connecticut, he learned that his

brother Heman had died the week before. Captain Heman Allen had fought at Bennington, where he had contracted a cold which he had been unable to shake off. Never the same after the battle, his widow said. He was the first of the Allen brothers to go. Ethan stopped at Salisbury only for a day.

Now for home and family. Home for Mrs. Allen and the children had been a small house in Sunderland on the Grants. Ethan found them well, if strange from his long absence, and they and the neighbors were shocked to see little more than a shadow of the man who had taken Ticonderoga but not Montreal.

Sunderland was still Sunderland; but the New Hampshire Grants were no more—at least in the vocabulary of most of the people who lived there. While Ethan swore and brooded in various English prisons, the men of the Grants had continued the work he had begun in 1770 and carried on for five years. In January of 1777 they had held a convention at Westminster, scene of the "massacre," and had proclaimed the district of land commonly called the New Hampshire Grants to be a "free and independent state capable of regulating their own internal police in all and every respect whatsoever, and that it should thereafter be known by the name of New Connecticut."

Happily, this dismal piece of unoriginal nomenclature was not permitted to stand. Learning that a district along the Susquehanna River already had appropriated the name of New Connecticut, the men of the Grants held a second convention, at Windsor this time, and on June 4, 1777, declared their country to be Vermont. This name, derived from two French words meaning "green" and "mountains," was suggested to the legislators by Dr. Thomas Young, then of Philadelphia, in a letter dated April 11, 1777. (Dr. Young had been involved with Ethan many years before in the small-pox inoculation difficulties. He never ceased to have an interest in Ethan Allen and his efforts to form a new government for the Grants.)

Although Vermont, when Ethan saw it again in 1778, was still very much the frontier, a little more of it had been tamed while he was away. Deserters from both British and American armies had begun what would soon become a trend by squatting on Vermont lands. The trickle of settlers, mostly of whole families, from Connecticut had never ceased. They now strung out along the shores of Lake Champlain, making tiny hamlets at Charlotte, at Shelburne, and on Burlington Bay. There was quite a settlement at the Lower Falls on Otter Creek.

But it was a long way between smokes. Homes were one-room huts built of logs chinked with moss or mud, and around the hut might be so much as an acre of ground to plant between the stumps. Corn was almost the only crop, and so distant were the few gristmills that most of the corn was ground in a samp mortar, in the yard. This was made by burning out a hollow in a stump, then attaching a weight or plunger to a near-by sapling which served as a spring pole in the hands of the operator. You could tell when you were approaching a cabin by the *thump-thump-thump*. The only sugar was that of the maple, made from sap caught in birch-bark lunkins. Potatoes were rare; wheat, almost nonexistent. A well grounded fear of Indians still prevailed, and somewhere on the inside wall of every cabin hung a rifle or smoothbore, loaded and ready.

Nor was this bastard Vermont yet a part of the United States of America. Congress had refused to recognize it. New York at present had its hands full, without worrying about the Grants. Ira Allen, his brother Heman, Jonas Fay, Thomas Chittenden, and others had called themselves a Council of Safety and had run the new republic after a fashion until March of 1778, when Chittenden was formally elected Governor. A sort of legislature called the Assembly had been elected, and a Council named to aid the Governor in his deliberations. Vermont had drawn up a constitution, with a radical prohibition of slavery, the first of its kind in the United States.

In the meantime Vermont had been doing its part in the general revolt of the colonies. Colonel Seth Warner's regiment had continued its service with the Continental Army. It had fought bravely to cover General St. Clair's retreat from Burgoyne, and it had played a heroic part with General Stark at the battle of Bennington.

When Ethan Allen arrived in Sunderland, then, he was in what most of its inhabitants liked to think of as the independent republic of Vermont. It really wasn't quite that yet, but it might be, given time and a few years more of life to Colonel Allen.

In the adjoining town of Arlington, just then, the Governor and his Council were in session. Ethan hurried over to see the boys. They gave him a reception to warm his generous heart. He sat in at the meeting, which turned into a small celebration, with Ethan relating his many adventures in far places and horrendous jails. And he told of his conversations with Generals Washington and Gates. He opined that Congress would not make trouble for Vermont.

He must have been happy to find that the chief business before the present session of Governor and Council was to plan the further confiscation of lands in Vermont owned, or at least claimed, by Tories who had fled the state. He discovered his young brother Ira was Treasurer of the new republic, and good old Matthew Lyon, the man who had fired the big mortar after Ti was captured, was Secretary of State. He was again among friends, and old one-eyed Tom Chittenden, who had been the first customer of the Onion River Company, was Governor of Vermont.

This Thomas Chittenden was a sort of original, too. Barely able to write his name and much older than most of the contemporary Vermont leaders, he had qualities of perception that seem to have been almost uncanny. He was, as related, a large owner of lands in the Onion River country of Vermont—which made him a pretty good man to be Governor, in the eyes of the Onion River Company. But his real estate interests were not the sole reason for his prominence. He was very keen, and his judgment of men and measures was unerring. Of him Ethan once remarked that, although for the life of him he couldn't tell how he did it, Tom Chittenden seemed always able to resolve the most complex question and to reduce it to its simplest parts.

Now Ethan watched while the Governor signed an order sending Captain Jesse Sawyer of the Vermont militia "in search of enemical persons," and another order directing a Vermont sheriff to take possession of the estate of a "Tory now with the enemy." Henceforth, as since the beginning of the Revolution, "Tories" and "Yorkers" in Vermont were dual personalities found in one and the same person.

Honors and cash came for the returned hero. A messenger arrived at Arlington with a letter from General Washington and a brevet colonel's commission in the United States service. This was granted by the Congress for "his fortitude, firmness and zeal in the cause of his country, manifested during the course of his long and cruel captivity, as well as on former occasions." In addition was a resolution from Congress granting Ethan a lieutenant colonel's pay during his captivity.

No man to let a courtesy stand without acknowledgment, Colonel Allen sent off letters to General Washington, General Gates, and the Congress. He said he was recruiting his constitution by a "regimen of diet and exercise" and was ready to act when called. He esteemed the approbation received "above gold and silver."

His old friends had selected Bennington for Vermont's welcome to her foremost man. The day had been set, and word had been sent to the remotest tavern and farm. Ethan rode out of Arlington and direct to the Catamount tavern on the Bennington hillside. It was a monster gathering, for the time and place. Crowds flocked in from neighboring towns, and men came afoot and on horseback from distant parts of Vermont, New Hampshire, Massachusetts, and Connecticut. Old Green Mountain Boys who had followed their great riot-raiser on scores of raids now came to drink and to pay him homage. The woods around Bennington resounded with the hoot-owl calls of the Boys as they approached the Catamount.

The welcome had been planned to coincide with the June session of the Vermont Assembly, and the combined affairs lasted several days. Three salutes were fired from a cannon the first evening, and next morning Sam Herrick, now a colonel, had the piece fired fourteen times—thirteen for the United States and one for young Vermont.

Landlord Fay's bar wenches worked as never before. Punch and stonewalls and flip went down the hatch. Colonel Allen looked around and saw that "rural felicity, sweetened with friendship, glowed in each countenance." This did him immense good. He had to retell the story of his long captivity, and he also took occasion to air his opinion of his many jailers—the worst of whom, it seems, was one Loring *

* Doubtless Joshua Loring, Jr., who left Boston with the British in 1776 and went to Halifax. He was soon appointed commissary of prisoners by Sir William Howe, a sudden and somewhat extraordinary promotion which was allegedly brought about through the friendship of Mrs. Loring with Sir William. He died in England in 1789, leaving a reputation for cruelty among Americans who had been incarcerated under his wardenship.

—and of the British commander-in-chief, Sir William Howe. "They are," he said, "the most mean spirited, deceitful animals in all God's creation below, and legions of infernal devils with all their tremendous horrors are impatiently waiting to receive Howe and Loring with all their detestable accomplices into the most exquisite agonies of holy fire." It was one of the colonel's best descriptive passages.

Toasts had to be drunk separately for each State in the Union, and one, unquestionably a double slug, for Vermont.

A serious yet pleasing feature of Vermont's first public celebration was to be the public hanging of a horrible Tory named David Redding. This man had been convicted of stealing muskets from the Vermont militia and of acting as a spy "for the enemy." The gallows had been erected, thoughtfully enough, in a field across the road, handy to the Catamount, and on June 4 the field was crowded with people.

In the meantime, John Burnham, counsel for Redding, had convinced the Governor and Council that his client had been convicted by an illegal jury composed of only six persons, whereas twelve jurors were required by law to convict in a capital case. Governor Chittenden had signed a reprieve of seven days and granted a new trial.

But here was a large crowd, gathered for the purpose of seeing a man hanged, and yelling for blood. When it was announced that the prisoner had been reprieved, the crowd reacted in the manner of mobs of all time: they felt they had been unjustly cheated of an amusement, and they began a movement to take the damned rascal and hang him, law or no law.

It looked as if a lynching were imminent, with the mob pressing hard on the sheriff and his prisoner, when Colonel Allen plowed through the ranks shouting for attention. He mounted a stump and, in a voice that all could hear, advised the mob to go home and return one week later. "By God," he bellowed, "you shall then see somebody hung at all events, for if Redding is not then hung, I will be hung myself."

Ethan's presence and action melted the bloodthirsty mob, and they went away laughing at his humor. On June 9 the Governor and Council passed an order making Colonel Allen the State's Attorney for prosecution of Redding. Exactly how much Attorney Allen knew of the case is not known. He didn't need to know much, anyway. Redding was a damned Tory, and twelve jurors, egged on by the eloquence of Prosecutor Allen, convicted him with surprising speed.

On June 11, Redding was beautifully hanged on the gallows that had been prepared for him the week before. The crowd was not quite so large, but it cheered the last agonies of the strangling Tory with gusto.

With the welcome to Colonel Allen and the hanging of Redding out of the way, the Governor and Council and the Assembly got down to business of state, sitting in the long main room of the Catamount. Ethan was invited to participate—which he of course did, although he had no official voice in the proceedings. He refused to let this formality stand in the way of any aid or counsel he might give.

On June 17 the Council granted what seems to have been the first Vermont divorce, to Lurania McLane against John, her husband, "for certain reasons mentioned" in her petition. The Council also held Lurania to have a good and lawful right to wed again, should she choose.

The Assembly voted a "premium for the destruction of wolves." It passed a bill regulating the Sabbath; expelled Zadock Remington and Esq. Brewster from their seats in the Assembly; voted to take the incorporated University of Dartmouth "under the patronge of this State" and appointed the Rev. Doct. Eleazar Wheelock to be a justice of the peace.

Like most such bodies, the Assembly also did pretty well by its members; it voted them three dollars a day while away from home, and fourpence per mile for horse travel.

How to raise money for current expenses of the State came up. To date Vermont had managed to get along fairly well by confiscating the estates of Tories who had fled to the British lines. But this revenue showed signs of drying up. Someone proposed in the Assembly that the people of Vermont be taxed.

This didn't sound very good to Colonel Allen. Taxes had caused enough trouble, anyway. The colonel stood up in meeting to say he thought he had a better suggestion than a tax. He proposed that Vermont confiscate the estates of known Tories who had not fled to the British but were now enjoying the immeasurable felicity of living in God's own country, alias Vermont. Banish these "enemical persons" from the State, he said, and sell their property for the good and glory of Vermont.

The idea went over with a bang. The Assembly promptly set up a board of commissioners to try persons charged with conduct unbecoming to a Vermonter. It was doubtless not by chance that Colonel Allen's name headed the commissioners. After reporting this action to Congress—which had not yet paid the least attention to Vermont—Commissioner Allen and his crew of jury-judge-hangman set out to clear the place of wicked Tories.

It was a dictatorial body, pure and simple, a sort of civil drumhead court-martial, from which there was no appeal. The first tribunal was held in Dorset, where the commissioners went at their work with a will. They found Asa Baldwin, the wealthiest man in town, to be guilty of every charge on the docket. They ordered him out of Dorset and claimed his property for Vermont. It was a rich haul. Several more Dorset men were convicted, but only in minor degree. They were permitted to go free and to retain their property on payment of the costs of trial, which in some cases appear to have been very extensive.

Moving on to Manchester the commissioners laid a heavy hand on William Marsh. He was found to be as guilty as suspected, and his great estate was forfeit, sold in parcels to the highest bidders. Commissioner Allen himself bought one hundred and fifty acres that lay on the Onion River.

From Manchester the commissioners moved on to other districts, letting a few suspects go free but always charging the costs of trial.

It would seem that in the mind of Commissioner Allen the word "Tory" had already become synonymous with that of "Yorker." He collected eight prisoners for banishment and took them to Albany to deliver to General John Stark for safe-keeping, and he wrote to a friend that "these enemical Persons are Yorkers as well as Tories." Along with the eight unfortunates he also forwarded a letter to General Gates, asking him to send them to the enemy's lines, for they were "atrocious villains."

During this period, as in the past, Ethan had little domestic life. Brother Ira owned a fairly large house in Arlington, and he invited Ethan to move in with his family. They did so, but Ethan did not see much of them. Governor George Clinton of New York was making a new attempt to seduce the Vermonters, and something had to be done about it.

Clinton had issued a proclamation offering to confirm titles of lands on what he still chose to call the New Hampshire Grants, if the New York jurisdiction would be admitted by the settlers. The quitrents were to be reduced to what they were in the original grants, whether by New York, New Hampshire, or Massachusetts. He also offered to repeal the Bloody Law of 1774, which prohibited men of the Grants from even meeting to discuss land titles or anything else. The tenor of the proclamation was conciliatory, even friendly.

But Governor Clinton was no longer dealing with the New Hampshire Grants, no matter what he called them. He had to deal with the roughly organized but rather determined republic of Vermont, and the leading spirit of that odd republic was Ethan Allen, a rude man but one who knew more about making and holding a republic than Governor Clinton, able man that he was, ever dreamed.

It is unquestionable that Ethan now feared disaffection on the part of Vermonters far less than he feared what action Congress might take one day soon in regard to Vermont. It should be remembered that so far as Congress was concerned, Vermont did not exist. Clinton knew this and was determined to keep the Vermont lands under the jurisdiction of New York. He was no doubt strengthened in this action by the same "junto of land thieves" that had backed Governor Tryon. Likewise, the determination of Vermont to remain Vermont was aided and abetted by the fact that the Governor of Vermont and most of its leading men owned doubtful titles to enormous tracts of Vermont land. Such was the condition of things in the summer of 1778.

Dipping his quill into a bottle of vitriol, Ethan returned to the propaganda writing he had done so well before his captivity. This time he felt he must not only show Vermonters and New York that Vermont was an accomplished fact, but make such a strong case that Congress would have to recognize the new State, or at least keep hands off. If Congress didn't—well, it was a large world, and Ethan Allen was a man of unlimited ideas.

He did some of his writing at home in Arlington, some in the Catamount at Bennington, the latter a place conducive to bringing out the best in a man, whether spoken or written.

A man, too, had to mix a modicum of rum with his ink, and on a number of evenings, so legend has it, Ethan returned home from Bennington slightly under the weather.

Whether his wife Mary had a hand in it isn't known, but one night a group of his friends decided to frighten him into sobriety. Wrapping themselves in white sheets, they hid under a bridge on the outskirts of Arlington. Ethan came trotting along on his horse. Suddenly the horse snorted and shied at an army of ghosts in the road. Ethan reined the animal. "Hallo!" he shouted. "If you're angels of light, I'm glad to meet you. And if you're devils, then come along home with me. I married your sister."

But the rum and the ink were merging into a red-hot pamphlet. It came off the press in August of 1778 and was titled "An Animadversory Address to the Inhabitants of the State of Vermont: with Remarks on a Proclamation, under the Hand of his Excellency George Clinton, Esq; Governor of the State of New-York." In it he strongly intimated that the truth was not to be found in New York officialdom. He had dealt with both New York and Great Britain, he said, and one was as bad as the other. Their word of honor meant nothing. He termed New York's claims to any lands in Vermont "romantic," under any conditions. He accused Governor Clinton of trying to fool "these woods people." He called the New York Legislature "wicked and depraved" and laughed that it should now offer to repeal the Bloody Law. That law, he pointed out correctly, had been repealed; by its own wording, which he took pains to quote, it had lapsed on the first day of January, 1776, two years previously. He gave it a sneer in passing.

Now he got down to the business of his "Animadversory Address" to the Vermonters themselves, which was patently meant not so much for Vermonters as for the Congress of the United States; but he hailed the Green Mountaineers in purple prose as patriots to a man, fit for Statehood on every count.

"You have experienced every species of oppression," he wrote, "which the old Government of New-York, with a Tryon at its head, could invent and inflict; and it is manifest that the new government are minded to follow in their steps. Happy is it for you that you are fitted for the severest trials! You have been wonderfully supported and carried through thus far in your opposition to that government. Formerly you had every thing to fear from it, but now little; for your public character is established, and your cause known to be just. In your early struggles with that government, you acquired a reputation for bravery."

Now he thought fit to point out how Vermonters had aided the United States in the great revolt:

"This [bravery] gave you a relish for martial glory, and the British invasion opened an ample field for its display, and you have gone on conquering and to conquer until TALL GRENADIERS are dismayed and tremble at your approach. Your frontier situation often obliged you to be in arms and battles; and by repeated marchings, scoutings and manly exercises, your nerves have become strong to strike the mortal blow. What enemy to the State of *Vermont*—or New-York land monopolizer, shall be able to stand before you in the day of your fierce anger?"

The answer, apparently, was Nobody.

All in all, the Animadversory Address was exactly the right combination of logic, bombast, and humor to invigorate backwoods Vermont and make it feel like a sovereign State, competent to deal with New York, with Congress, or with the Devil himself—whom many pious people seriously believed to be in league with Ethan Allen.

The pamphlet was hardly off the press before new complications arose, this time on the eastern border of Vermont. Over there, on the eastern side of the Connecticut River, long called New Hampshire, were sixteen towns which, for one reason or another, thought they should like to withdraw from New Hampshire jurisdiction and become part of the new State, or republic, or whatever it was, of Vermont. They had so petitioned the Vermont Assembly and had been encouraged.

Now came a letter from Meshech Weare, "President of New Hampshire," to the Governor of Vermont. But the letter, to begin with, was addressed to the Hon. Thomas Chittenden. His title was ignored. The letter explained that no slight was meant, but that New Hampshire could not properly use the word "Governor" when addressing a district that did not exist as a State. Going on from there, the letter pointed out frostily that Vermont was hardly in a condition to be annexing sixteen towns that belonged and always had belonged to New Hampshire—a State, by the way, that was a part of the United States of America.

Governor Chittenden was pretty mad to be addressed simply as "Honorable." He thought he was as much a Governor as anyone. He and the Council hardly knew what to make of this state of affairs. They could readily see New Hampshire's side of it, but the sixteen towns had asked for admittance to Vermont, and Vermont was a hospitable place. Still, how would such doings look in the face of Vermont's fight with New York? Ethan Allen had just got his wind after pointing out what a mob of depraved villains were running New York. Was the kettle, like the pot, rather black?

Ethan had just arrived in Arlington from his printers at Hartford when the New Hampshire letter came. He read it over carefully, and by the time he was done he had a plan ready. With a swiftness that took the plodding Governor and Council off their feet and left them wondering, he proposed to go as fast as possible to Philadelphia to see what an able man could do with the illustrious Congress of the United States.

In those days, a Hero could not rest long on his honors—not if Vermont was going to survive. Before night Ethan was astride a fresh horse, heading southwest out of the pine trees.

"*I can upset his Blackstones, his whitestones, his gravestones and his brimstones.*"

CHAPTER IX

The Great Infidel Takes Charge

Arriving in Philadelphia, Ethan discovered he had no time to lose. The New Hampshire delegation had already laid a remonstrance, done in pretty stiff language, before Congress, and were lobbying among members for support of their contention that the pretended state of Vermont had no business in the sovereign state of New Hampshire. The remonstrance was to come up for consideration the next day.

The Vermonter sought out the New Hampshire delegates. He asked them to withdraw their protest until the Vermont Assembly had met, a fortnight hence, when he was positive Vermont would rescind its previous action in admitting the Sixteen Towns, now become a major *cause celèbre* and spelled with capital letters.

The New Hampshire men must have had great faith in a man who had no official vote in Vermont's councils, and who, as would presently be clear, wasn't likely to. They complied with Ethan's request, asking that the Sixteen Towns matter be deferred.

Lobbyist Allen now proceeded to work on Congress with a finesse that showed how well he understood the niceties of fancy diplomacy. He needed to move warily, for Congress was in a cockier mood than it had ever known. France had come into the war with eighteen ships and some four thousand troops. An American retreat at Monmouth had been turned into an American victory. But Ethan saw Henry Laurens, president of Congress, in private, and got from him a promise that if the union of the Sixteen Towns were dissolved, he, Laurens, would use his influence toward admitting Vermont as a state of the Union.

This was all Ethan wanted, right then. He distributed copies of his Animadversory Address to Congressmen and lobbyists, then returned to Vermont to make his report. While away on this trip he had been elected to the Vermont Assembly by the men of Arlington, an office he immediately refused. Matthew Lyon was elected in his stead.

The Assembly met at Windsor in October of 1778. It found some irregularity or other—nothing crooked—in the credentials of Delegate Lyon and he was refused his seat. Ethan was then asked to take Lyon's place. Always accommodating, the genial colonel would have taken the vacant place except for the new test creed Vermont had drawn up.

Every member of the Assembly, before taking his seat, was obliged to vow: "I do believe in one God, the Creator and Governor of the universe, the rewarder of the good and punisher of the wicked. And I do acknowledge the scriptures of the Old and New Testament to be given by Divine inspiration, and own and profess the Protestant Religion."

Ethan looked the creed over. He said he was ready to admit a belief in a First Great Cause, which he usually termed "Nature," but he denied all "ministerial damnation-salvation and the merchandise thereof"; and as for formal religion and its Bible, they were "this Ghostly Tyranny."

"I will not, sirs," he said heartily, "subscribe to this oath."

This matter stumped the Assembly only briefly. Oath or

Catamount Tavern, always the favorite meeting place of Ethan Allen and the Green Mountain boys.

no oath, the boys knew they needed the Great Infidel as never before. He took no oath of any kind, but attended all the sessions and was even placed on important committees.

Making his report on the visit to Congress, he said that unless Vermont dissolved the union with the Sixteen Towns, then "the whole power of the United States of America will join to annihilate the state of Vermont." He went to some length in this matter, stressing the fact that all states must be sovereign powers within their limits and that it would not do for Vermont to get mixed up with New Hampshire. He added casually that President Laurens of Congress had told him that if Vermont would squarely reject admittance of the Sixteen Towns, he, Laurens, could see no reason why Vermont should not become a state in the Union.

This was all very well from Vermont's viewpoint; but the Sixteen Towns were not going to give up without a fight. One of their delegates, Elisha Payne of Cardigan, arose to ask Colonel Allen an embarrassing question about his horse-trading in Congress. "Colonel Allen," he said pointedly, "did the New Hampshire Congressmen agree to aid you in disputing New York's claims to Vermont if the union with the Sixteen Towns was dissolved?"

Colonel Allen was much put out at this keen question. Angry, too, but honest still. "Yes, upon my honor they did," he admitted, and by the admission gave strength to the desire of the orphan towns to remain in Vermont. It also gave them what amounted to being a perfect slogan, beloved then as now by all good Americans: "Are we of the Sixteen Towns being sold by Vermont for aid to fight the Yorkers?"

The men of the Sixteen Towns had a strong lobby in the Vermont Assembly. They prevented any action toward dissolution, just then, and a committee was named to carve the state into four counties. This action, however, was defeated when the Assembly voted to let the counties remain as they were—which precluded any territory east of the Connecticut River and left the sixteen orphans in New Hampshire, where they had been since the beginning of time. The action amounted to being a declaration against union with the towns.*

The "President" of New Hampshire was officially notified that Vermont was done with the Sixteen Towns and would have nothing further to do with them. Along with the official notification, Colonel Allen was pleased to send a note of his own. He hoped, he said, that New Hampshire would forgive the imbecility of Vermont. The ruckus had been occasioned, he averred, by designing men who did not have the good of the country at heart. But it was now all "desolved" and settled. He added that he had been appointed as Vermont's agent to the Congress, and, seeing that the matter of the towns had been settled favorably for New Hampshire, he would of course expect New Hampshire's Congressmen to accede to Vermont's claim to be a part of the United States.

Lobbyist Allen was overlooking no bets.

Presently Ethan made another visit to Congress, submitting to that body the minutes of the Assembly showing that Vermont had left the Sixteen Towns out of its (doubtful) jurisdiction. The towns, however, were stubborn as Vermonters, and now John Wheelock, who represented them, told Congress that Ethan Allen had virtually traded the towns for a promise to get Vermont into the confederacy of states, a thing he had no authority for doing. Moreover, said Mr. Wheelock, the Sixteen Towns were still in full revolt against New Hampshire. If they were not to be a part of Vermont,

---

* The New Hampshire towns which wanted to be part of Vermont were Cornish, Lebanon, Dresden (Hanover), Lyme, Orford, Piermont, Haverhill, Bath, Lyman, Apthorp (Littleton and Dalton), Enfield, Canaan, Cardigan (Orange), Landaff, Gunthwaite (Lisbon) and Morristown (Franconia).

then they would set up independently of all states—just as Vermont had done. Sauce for the goose, he said.

This was highly dangerous stuff for Vermont's cause. If every handful of towns in the country attempted to set up a new state, Congress might well crack down on all of them—including the so-called state of Vermont. Lobbyist Allen worked his head off "seeing" the right men to put down the revolt of the Sixteen.

Congress decided to ponder the question. Colonel Allen started back for Vermont, satisfied he had done everything possible at present to hold his lines. He learned now that in the meantime an old danger from an old quarter had been revived. Governor Clinton of New York had got out another of those proclamations of his. This time he suggested that if the people of the New Hampshire Grants—he still wouldn't term them Vermonters—would acknowledge allegiance to New York, the matter of land titles might be submitted to Congress for arbitration.

Ethan sat down and tore off a reply to the Governor, sending it to Hartford for printing in the *Courant*. It was in his usual style, which fitted the purpose very well, and it damned New York up one side and down the other. Yorkers were simply "malcontents," he said, dogs in the manger, and worse.

On top of the public rows and alarms, trouble now broke out within the lively Allen family. Levi Allen had bought into certain Vermont lands, although not into the Onion River Company. He seems to have been a man who took nothing very seriously, and certainly not Vermont's preposterous claims to being a state. To him, New York was the state that would win out and take title to all of Vermont. So, after thinking the matter over, he had sold his land rights to Ira and Ethan. Because of some muddle or other, Levi had refused to deliver his title at what Ethan and Ira thought was the proper time. When Ethan returned from Philadelphia this trip, he went before the Vermont Court of Confiscation, which had already done a big business in converting Tory lands to the state's use, and charged that Levi Allen was a miserable Tory, that he had been detected in supplying the usual "enemical persons" and worse, that he had circulated counterfeit Continental money.

The court seized all of Levi's property within the state and ordered him to appear at Arlington to show cause why it should not be confiscated. This was done in an advertisement in the *Connecticut Courant*. Levi wrote a blasting letter which he sent to the same paper for publication, and then repaired to Arlington to defend his case. For reasons now not clear, the court failed to put in an appearance at the appointed time, and no hearing was then held.*

Levi was hot around the collar, what with being called a Tory and all, and one day soon the *Courant* had a piece of doggerel in its columns. It was titled "The Three Brothers" and has been attributed to Levi, who sings thus:

ETHAN:
    Old Ethan once said over a full bowl of grog
    Though I believe not in Jesus, I hold to a God,
    There is also a devil—you will see him one day
    In a whirlwind of fire take Levi away.

IRA:
    Says Ira to Ethan it plain doth appear,
    That you are inclined to banter and jeer,
    I think for myself and I freely declare
    Our Levi's too stout for the prince of the air.
    If ever you see them engaged in affray,
    'Tis Levi who'll take the devil away.

* Despite this litigation, which continued for several years and was finally settled in Ethan's favor, the two brothers appear to have been good friends to the last. At least they were later partners in business deals.

LEVI:

> Says Levi, your speeches make it perfectly clear
> That you hath been inclined to banter and jeer,
> Though through all the world my name stands enrolled,
> For tricks, sly and crafty, ingenious and bold,
> There is one consolation which none can deny
> There's one greater rogue in this world than I.

ETHAN & IRA:

> "Who's that?" they both cry with surprise.

LEVI:

> " 'Tis Ira, 'tis Ira, I yield him the prize."

Which would indicate that although Ethan had filed the charges against him, Levi considered Ira to be the instigator —and a plain slicker to boot.

A few days after the above strophes appeared in print a friend, meeting Ethan, pleasantly remarked that he had recently seen Levi. "Seen Levi?" said Ethan. "Well, how was he? God damn his lukewarm soul." Hearing of this remark, Levi sent him a challenge to a duel; but Ethan refused, saying that it would be disgraceful to engage in an affair of honor with a Tory.*

Ethan was present at the next sitting of the Vermont Assembly, held in Bennington. Up one sleeve he held what he thought might be a trump card in the dangerous game he was playing with the Congress of the United States and the Governor of New York. This trump card appears, in his own handwriting, in the form of a petition to the Vermont Assembly, asking for forty-eight square miles of free land in the northern part of the state, around Lake Memphremagog and elsewhere. The petition carried sixteen names, and the

---

* Ethan always sought to keep the idea of "wicked Tories" very much alive. One time Landlord John Norton of Westminster was discussing with him the recent introduction into Vermont of the religious doctrine of Universalism, which contains no hell. "That religion will suit you, will it not, Colonel Allen?" he asked. "No, no," the Colonel replied, "there must be a hell for the punishment of Tories."

chief reason for it becomes apparent at once from the fact that only three of the sixteen names were of Vermonters. The others were members of the Congress or officers of the Continental Army.

This petition for free land was diplomacy, or chicanery, of the first water. General Horatio Gates, for instance, whose name was on the petition, would not be overly anxious to lead Continental troops to crush the pseudo state of Vermont and thus invalidate its titles to lands. Nor would Congressman Lovel, Congressman Wolcott, and others—all on the petition—be backward in supporting the attempt of Vermont to become a state.

Vermont was still just the New Hampshire Grants to Congress, but its Assembly went ahead as though it had complete authority to regulate its internal affairs. It had previously adopted a very radical constitution, frowned upon by many of the original states, and had passed several statutes. Now it considered, as all states must, the matter of Sex. Polygamy, rape, and even "lascivious carriage and conduct" were prohibited. Marriages were regulated. Adulterers were put down for a whipping, plus the branding with a hot iron of a capital A on the foreheads of both the lusting participants.

Henceforth, common drunks would pay eight shillings for each offense. What Colonel Allen thought of it isn't of record, but the use of "profane swearing & cursing" was assessed at six shillings per curse. The importance at the time of canoes was made apparent by a special law providing punishment for the stealing, or the using without permission, of canoes and boats.

In the field of diplomacy the Assembly voted to appoint a committee to manage Vermont's affairs at Congress—which Ethan seems to have anticipated—and Colonel Allen, Jonas Fay, and Paul Spooner were named. Ethan was also appointed a special messenger to confer with General George Washington about defending the northern frontier of Vermont against the British.

But this was one trip Ethan Allen did not make. General Washington had learned of the tactics being used in Congress by Colonel Allen, and he did not approve. Joseph Fay of Bennington, instead of Ethan, went to see the General. And in the brief interval of quiet Ethan sat down and wrote what was soon to be the best seller of the period.

This was titled "A Narrative of Colonel Allen's Captivity, Containing His Voyages and Travels, With the most remarkable Occurrences respecting him and many other Continental Prisoners of different Ranks and Characters. Interspersed with some Political Observations. Written by himself, and now published for the Information of the Curious in all Nations. Price Ten Paper Dollars."

Right off the bat, in the first long sentence of his Introduction, he went to work on the British. "Induced by a sense of duty to my country," says he, "I have concluded to publish the following narrative of the extraordinary scenes of my captivity, and the discoveries which I made in the course of the same, of the cruel and relentless disposition and behaviour of the enemy, towards the prisoners in their power; from which the state politician, and every gradation of character among the people, to the worthy tiller of the soil, may deduce such inferences as they shall think proper to carry into practice."

Following this salute, he went on to lambaste those unnamed but damnable persons who were "preferred to places of trust and profit by tory influence." Then he asked the critical reader to excuse any mistakes in grammar, "as the author has, unfortunately, missed of a liberal education."

The Narrative itself is a racy and fast-moving story of what happened at Fort Ticonderoga and for more than two years afterward. Bombastic and modest by turns, it shows humor on almost every page. Its studied understatements and irony read as well today as when written, and the quaintness of the author's style, which was considered unique even in its day, gives it a zest that many contemporaneous narratives sadly lack.

Those English officers who displayed any kindness to Ethan or to other prisoners come in for high praise; those who did not are abused in a manner at which the author was adept. Ethan was a rebel against the Crown, and throughout the Narrative the rebel Irish are honored. There is the unnamed Celt who saved Ethan from death at the hands of the gigantic savage at Montreal; the ship's petty officer Gillegan who generously permitted the prisoner to share his quarters; and the open-handed gentlemen of Cork who came aboard and loaded Ethan with clothes, provisions and rum.

The Narrative, as already pointed out, shows clearly the generosity of spirit of the author. Here was an opportunity, if he had chosen, to tell the world that he had been shabbily treated when command of the Grants regiment was given to Seth Warner. It was also an opportunity to crack down on Major Brown and Warner for leading him to attack Montreal and then not supporting his own spirited attempt. Montreal would doubtless have fallen into American hands, had Warner and Brown done their part.* Yet, there is no criticism of either in the Narrative. Indeed, the author goes out of his way to praise the bravery of Colonel Warner and his men at the battles of Bennington and Hubbardton.

The Narrative was completed late in March of 1779, and the author sent it to the *Pennsylvania Packet*, of Philadelphia, which ran it serially. It was an amazing success from the first installment, and was reprinted in book form as soon as the

---

* According to J. E. A. Smith, in his *History of Pittsfield* (1869), Brown thought that the St. Lawrence was too rough for crossing, and that Ethan, too, would not attempt it. It must have been rough, indeed, for Brown was not known for excessive prudence. He died with his boots on, facing the British, in 1780.

last chapter had appeared. The public promptly bought every copy, and the Philadelphia printers brought out a second edition, and a third. At the same time, in Boston, Draper & Folsom got out an edition, to be followed shortly by another.

Three printings were made in the following year, one each in Newbury and Danvers, Massachusetts, another in Norwich, Connecticut.*

Both the high and the low read Ethan's Narrative. The Reverend Jeremy Belknap, New Hampshire's early historian, said of the author that he was "an original in his way, but as rough and boisterous as the scenes he has passed through." But it was on *hoi polloi* that the book had the greatest effect. Painting as it did a truly horrible picture of most British officers and men, it was fine propaganda and had the added value of being a highly readable story. No historian has attempted to trace its influence, but it may well have had something of the effect, on lukewarm patriots, of the better known writings of Tom Paine, another "infidel."

Writing a book is an enervating job, and when the Narrative was out of the way Ethan felt the need for a little refreshment and relaxation. Another good excuse was that the 3rd of May was the anniversary of Colonel Allen's exchange as a prisoner. So, on May 3, 1779, dressing in his best silk suit—the one presented by the gentlemen of Cork—he laid away the cares of war and literature and began a round of visiting with his friends. Punch and stonewalls flowed with what one of the celebrants said was "an over abundance," but he was likely of weak stomach. Colonel Allen related additions and footnotes to his Narrative, and he and old Green Mountain Boys recalled the stirring days when they rode roughshod through the Grants to chastise the Yorkers. They didn't know it, but they were soon to ride again.

* At least nineteen editions of the Narrative appeared in the seventy-five years following publication.

At its February meeting the Vermont Assembly had passed an act for forming and regulating a state militia. To encourage "military skill," power was given to each captain of a company to draft men within the district he commanded. Any soldier who refused to serve, was to pay eighteen pounds with which to hire a substitute. If he didn't have eighteen pounds, the fine was to be raised by selling his goods or property to that amount.

Early in April the Continental Army, through its new commander of the Northern Department, Brigadier General Clinton, brother of the New York Governor, ordered "the pretended state of Vermont" to furnish troops to defend the frontier settlements.

Vermont was willing. What it called its Board of War convened and ordered the drafting of militia to begin. The various captains of companies listed the men they desired for service. It is just possible that the captains, all of whom were strong for Vermont, picked for service many of those men whose sympathies were known to be with New York. In any case, there was no trouble so far as patriot Vermonters were concerned; they either responded to the draft in person, ready to serve, or they paid their forfeits to the state.

In the town of Putney were a number of men who said they would not serve in the militia of a pretended state, nor would they pay a forfeit for the hiring of substitutes. This was the condition faced by Sergeant William McWain, draft officer for a militia company, when he arrived to induct draftees into service. Sergeant McWain tried the force of peaceful argument. He told Putney folks that they were defying the lightning, plus Ethan Allen, when they defied Vermont's authority. Putney folks damned the sergeant's eyes and told him to run along.

A resolute and patriotic man, Sergeant McWain proceeded to levy on the estates of the draftees, according to law. He took possession of two cows, one belonging to James Clay, the other to Ben Willson, and posted a notice that the animals would be sold one week hence "at public outcry." The sale never came off. On the morning of the day set for the sale, more than a hundred men, all unarmed, assembled in Putney. This was too much for the lone draft officer. The mob took the cows from him and returned them to their owners, while Sergeant McWain rode like Revere to Arlington, to warn Governor Chittenden and Council that red treason was afoot in Putney.

The Yorkers (Tories) of Putney and near-by towns were not done with their treason. While Vermont's Governor and Council were deliberating how best to proceed on Sergeant McWain's report, committees were formed in Putney, Hinsdale, Guilford, Brattleboro, Westminster and four other towns for the "purpose of opposing the pretended state of Vermont." They met openly in Brattleboro and drew up a letter which was sent to the Governor of New York. It related the outrages they suffered by reason of living in a region that had no well regulated government. They deplored the fact that Congress was temporizing in putting down the Vermont upstarts and outlaws. And they demanded, nothing less, that New York prepare to send troops to support their own poorly armed men who sought to shake off the "lawless rule" of a mob of "riatous men"—by which they referred to the duly constituted officers of the independent republic of Vermont.

Governor Clinton sent his reply by express, saying that if "Green Mountain Boys or other parties," pretending to carry out execution of pretended laws, should further trouble the honest Yorkers, he would dispatch New York troops, to lay once and for all the pretensions of Vermont authority.

These doings of the Putneyites and others were naturally considered high treason by the elected Governor of Vermont and his Council. It was a revolt that would have to be put down promptly and with vigor. In Vermont at the time no man was more prompt and vigorous than Colonel Ethan Allen. To him, as always, the Governor and Council turned again. Colonel Allen was ordered to raise one hundred volunteers and see what he could do about draft riots in the hills.

Legend has it that Ethan mounted a horse and rode hurriedly out of Arlington with fewer than twenty men. Along the way, as in times past, he stopped to sound the old Green Mountain call to arms. "We're going on a big wolf hunt," he rumbled at farms, at saw mills, and trappers' cabins. The record and not legend shows that *he* needed no draft laws, no forfeits or bonuses. By the time his force emerged on the east side of the mountains, more than a hundred armed men marched with him. Just to let the Yorkers know what to expect, he sent runners ahead into the affected territory to announce that Ethan Allen and *"five hundred soldiary"* were advancing with terrible tread.

Thirty-six men were arrested in Putney, Brattleboro, and the other Yorkish places, and taken to the jail at Westminster. During this affair Colonel Allen was unusually severe. He hurled insulting language at his prisoners and seems also to have struck a number of them across the buttocks with his huge sword. Throughout the business he reiterated that the arrests were not being made to distress individuals, but were intended to be a challenge to New York to turn out and fight Vermont. He wanted a trial by arms.

Friends of the prisoned Yorkers wrote Governor Clinton for immediate aid, saying that "otherwise our Persons and Property must be at the disposal of Ethan Allin which is more to be dreaded than Death with all its Terrors."

That was how Colonel Allen looked to Yorkers, and Tories.

The court town of Westminster seeming to be a hotbed of

these Tory vermin, old Death-and-Terrors Allen took measures. He had his men seize a large stock of gunpowder which had been sent the Yorkers by the state of New York, apparently with the idea of an armed revolt. He placed strong guards around the courthouse and jail to prevent any attempted delivery.

Moses Robinson, an old friend of Colonel Allen, and chief of the superior court of Vermont, was the presiding judge. The trials began.

State's Attorney Noah Smith told the court right off that he was unable to sustain charges against three of the prisoners, and withdrew the indictments. Next, Attorney Stephen Bradley, for the accused, asked the court to quash the proceedings against three other defendants, who were under age. The court granted this motion after Attorney Smith had consulted his Blackstone's Commentaries and conceded the point, and was about to proceed to trial of the remaining prisoners when "a vast commotion" broke out at the back of the courtroom.

The commotion, naturally enough, was Colonel Ethan Allen, a man who didn't go to the trouble every day of arresting men only to have them turned loose—law or no law. Attired in his well worn regimentals, waving his cocked hat, and with his sword clanking at every step, the tall Green Mountain Boy strode down the aisle. "What goes on here?" he shouted.

The startled court and spectators saw that the Colonel was breathless. He had not been in the room when the trials began, but word was brought to him—likely in Landlord Norton's place—that prisoners were being discharged without trial. Now he came to teach the court its duty toward all Yorkers, and Tories. Reaching the front of the room, he bowed to Judge Robinson, and before that surprised justice could speak he turned on State's Attorney Noah Smith.

"I would have the young gentleman know," he said in his best sonorous tone, "that with my logic and reasoning from the eternal fitness of things, I can upset his Blackstones, his whitestones, his gravestones and his brimstones."

Spectators got a laugh out of that one, but not so the court. The presiding justice, as soon as he could find voice at all, informed Colonel Allen that he would gladly listen to his remarks as a private citizen, but would not allow him to address the court, either in military attire or as a military man.

Ethan acknowledged the rebuke with a nod of his head. He threw his cocked hat on the judge's bench. He unbuckled his sword and slammed it down beside the hat. Then he turned to the judge and in what one present described as "a voice of Stentor," he ripped out two lines from Pope's *Essay on Man*:

> For forms of government let fools contest;
> Whate'er is best administer'd is best.

The reaction of the court and audience to this dramatic effort is not of record, but Ethan didn't give them much chance for reaction. Turning to Judge Robinson, he let the judge, the court, and all present know how he felt about eminent counsel for both the state and the defendants.

"Fifty miles I have come through the woods with my brave men," he said, "to support the civil with the military arm; to quell any disturbances should they arise; and to aid the sheriff and the court in prosecuting these Yorkers—the enemies of our noble state. I see, however, that some of them by the quirks of this artful lawyer, Bradley, are escaping the punishment they so richly deserve, and I find also that this little Noah Smith is far from understanding his business, since he at one time moves for a prosecution and in the next wishes to withdraw it. Let me warn your Honor to be on your guard lest these delinquents should slip through your fingers, and thus escape the rewards so justly due their crimes."

Bowing again to Judge Robinson, Ethan buckled on his sword, put on his hat, and strode straight out of the court-room without a word.

It had been as remarkable a five minutes as any Vermont court was likely to see. What effect the colonel's intrusion may have had on the court, if any, cannot be known; but it is of clear record that the next thirty defendants were tried and found guilty, one after another, and fined a total of £1477, 18 s., including costs of the court.

Colonel Allen did not return to the trials. Knowing the Vermont Assembly was about to sit in Windsor, farther up the Connecticut, he rode there to see if anything required his attention. Meanwhile, the enraged Yorkers, fined and freed by the court, were hurrying to New York to tell Governor Clinton that the time had come to take punitive measures against the pretended state of Vermont.

When the details of the arrests and fines had been laid before him, Governor Clinton decided that action on a large scale was necessary. He sent affidavits of the Westminster trials to John Jay, new president of Congress. He also wrote the New York Congressional delegation that he felt it his duty to order a thousand men of the New York militia to proceed to Brattleboro and put down the pretended officials of the pretended state of Vermont. He wrote General Washington that, as Congress had taken no action to do so, he was preparing to march on the riot-rousers and crush them. To Washington he pointed out that although Ethan Allen had been commissioned a brevet colonel by the Congress, he had seized and imprisoned without authority citizens of New York—or what Governor Clinton still called New York. He intimated that such actions on the part of a Continental colonel constituted high treason. And he added that he wished General Washington would return the "six brass six-pounders, together with their apparatus" which New York had loaned to the United States.

Clinton's letter showed how respect for Colonel Allen's abilities had mounted in New York. A former Governor of that province had sought to lay him low with an offer of one hundred pounds on his head. Governor Clinton felt that at least a thousand men and a train of artillery were needed to turn the trick.

> *"Rather than fail, I will retire with hardy Green Mountain Boys into the desolate caverns of the mountains, and wage war with human nature at large."*

CHAPTER X

Dangerous Horse Trading

———— ◆◆◆ ————

Ethan Allen knew nothing of what the outraged Yorkers would do after they had been .released. He cared less. Thoughts of an enemy's retaliation, if ever he had any such thoughts, never troubled his sleep. Arriving in Windsor on the 3rd of June, 1779, he received a great welcome from his old cronies in the Assembly; nor did they stop there with their appreciation. They voted pay for the volunteers who had arrested the Putneyites and others, and they elected their leader to be brigadier general of the Vermont militia.

At last the men of Vermont had recognized officially the one among them who had fought with no holds barred to make a state out of the Grants. It did the old soldier's heart good. He beamed over a dozen or so stonewalls and could see nothing but rural felicity on every hand.

The Assembly now appointed Ira Allen to be surveyor-general of Vermont. He was already its treasurer and a member of the Council, and this new office was destined to be even more important, at least so far as the Onion River Company was concerned.

General Allen, in fine fettle but in the same old regimentals, attended all the legislative sessions, without a vote. He needed none, for by force of action and personality he was now recognized as the most powerful man in Vermont, civil or military. At the same time, he was being attacked privately —very privately, indeed, for he was known to be a violent man—by certain Vermonters who disliked the way he ran things. They were nursing their enmity until they should see a chance to strike openly.

Governor Chittenden presently issued a proclamation pardoning every convict in the state except those (there were none) guilty of capital offenses. Just to make sure that this Christian gesture was not interpreted by Yorkers to indicate weakness, the Assembly, in which General Allen might be said to have considerable influence, passed a statute. It was significantly directed only at persons who should claim authority except "as shall be derived from this state," and the penalties read somewhat as though General Allen himself had dictated the statute. They promised to breakers of the law a stiff fine for the first offense; and not more than forty stripes for the second offense. If the person was still alive and able to commit a third offense, he got the works: "His right ear shall be nailed to a post, and cut off," and further, he "shall be branded in the forehead with a capital letter C on a hot iron."

General Allen viewed these measures with much satisfaction. "By God," he said, "they'll think twice."

Down in Philadelphia, Congress was fighting a war with Great Britain. Things weren't going so well. Georgia had been lost. The coasts of Virginia and Connecticut had been plundered by the British. A sizable army still threatened the northern frontier. Congress thus had little time to devote to squabbles among the thirteen legitimate states and Vermont. But the Congressional delegation from New York managed to offer a resolution the object of which was to get from Congress an acknowledgment of the right of each of the states to retain in its possession all the lands it held while a colony.

Congress dawdled over it. When news came that the men of the New Hampshire Grants had gone so far as to imprison, and fine, New York citizens who had refused to serve in a nonexistent militia, Congress acted with typical vigor: it voted to send a committee to investigate. The committee was also instructed to look into the business of "the conduct of Colonel Ethan Allen, now in the pay of the United States, concerning the charges exhibited against him by Governor Clinton." *

Committeemen Atlee and Witherspoon met with Governor Chittenden of Vermont in Bennington. All parties were very polite and conciliatory, but the Governor said the people of Vermont would as soon be under the jurisdiction of Great Britain as of New York. He told the committee that if the Yorkers in his state would only consent to turn out and serve with the Vermont militia against the British, he would be content to let the matter of jurisdiction rest until the common enemy, England, had been put to rout.

After much more talk, all of it comparatively pleasant, the two committeemen returned to Philadelphia—where Congress refused to hear their report because only two of five members had conferred. The one attempt of Congress to settle the Vermont question had, characteristically, failed in committee.

While the futile Congressional committee was performing in Vermont, Ethan Allen and Jonas Fay slipped away to Philadelphia and were admitted to Congress, which even then was wondering about this fabulous giant whose wild doings were creating almost as much talk as the Revolution itself.

* This latter instruction to the committee was dropped, and a line drawn through it in the Congressional Journal—a line, as John Pell points out in his *Ethan Allen*, that can be accounted for only "by the desire of certain Congressmen to refrain from hurting Ethan's feelings."

Allen and Fay laid Vermont's side of the riotous cow troubles before Congress, but they got little or no official encouragement from that body. Ethan returned to his home in Arlington, but not to loaf. He whacked out another pamphlet, called "A Vindication of the Opposition of the Inhabitants of Vermont to the Government of New-York, and of their Right to Form into an Independent State, Humbly Submitted to the Consideration of the Impartial WORLD, By Ethan Allen." For the first time one of his pamphlets could announce: "Printed by Alden Spooner, *Printer to the State of Vermont.*"

That, as General Allen might have said, would make them think twice.

The Vindication was simply a few new and stirring chords of the same old tune. Author Allen hewed straight to the line: Vermont was a state fully capable of handling its own affairs. It had proved as much. All Yorkers were land jobbers. All Vermonters were poor but very honest and worthy people. The author, as in the past, mixed poetry, bombast, documents, and common sense to prove his case. Soon as they were off the press, Ira Allen distributed pamphlets to the legislatures of New Jersey, Pennsylvania, Delaware, and Maryland.

John Jay, one of the great legal minds of the day, read the Vindication and said, "There is quaintness, impudence, and art in it." Indeed there was, and although it of course settled nothing, it did serve to let Congress and the various states know that Vermont was operating under a full head of steam.

Congress paid no official heed to the Vindication. It passed resolutions ordering the so-called State of Vermont to refrain from attempting to exercise jurisdiction until the first day of February, 1780, when, it intimated, the whole matter would be gone into thoroughly by Congress, and settled.

When this news reached the Vermont Assembly, a majority of the members stated they were willing to accede. General

Allen was aghast at such poltroonish feelings. He pounded the table. Didn't the simple Vermonters know that, if they conceded so much as an inch in the controversy, Congress by the influence of New York would "annihilate their state"? Couldn't they see that now, when Congress had a foreign war on its hands, was the time to present a resolute front? By the Eternal! Congress, with the war over, would do as it damned pleased about Vermont—and it would serve Vermont right, if its people were nothing but a lot of dillydally, white-livered, Tory-loving lackeys.

General Allen swore even more roundly than usual, and had himself appointed, wholly illegally, to a committee of the Assembly to outline a defense against any such annihilation as he viewed. He must have worked hard on the members, for five days later the Assembly voted to support Vermont's right to independence. And with a truly sovereign gesture, it voted to make grants of unappropriated lands in the state.

Applications for lands were soon forthcoming, among them one from General Ethan Allen, Colonel Sam Herrick, and Jonas Fay who, with some three hundred associates, asked for two large islands in Lake Champlain. This grant was made, and the islands became known as the Two Heroes, supposedly for Ethan Allen and Sam Herrick.*

The Allen boys thought the new crisis in the affairs of Vermont called for special efforts. Ira went south to see what he could do in the way of raising sentiment in the states beyond New York, while Ethan went to Boston for the same purpose. Here he appeared before the General Court to ask Massachusetts not to oppose Vermont's claims at the coming hearing before Congress. Finding that Massachusetts itself was planning to revive its ancient claim to parts of land in south-

* Historians do not agree as to the heroes for whom the islands were named. All name Ethan, but instead of Herrick certain writers have named Ira Allen and Seth Warner.

ern Vermont, and that the New Hampshire cabal was working in Congress for Vermont's return to New Hampshire, Ethan hurried back to Bennington to get out still another pamphlet. This one was to head off these new and upstart claimants. He titled it "A Concise Refutation of the Claims of New-Hampshire and Massachusetts Bay to the Territory of Vermont; with Occasional Remarks on the long disputed Claim of New-York to the same."

The pamphlet, which appeared in January of 1780, was signed jointly by Ethan and Jonas Fay, and it didn't give a fraction of an inch to anybody's claim to Vermont. It wasn't even conciliatory in tone, but stated it would be idiotic to submit Vermont's "Heaven-Born Freedom to the arbitrament of any tribunal below the stars." This was the first time that either Heaven or the stars had appeared in a pamphlet by General Allen, and it must have surprised his readers to read such a phrase. Apparently he well knew the laws of good propaganda, one of which is that God must be brought into the business somewhere, but he was unwilling to go further in the matter of Divinity than Heaven and stars.

Having called on Heaven as the only tribunal fit to pass on Vermont's legitimacy, the two authors wound up by saying Vermont would resort to arms rather than submit its case to Congress. This, patently, was high treason—an absolute challenge to the Congress of the United States. It was also first-class diplomacy, or statecraft. The dreaded first day of February passed without so much as a mention of Vermont in Congress.

By his swearing, his table pounding, his pamphlets and his all-around courage, Ethan Allen had won again, in spite of Vermont's easy-going Assembly, which didn't want to irritate Congress but was literally forced to vote its own independence.

A week later, however, the leading men of Vermont re-

ceived a rude shock. Governor Chittenden had written the
Continental Commissary in charge of military stores at Bennington, requesting him to send certain supplies to Vermont
troops quartered at Rutland. The Commissary sent no supplies. Instead, he wrote the Governor that the Commissary-
General of the United States had ordered that Vermont was
to receive no supplies of any kind out of Continental stores,
in Bennington or elsewhere.

This action sounded ominous, but it gave the wild Vermonters no pause. At least one of them was not daunted.
General Allen went right down into Connecticut on his horse,
and there, and in Boston, he bought gunpowder and lead to
the value of £5,174,* which was an awful lot of powder and
lead. He gave his personal note in these purchases and had the
ammunition started for Vermont at once. Heaven was all right
in its way, according to General Allen, but he liked to see a
full magazine of powder.

And now the Vermont Council took steps. They passed
what amounted to being a wartime act prohibiting the transportation out of the state of wheat, flour, pork, and other provisions. Neither Ethan nor the other leaders could know exactly what the Continental Congress and its Army had in
mind in refusing supplies, but they determined to be prepared
for any emergency, war with the United States included.

A little later Governor Chittenden signed a letter, no doubt
written by Ira Allen, to the president of Congress. He referred to the "future tryal by Congress" of the Vermont question, saying he doubted not that, if Vermont submitted, New
York, New Hampshire, and Massachusetts would divide Vermont among them "the same as the King of Prussia, the Empress of Russia, and the Empress of Hungary divided Poland

---

* It is impossible to know how much money this figure represented in
Sterling, for the Continental currency of the time was notoriously erratic
in value.

between those three powers." The only difference he could see, said Vermont's Governor, was that Vermont was far from being in the possession of the bordering states.

With lead in the bag and powder in the horn, the Green Mountain men were beginning to talk tough to Congress.

This was the line General Allen had so long hewed to; but now an entirely new note was sounded. In his letter to the President of Congress the Governor went on to say that Vermont, if she chose, might accept terms of cessation of hostilities with Great Britain "without the approbation of any man or body of men." He pointed out that he could see no reason why Vermont should maintain a defense of the northern frontier for the benefit of a United States which refused to recognize her. It was fair warning of a policy the embattled Green Mountain men were about to adopt as a last defense of their autonomy.

The British had long been aware of the feelings of Vermont, which, bluntly, were that every step she took to support the United States only rendered her own position the more precarious. If the war were brought to a successful conclusion, the claiming states of New York, New Hampshire, and Massachusetts would leap at Vermont, as Ethan Allen said, and rend her limb from limb.

Sir Henry Clinton was in command of the British army in America. For a major general's commission and several thousand guineas, he had bought Benedict Arnold, who proved to be high at the price. Sir Henry, taking the Vermont question into consideration, now laid plans to buy Ethan Allen for a good deal less. The first move was made through Colonel Beverly Robinson, commander of a regiment of Tory Americans serving with the British troops.

On the street in Arlington, Vermont, one day soon, a man dressed in rough civilian clothing accosted General Allen and gave him a letter from Robinson. It was carefully written, but it finally came to the point; and the point was that Sir Henry Clinton was prepared to negotiate a separate peace with Vermont. Robinson said that he himself could not make any definite proposals, but that he was assured Vermont could obtain a separate government under the Crown. He spoke of the "wild and chimerical scheme of the Americans," by which he meant the Revolution; and closed with the expressed hope for a restoration of peace and happiness to America, under British rule.

This was hot and dangerous stuff, and Ethan Allen knew it. He sent the messenger back to Robinson without a reply and immediately placed Robinson's letter before Governor Chittenden, Ira Allen, and a few other leading men who happened to be in Arlington. This small group, not more than eight men, decided not to have any written correspondence with Robinson. They also thought it would be well to keep the door open; Governor Chittenden wrote General Haldimand, British commander in Canada, proposing a cartel for the exchange of prisoners, and the letter was sent to a British ship then on Lake Champlain.

While these intrigues were being prepared, the British made a show of force on the lake. Scouts of the Vermont militia reported great activity, and that troops were being landed to attack the northern settlements. General Allen set up headquarters at Castleton. A party of Indians, led by British officers, raided the town of Royalton, killed a few men and burned the place. This, however, was the only attack made; and many a Vermonter not in the know was pleased, but curious to know why a supposedly hostile army of ten thousand British did not march into Vermont whose sole protection was a small militia.

But the British did not attack, and now began a long and complicated exchange of messages and conversations between Generals Haldimand and Carleton and agents of the British on one side, and about eight leading men of Vermont on the other. Justus Sherwood, a Tory who had known Ethan well in former days, presently came from Haldimand with a flag of truce and a reply to Chittenden's request for a cartel. It was favorable, and it also promised that during the negotiations and exchanges, no attacks would be made on Vermont. Ethan accepted the letter and laid it before a council of militia officers, who discussed it.

Ethan would give no written reply to Sherwood, but he talked long with him. He made it clear at once that he would have no part in "a damned Arnold plan to sell his country and his honor by betraying the trust reposed in him." Sherwood replied that, while that was all very well, now was the time for Vermont to shake off the yoke of Congress and New York and New Hampshire and Massachusetts and resume its former allegiance to Great Britain. He said he was authorized to promise that if Vermont would join the Crown she should be formed into a separate province, and that General Allen should command a force of Vermonters to serve with the King's troops.

Ethan said he was not empowered to speak for Vermont—he would have to take the matter up with the Governor and other elected representatives; further, that if any declaration of a proposal were made at present to join the British his own people would cut off his head.

The Vermont militia officers were satisfied with the proposed truce during the cartel, but one of them pointed out that the truce would still leave northern New York open to attack by the British. To this Sherwood replied that he would pledge that no offensive against northern New York would be made while negotiations were being carried out.

Ethan proposed that Vermont circulate further manifestoes complaining of its treatment at the hands of Congress. Then, if Congress did not recognize Vermont as a state, he thought they should issue an invitation to all peoples and nations on earth to a free trade with her as a sovereign state. He shied away from the idea of making Vermont a British province, and told Sherwood that any revolution of such a nature must be the work of time. And he concluded with his usual honesty: he told Sherwood that, if Congress granted recognition to Vermont, all negotiations with the British were to be at an end and were to be kept secret on both sides.*

Sending an officer to see Sherwood safely out of the lines, General Allen issued orders disbanding his militia. Get on with the farm work, he told them. He also sent word to Colonel Webster, commander of American troops on the northern border of New York, asking him to cease hostilities.

The Vermont Assembly was then sitting at Bennington. General Allen laid the Haldimand proposals respecting a truce during the cartel before the legislators, who passed a resolution of approval. Some of the boys in the Assembly, however, smelled a rat. It didn't seem to make sense that a large British army should suddenly cease all operations against Vermont, just because a few prisoners might be exchanged. Assemblyman William Hutchins felt so keenly about it that he presented a remonstrance aimed at General Allen. The General heard it read; then he stood up and said he wanted to hear no more of such talk. (The exact nature of the charges cannot be known, for the papers were destroyed.) The General said he noted an uneasiness among some of the people on account of his conduct in dismissing the Vermont militia. He was ready to resign, he said, but it was beneath his character to sit there and hear "such false and ignominious assertions." He walked out of the house.

---

* The exact nature of these discussions between Ethan Allen and his officers and Justus Sherwood were unknown to historians for well over a century, or until H. S. Wardner discovered the private journal of Sherwood in the Canadian Archives at Ottawa, and gave them light in his *Birthplace of Vermont*, published in 1927.

The remonstrance was withdrawn, and destroyed. The legislature observed that with a truce in effect Vermont needed no militia, and they accepted General Allen's resignation. They resolved a vote of thanks for his good services and backed it up with a grant of land. To Ethan Allen and associates they gave the town of East Haven.

During November of 1780, messengers exchanged lists of Vermont prisoners held in Montreal. It was considered too late in the season to make the exchanges. They could wait until the ice went out of the rivers and the lake in the spring.

If many Vermonters were puzzled because the British suddenly stopped a long-planned attack on their frontier, men of the states were not only puzzled but alarmed. Ethan Allen did what he could to alarm them even more. He wrote to General John Stark that the truce of Vermont with the British "has considerably engrossed the attention of the public." He mentioned certain mysterious manifestoes which Vermont might soon proclaim. It all had a sinister sound.

Rumors flew everywhere through the states. It was said that Ethan Allen had at last become thoroughly disgusted with Congress and was preparing to join the British. Another story had it that Ethan was raising a regiment of Tories, that he was collecting vast stores of grain in the Cohasse country on the Connecticut River, that he had been seen in Quebec in company with British officers.

Contacts by messenger with the British were continued by the Vermont men, and Colonel Beverly Robinson in a letter pressed the Vermonters to declare their state a Crown colony. But General Allen would declare nothing to the British. Thinking, no doubt, it was time to let Vermont's stand be known again, he wrote to the President of Congress and enclosed the two letters from Robinson. Once more he put his still independent republic on record.

"I do not hesitate," he wrote, "to say I am fully grounded in opinion that Vermont has an indubitable right to agree on terms of cessation of hostilities with Great Britain, provided the United States persist in rejecting her application for a union with them, for Vermont, of all people, would be the most miserable, were she obliged to defend the independence of united claiming states, and they, at the same time, at full liberty to overturn and ruin the independence of Vermont."

It was another threat, the boldest of them all so far, and Ethan closed on a typical and resounding note, one of his truly classic efforts.

"I am resolutely determined," he wrote to him who was as good as President of the United States, "to defend the independence of Vermont as Congress are that of the United States, and rather than fail, will retire with hardy Green Mountain Boys into the desolate caverns of the mountains, and wage war with human nature at large."

When Congress heard that letter read it must have come to the conclusion, if it had not already done so, that it was dealing with a wild as well as a determined man. It should be recalled that this period was a most trying one for the United States. Arnold had tried to sell them down the river. Major André had been hanged. The country was seething with rumors of further and worse treacheries. General Allen's conduct and that of Vermont appeared highly treasonable to many; but no one could say that the "treason" was being done in the bushes, behind the barn. This was the second time General Allen and his men had warned the highest American officials what was afoot in the Green Mountains.

Presently the Vermonters made a move in another direction. They had discovered that the people who lived in the strip of New York territory between the Vermont border and the Hudson River were in favor of coming under Vermont jurisdiction. These particular Yorkers had noted with considerable awe that the Green Mountaineers had somehow re-pulsed the British, that Vermont farmers were free to go about their plowing without fear of invasion—or so it seemed, any-way.

So these wondering Yorkers held a meeting in Cambridge, New York, and sent a petition to Vermont, asking to join the republic. This pleased General Allen immeasurably. He rode to Cambridge at once, and he must also have lost no time in getting into action; a few days later New York's Governor Clinton was writing that "this Allyn is going about persuading and deluding the people."

It was a move bold enough to make rashness seem an under-statement. Here was Vermont, not even sure of its claimed borders—if any—advancing into New York with the intention of cutting off a slice of territory eighty miles long and twenty miles wide, to add to its own doubtful state. No one but Gen-eral Allen would have attempted it.

While Ethan was "deluding" the Yorkers, Ira Allen was instigating a revival of the old plan to join the sixteen orphan towns of New Hampshire to Vermont. Vermont had form-ally and officially rejected the sixteen towns, but now, if she was not to become a state, she would take what territory she could from both sides, and go it serenely alone. Writing later of this period, Ira Allen saw it as a time when "the genius of Vermont was Fruitful in Resources"—which was understate-ment. He noted that "even in the gulph of difficulties, and on the Verge of Ruin, she waxed Strong, extended her wings and made herself known to the Nations of the Earth."

General Washington was now writing that he wished Con-gress would decide the Vermont question and add the strength of Green Mountain men to the United States. He noted that many deserters from his army had fled to Vermont, where there were no taxes and no danger of arrest, and he feared that if something were not done most of his troops would be

General Allen in gold lace.

Page 189

found living in the Green Mountains. Apparently it was not thought advisable to send provost guards into Vermont after Continental deserters.

Ira Allen and Joseph Fay conducted an exchange of prisoners with the British at Skenesborough. The British commissioners, losing patience because Vermont had made no move to join the Crown, now pressed Allen and Fay for a decision. Ira responded that the people were not prepared for such a revolutionary proposal. It would take time, he said—and time was exactly what he most wanted. He knew that Washington and Lord Cornwallis were then locking horns, and he hoped that any hour would bring news of his Lordship's defeat.

After using every objection he could think of or invent, Ira Allen agreed to a plan: General Haldimand should issue a proclamation offering officially to confirm Vermont as a colony under the Crown; the British forces should sail up Lake Champlain in full force in October, when the Vermont Assembly would be in session, and the British should then send an agent to distribute copies of the proclamation to the legislators.

October came. So did the British. They sailed up the lake under General St. Leger, and garrisoned at Fort Ticonderoga. The Vermont Assembly convened.

Acting as liaison man for the British was the same Justus Sherwood who had previously discussed with Ethan Allen the matter of a truce and cartel. Now Sherwood was impatiently waiting for word from Ira Allen, to tell him that the Assembly was meeting and the time was ripe for the British proclamation.

It is apparent that Sherwood was suspicious of Ira, as well he might have been. Hearing no word at the appointed time, nor for days afterward, Sherwood decided to send a letter direct to the Governor of Vermont. Needing a means to send it, Sherwood dispatched a party to capture a Vermont scout and bring him to the British camp, where he could be given the letter and released.

Taking a Vermont scout without trouble, even during a truce, was apparently impossible. The British party soon ran across one Sergeant Tupper and nine men who didn't wait to hear what it was all about but started shooting. The fire was returned, and Tupper was killed. His party surrendered.

Here was one of those incidents, unplanned, unfortunate, and fraught with trouble. General St. Leger acted promptly to undo the harm. He dined and wined the captured Vermont scouts, then sent them with a flag through his lines with the dead Tupper's clothes and arms and a letter of regret to Governor Chittenden.

The return of a dead soldier's clothes and arms from a supposed enemy created a sensation in the Assembly that almost grew into a riot. One Runnals (or Reynolds) wanted to know why a British general should be so polite as to return a dead Vermonter's arms and clothing. Ira Allen answered Runnals heatedly, saying that the present was no time for what Ira termed "impertinent questions." Governor Chittenden and Ira then secretly rewrote St. Leger's letter, holding out "everything which prudence and policy dictated." Then the "revised" communication was read to the Assembly. Whether or not the legislators were much fooled by the substitution is a question.

Before anything further could be done about the British proclamation, St. Leger received news of the surrender of Cornwallis at Yorktown. He must have felt that the Vermonters would not be interested in further proposals from the British, for before night he broke camp and started moving his army of ten thousand men to St. Johns on the Sorel (now the Richelieu River), in Canadian territory.

The surrender of Cornwallis just at this time was a mighty fine thing for the horse-trading Vermonters. That proclamation by General Haldimand could have become most embarrassing, and might well have led to the invasion of Vermont both by British and by Continental troops.

Ethan Allen had not been inactive during these weeks. He was over there in York State doing a job at which he had no equal; he was "raising the riatous crew" who lived between the Vermont line and the Hudson and thought they wanted to be part of Vermont.

Exactly what commission Ethan held in these proceedings, if any, is not clear. Some time after his resignation as General of the Vermont militia, the Assembly had voted him a new commission as brigadier general. But this he had refused. Commissioned or not, eyewitnesses to the trouble now brewing in York State reported that "General Allen is bound up in gold lace and feels himself grand as the Great Mogul." This would indicate he had substituted some sort of fancy uniform for a commission, the lack of which had never troubled him in the past, anyway. He had also toted in an old field gun to aid his "liberation" of a goodly hunk of the state of New York.

> *"Unless the inhabitants of Guilford peacefully submit, I swear that I will lay it as desolate as Sodom and Gomorrah, by God!"*

CHAPTER XI

Ethan's Republic Totters

A minor civil war naturally broke out in the wake of General Allen's ride through the eastern strip of New York. He enjoyed hugely this taking an offensive in his old enemy's own territory, and seeing his fire spread for eighty miles or more.

Loyal Yorkers, who hated the very names of Allen and Vermont, were hurriedly taking steps to put down the uprising and calling for troops to aid them. More than a hundred families fled out of New York to Bennington, in fear of their loyal neighbors. John Williams of White Creek wrote his Governor Clinton in December of 1781 that the situation grew worse daily as Ethan rode. "Nothing but Yorkers and Vermonters is talked of," said Williams, "even by boys and youngsters. . . . If nothing is done by this state [New York] soon, we shall be compelled to submit ourselves to the jurisdiction of Vermont. . . ."

General Allen in gold lace, and one cannon, were giving New York a taste of the old medicine New York had so often prescribed for others. Governor Clinton roused himself and sent two hundred militiamen to reconquer his lost territory. Governor Chittenden sent about the same number of Vermonters to aid General Allen and his army of Vermont-Yorkers to hold the line won. The two armies camped on opposite sides of the Wallumscaik River.

The Governor of Vermont took this opportunity to send Congress a letter about the current Vermont-New York war, saying that when these little matters were settled, there could "remain no obstacle to bar Vermont from a seat in Congress." The Wallumscaik war continued, but with little real violence. There were a number of brawls and small riots in taverns, and several prisoners were taken. New York tried to get General John Stark, camped with troops at Saratoga, to take the field against Vermont, but that old warhorse, whose courage no man ever questioned, did not think it advisable.

Vermont sent strong re-enforcements to its army, and the Yorkers began melting away without firing a shot. Ethan Allen, the well known author, fired a verbal shot after them. He sat down and turned out another of his popular pamphlets, this one titled "The Present State of the Controversy," by which he referred to the rather chaotic relations between his own homemade republic and the states of New Hampshire and New York.

Author Allen had a good time writing this work. On every page one finds robust humor, even irony and satire, at which he was getting better all the time. He "proved" Vermont's right to those parts of New York and New Hampshire which wished to be under her wing. For the benefit of Congress and the United States he bragged a bit over the manner in which his republic had prevented an army of ten thousand British from invading the United States from the north. And he laughed like hell at the claims of New York and New Hampshire. For them to stand there "griping their respective claims fast hold on Vermont," he said, "and at the same time make such a hedious outcry against the gripe of Vermont upon them, is altogether romantic and laughable."

All of which made perfectly good sense in Vermont but not elsewhere.

The latest Allen pamphlet was hardly dry before a weighty letter came to Governor Chittenden at Bennington. It was from none other than General George Washington, and it seemed to promise what Vermont had been fighting for since before the start of the Revolution. After rehearsing the various controversies, General Washington went on to recognize Vermont's claims as just.

"It is not my business," wrote the greatest figure in the land, "nor do I think it necessary, now to discuss the origin of the right of a number of inhabitants, to that tract of country, formerly distinguished by the name of the New Hampshire Grants, and now by that of Vermont. I will take it for granted that their right was good, because Congress, by their resolve of the 7th of August, imply it; and by that of the 20th are willing fully to confirm it, provided the new state is confined to certain prescribed bounds. It appears therefore to me, that the dispute of boundary, is the only one that exists; and *that* being removed, all other difficulties would be removed also, and the matter terminate to the satisfaction of all parties.

"You have nothing to do," went on the Father of his country, "but to withdraw your jurisdiction to the confines of your own limits, and obtain an acknowledgment of independence and sovereignty."

Here was something you could get your teeth into. None of the vaporings, none of the temporizing, none of the futile committees of a Congress, but plain honest talk from the most revered man in the United States. The letter seemed to Vermonters to settle everything for once and all. If dissolving the unions with parts of New York and New Hampshire would bring Congress to admit Vermont, then it should be done, and promptly.

Both Vermont and New York had been satisfied with the

boundaries laid down in the resolution of August 20th to which Washington referred; but Vermont had failed to accept the resolution because of lack of faith in Congressional promises. The letter from General Washington, however, put an entirely different face on the matter. The Vermont Assembly went into action and after ten days of debate voted to relinquish, without asking their leave, those parts of the two adjoining states which had joined Vermont.

And now, having complied so promptly and handsomely with the requirements, Vermont was confident of immediate recognition. With understandable elation she held an election and named her delegates to sit in Congress.

The proud delegates did not take their seats. Southern states did not now want Vermont admitted, fearing that New England would then control the Congress—a thing to be abhorred. Then, too, Kentucky was trying to break away from Virginia to become a state, which Virginia viewed with alarm. The condition of Kentucky, in fact, was somewhat analogous to that of Vermont.

And Congress, in general, was in a cantankerous mood, not to say imperial. The Revolution was over, even if peace had not been declared, and the Congressional body was beginning to feel its oats. Vermont had voluntarily renounced its claims to territory in adjacent states: *that* matter was settled. And now Congress turned a frosty gaze on the would-be delegates from the green hills, and made no move to legitimize their state.

Instead, Congress went into a fury. It passed resolutions of severe censure on Vermont's officials. It resolved that Vermont be required to make full restitution to the many persons condemned to banishment or confiscation of property, and that they not be molested on their return to their former homes; and it closed the subject with a threat: "that the United States will take effectual measures to enforce a compliance with the aforesaid resolutions, in case the same shall be disobeyed by the people of the said district."

This blow, many people in Vermont felt, was mortal. Vermont seemed to be tottering to a quick fall and the "annihilation" against which Ethan Allen had so often warned and fought. It was freely predicted both by Vermonters and by others that the pretended state had come to the end of its rope, and that presently it would be sliced into pieces, to be gobbled up by the claiming states of New York, New Hampshire, and Massachusetts.

In this period of gloom, however, a few spirits glowed like coals. Governor Chittenden and his Council promptly prepared and sent to Congress a sizzling remonstrance, telling that body that by their own Articles of Confederation they were prohibited from meddling with the internal policy of any state. The protest bluntly refused to revoke the legal decisions of Vermont in respect to the "criminals" already mentioned: banishment and confiscation had been Vermont's own business, not that of Congress.

New York and New Hampshire were in high glee at the welshing of Congress, and sneering editorials appeared: Vermont was and always had been a pretended state and nothing more. The savage, cruel, abusive, horrendous, and awful infidel, Ethan Allen, had ridden to the fall he well deserved.

Ethan and Ira Allen, together with Chittenden and the other real leaders of Vermont were now thoroughly disillusioned about Congress and the United States in general. So were most of the citizens. Colonel Stephen R. Bradley of the Vermont militia reported that all over Vermont men were damning the Congress and, as a toast, drank confusion to it. Other toasts, he said, were being drunk to the health of King George the Third of England. Sam Robinson of Bennington, one of Vermont's leading men, said publicly that "the Vermonters are a-fixen a pill that will make the Yorkers and Congress hum."

Citizens of Berkshire County, Massachusetts, sent word that they would assist the embattled Green Mountaineers, by arms, to defy Congress and New York.

The Governor of Vermont, with his Council—plus Ethan Allen—met in a heated session. Congress would have none of Vermont, would it? Then by the Great Jehovah, by the Devil himself and all the various "little insipid devils of hell," Vermont would have none of Congress. Becoming a state in the Union looked hopeless, wholly out of the question. From this time onward General Allen and his men devoted their energies to making Vermont an independent republic, in name as in fact. If that did not prove feasible, then it should be a province of Great Britain.

General Allen knew that the Green Mountain republic must keep the British from attacking. It must also so order its internal affairs that the minority party of York sympathizers would not get out of hand and bring both Congress and the state of New York to aid them. The republic was sitting on two baskets of eggs, or on two kegs of powder, as one Councilman remarked.

The Vermont militia and sheriffs were told to be closely on guard for local Yorker uprisings, especially in the town of Guilford.

And now the flow of letters was resumed between Vermont officials and the British in Canada. Justus Sherwood, who had arranged the cartel for exchange of prisoners, again acted as chief liaison agent for the British. Many people in Vermont had come to suspect the intrigue but knew nothing definite.

During the intervals of waiting for letters from the British, Ethan turned his hand to completing a book he had planned for almost twenty years. It was to be on Philosophy, which he always spelled with a capital letter, and it had had its inception in the long talks he and Dr. Thomas Young of Salisbury had enjoyed in Connecticut taverns before the Revolution.

Dr. Young had died in the meantime, and Ethan, on one of his many trips to Philadelphia, had got the notes left by the doctor. Originally it was planned to be a collaboration.

Ethan did most of his writing at home in Sunderland where, so tradition has it, he was aided by a young college graduate, said to have been a Harvard man. The Allen library at this time included Pope's *Essay on Man*, one of Ethan's favorite books; Salmon's *Geographical Grammar*, which was doubtless more correct but hardly so extensive as Ethan's own; Rathburn's *Account of the Shaker Sect;* a Bible, and two dictionaries, one of which was Dr. Johnson's.

The young Harvard man must have put in a few hectic weeks. It was Ethan's custom to dictate his thoughts on philosophy, walking up and down the room, swinging his cane and pausing to roar especially loud when some fine idea or turn of speech hit him fair. Sunderland folk, passing by the Allen house, often heard shouts that sounded like fearful "infidelity," and endless arguments. The college youth, it is said, would interrupt on occasion with a point of grammar, probably of syntax, things that never troubled General Allen in the least. The General would then swear most horribly, pounding his cane until all in the village could hear, and became aware that Literature, no less than War, was not to be had without clamor and struggle.

It was a trying period for Sunderland. If a cow failed to give down her milk, citizens were sure it was because evil spirits were all about, attracted by the awful infidel, at work in his sulphurous den. The very eaves dripped brimstone. Every thunderstorm was laid to the same cause. So were unseasonal rains which wet the hay. Almost every known act of God except an earthquake was visited on Sunderland that spring, and townsmen were glad when the General was done.

The manuscript was completed early in July of 1782. Ethan put it into his saddlebags and rode down to Hartford, where

Watson & Goodwin had been pleased to publish his political pamphlets. Here he ran head on and all unsuspecting into a snag many authors have met, before and since. Watson & Goodwin looked over the work and refused politely but positively to have anything to do with it. "Why," said they in horror, "this is an attack on religion!"

"It's damned well nothing of the kind," roared the Green Mountain philosopher. "It is an attack on superstition and error, on the ghostly tyranny of the clergy."

Messrs. Watson & Goodwin hemmed and hawed. Ethan pleaded. He swore. He abused the printers roundly, calling them poltroons; apparently he hoped to frighten or shame them into printing his book.

Whether or not he would have been successful will never be known. Vermont was sizzling again. As so often in the past, the republic needed its strong man. A horseman galloped into Hartford to say that General Allen was wanted at home and quickly. Leaving the manuscript with the embarrassed printers, he hurried to Vermont.

It was the damned Yorkers again, but this time it was more serious business than ever before—trouble that had been brewing in the aforementioned town of Guilford, brewing for five years and now, apparently, come to a head.

Since 1772 Guilford had existed practically as a tiny republic by itself. It had a New York charter. When Vermont declared its independence in 1777, Guilford refused to acknowledge its authority and continued to govern its village by town meetings. It seems to have governed well, but that was beside the question. On occasion, as has been shown, Vermont had cracked down, with arrests and fines and confiscations, but now the Guilfordites had taken new heart at the recent action of Congress. They were determined to resist. Governor Clinton of New York, whom they recognized as their titular head, had encouraged them to strike now when Vermont was tottering and seemed about to fall apart. He wrote them that resistance by force was wholly justifiable.

Guilford citizens held a meeting and voted to "stand against the pretended state of Vermont, with lives and fortunes." They secured a sizable store of powder and lead, and began drilling. The open break had occurred while Ethan was down in Connecticut. Jonathan Hunt, a Vermont sheriff, had gone to Guilford to execute a writ against Timothy Church. Church raised his neighbors and defied Hunt to arrest him. Outnumbered forty to one, the sheriff withdrew and went to Bennington to report the outrage to Governor Chittenden and his Council.

Apparently that body felt entirely inadequate when Ethan Allen was absent. It sent the horseman to bring him home.

General Allen washed the ink off his hands and got into his fine uniform, the one with gold lace he had worn when he frightened the Yorker army away from the Wallumscaik River. He buckled on his noted sword, got astride a black horse, and let it be known he was going on another wolf hunt. Within a few days he had an army of more than two hundred men, all volunteers, gathered at Bennington.

The General sent Colonel Ira Allen and a party of twenty men ahead as an advance guard. "And Colonel Allen," said General Allen, "while you are about it, you might arrest that eternal Tim Phelps who has been calling himself a sheriff."

"Yes, sir," said Colonel Allen, and with his party started over the mountains, followed at a proper distance by the main body of troops.

Timothy Phelps, it is true, had accepted a commission as sheriff from New York, and was therefore hated by honest Vermonters. Phelps was also an able and a violent man, and many feared him. Not long before, he had felled a Vermont sheriff with a pitchfork handle, and he was loud-mouthed, to boot.

It is not clear from the record just how Phelps was taken, but taken he was on the first day the Vermonters rode. They brought him before General Allen.

Before the General had a chance to open his mouth, Phelps shouted that he himself was the true sheriff; all Vermonters were mere pretenders. He abused General Allen and his men, calling them a pack of rioters and outlaws. He even commanded them, in the name of the state of New York, to disperse.

General Allen did not say anything, but he acted promptly and, for him, with unusual gentleness. Sitting on his black horse, he quietly unsheathed his sword. When the pseudo sheriff paused for breath, the General reached out and with one mighty swipe cut Phelps' hat neatly from his head. "Take the damned rascal out of the way," he told the guards. Then he "galloped off to superintend the operations of other portions of his forces."

Ethan's forces grew as the march proceeded, and he was glad. He knew that this expedition was perhaps the most important he had commanded since '75. If Guilford were permitted to defy Vermont, the republic was done. If the Guilford trouble managed to gain the attention of Congress, Continental troops might march into Vermont to put it under martial law. So, the General wanted a show of such force that Guilford would give in without bloodshed.

As the troops approached the village they numbered more than four hundred men, most of them mounted. Detachments had been sent to near-by Halifax to arrest Yorkers there, and these were brought to Guilford. The arrests in Guilford village were made without bloodshed and with little violence.

Late in the afternoon General Allen, a part of his troops, and all the prisoners set out for Brattleboro. A little way out of Guilford, the advance guard was surprised by an ambush. Volleys of gunfire rattled across the road. Several Vermonters were wounded, and the others turned and ran back to the main body of troops, leaving men bleeding on the ground.

General Allen paused briefly for a council of war. Many of his men, now much excited, asked him to kill a Guilford prisoner for each man killed by the enemy (none had died so far); but General Allen wanted no more bloodshed than necessary, and he had another idea. Leaving his horse with his troops, the tall General strode afoot into the village at the head of a squad of his men. Coming to the center of the settlement he paused and delivered a brief proclamation that went ringing straight into Vermont history.

"I, Ethan Allen," he roared loud enough for all the townsfolk to hear, "do declare that I will give no quarter to the man, woman, or child who shall oppose me, and unless the inhabitants of Guilford peacefully submit to the authority of Vermont, I swear that I will lay it as desolate as Sodom and Gomorrah, by God!"

It was an ear-filling threat, uttered by one whose very name was a terror to Yorkers. The threat also was cannily worded by a master of bombast who knew that Guilfordites were pious people who read their Bible and knew well enough what had happened to Sodom and Gomorrah.*

Once delivered of his frightful oath, the General glowered hard at the town and all in it. The terrified citizens dispersed quickly and quietly, to hide until the tough though classic General had gone.

General Allen and his troops took twenty Yorkers to Westminster for jailing and trial, but it is obvious that the General did not write the charges against them. These began, "Not having God before their eyes, but being moved and seduced

---

* This awful threat of General Allen's at Guilford entranced all early historians of Vermont. In the indexes of their books, under *Allen, Ethan,* appear the notations "his terrible proclamation," "his awful proclamation," etc.

by the instigation of the Devil," and went on to lay charges of treason, insurrection, and rebellion.

All the prisoners got something—a fine, jail, or banishment; but before any of them were released General Allen gave them a piece of his mind and loaded it with propaganda. "Had I but the orders," he told them, "I could go to Albany, New York, and be head monarch in three weeks. And I have a good mind to do it."

He damned Governor Clinton with "blatant and vulgar oaths" and wound up with his current and final opinion of both Clinton and the Congress of the United States. "You have called on your God Clinton," he told the jailed Yorkers, "until you are tired. Call now on your God Congress, and they will answer you as Clinton has done."

General Allen wanted them to know that Vermont was now too strong to be intimidated by outsiders, but he must have wondered if the Guilford affair would not bring Continental troops.

Laying Yorkers by the heels was just good clean fun for General Allen. The business of carrying on the intrigue with the British in Canada was no fun at all. It had to be done furtively, and furtiveness was no part of Ethan's character. He liked battle in the open, where the man with the most courage, the longest sword, and the most terrible voice could display his talents.

Even in his contacts with the British agents Ethan Allen found it difficult to be as circumspect as conditions warranted. Many of his letters to General Haldimand, British commander in Canada, were signed with eight crosses, but others were signed boldly with his own name, and dated to boot. At times he warned the British they must be more careful in selecting their messengers, one of whom, named Holleburt, according to Ethan, had been attending public dances and "is much given to drink."

Most of the horse trading devolved upon Ethan, for Ira Allen was ever a careful man, not liking the appearance of halters, and Governor Chittenden was more or less dominated by the two brothers. Congress now knew about the intrigue, and if it pushed the matter with an investigation Ethan Allen would most assuredly be hanged by the neck; and although Ira, Chittenden, and a few others were just as deeply involved they had played their cards so closely that they might have been cleared. Ethan Allen, in short, was always the man who exposed himself most.

The intrigue continued. Meanwhile the real fighting of the Revolution ceased altogether, and General Washington proclaimed the 19th of April, 1783, as the official date for the cessation of all hostilities. Such a notable event appealed to Ethan as a good excuse for a party, and he went on a party on the night of the 18th, in Manchester, Vermont. He did not, however, forget the cares of state, for he dashed off a letter to Justus Sherwood, the British agent. Heading it "At a Tavern at Manchester, half seas over, the 18th of April, 1783," he went on to say:

"The sudden alteration of political matters in America makes it needless for me to expatiate on policy. The die is cast, the peace is taken place and the United States are acknowledged independent of Great Britain. How Vermont as a body politic or as individuals will fare, time and future scenes must determine.

"In the meantime, I assure you that Vermont are determined not to unite or confederate with Congress. At all events they keep an eye on the accumulated debt, and good people are flocking to the State. But our enemies are busie and so are our friends, which will produce something by and by. . . . The scene is changed and Vermont must do as well as she can and in the mene time feel the highest obligations to their friends and will not confederate with Congress come on what will but will be Independent of Independency."

Half seas over he may have been, but the feelings expressed in this letter were to be consistent in Ethan Allen for the rest of his life. Congress stank in his nose. Vermont would go it alone if she could; and if she couldn't she should be British.

With the letter to Sherwood, Ethan sent a verbal message. It was to the effect that Vermont would encourage settlement by Tories and other disaffected Americans who had fled to Canada. He saw the "northern parts of Vermont" as especially suited for this settlement and suggested that the "private cabinet of Vermont" would do everything possible to make life safe and pleasant for settlers. The old Onion River Company, dealer in fine lands, was about to come to life again, after lying dormant while its officers carved an independent republic out of the New Hampshire Grants. And the officers of the Onion River Company, it will be recalled, were approximately the same as those of Vermont—Chittenden, Ira, and Ethan Allen.

Whether Ethan had just happened to think it was time to dust off the Onion River enterprise, or whether he had been giving it thought right along, is not known. He had been a very busy man, anyway, and so had the other Company officials. It would seem from the record that his next move, like so many he made, was made on the spur of the moment. He collected Chittenden, Ira, and Joseph Fay, and led a private tour of the Onion River lands which they owned, or at least claimed. They found them very good to look upon, and Ethan sent another messenger to Sherwood, urging the policy of crowding into northern Vermont as many settlers from other states and the Canadian provinces as possible He believed the Revolution would break out again, he said—in which case Vermont would take no part in it "until a favorable opportunity should present for the King." Then, said he, the new settlers in Vermont would make just so many more soldiers to take up arms for that party which Vermont should espouse. He didn't say which "party" it would be.

The proprietors of the Onion River Company and the head officials of Vermont continued their tour of the northern lands, and Ethan, always full of good ideas, dispatched still another letter to Sherwood. This time he "supposed" that the recent settlement of the war would admit of a free trade, and he suggested that the British might like to purchase a quantity of fine fresh beef which could easily be "procured in these parts." It should be noted again that it is always Ethan's neck that is nearest the halter.

At this point the real estate and trading tour was interrupted. Word came from Sunderland that Mary, his wife, was dead. He returned for the funeral and the burial, which was in the Sunderland graveyard across the Batten Kill from the Allen home. Consumption had carried Mary off before she was fifty.

The Vermont Assembly met in October and, among other things, authorized Ira Allen, surveyor-general, to hire a force of men to lay out town lines. It went into the matter of prohibiting Yorkers from bringing civil suits in Vermont. Then it returned to the almost as fascinating subject of real estate and passed an act declaring the first of May "a lawful time to begin the settlement of new lands that have been prevented by the late war betwen Great-Britain and America." It is barely possible that the hand of the Onion River Company can be seen in this last legislation.

During this period real estate went into a boom not unlike that of more than a decade before. Ira Allen was the largest owner of land in the state. He was buying and selling. So were Chittenden, the various Fays, and others. Ethan was never much good as a trader, but he managed to get in a few deals, buying rights for six pounds each and selling them for forty pounds.

Settlers from Connecticut were coming in, too; and Ethan's proposal for trade with Canada was bearing fruit. Cattle from Vermont's northern towns were taken to Quebec and sold. Canadian traders appeared in Vermont. Deserters from both British and Continental armies were coming in to clear farms. Sawmills could not meet the demand for boards and planks. The republic, in fact, was doing very well.

But the Yorkers had one more gasp in them. A gang of them attacked the home in Newfane, Vermont, of Luke Knowlton, a Tory who had played an active part in the negotiations with General Haldimand. At two o'clock of a cold November morning Knowlton's door was battered in by men armed with clubs, guns, swords, pistols, and bayonets. They took him prisoner and hustled him across the state line in the dead of night into Massachusetts, where he was held.

The alarm was sent to Governor Chittenden, and he, as usual, turned to General Allen, the uncommissioned but ever ready military man.

Luke Knowlton was an old friend of General Allen's. The General went direct to the Catamount Tavern's taproom. His call had the very same appeal as of yore. Men rallied quickly, and the General sent word ahead that he was starting for Massachusetts with blood in his eye. He didn't have to march, for his announcement was enough. Luke Knowlton was released and returned to his home in safety. Vermont was the only place this side of Canada where he *could* be safe, for General Washington had condemned him as a traitor and issued orders for his arrest.

Except for a few minor alarms, which required little attention from General Allen, the Luke Knowlton affair was the last in which he was called to defend the republic from enemies within. He himself said of the actions against the Yorkers of Guilford and elsewhere that they were "a savage way to support government," but seemed to be the only way by which to implant a respect for Vermont authority.

Gradually General Allen's neck was coming out of the loose halter of the intrigue with the British. They were fast losing interest in Vermont, now that they had lost the war.

True enough, Vermont was in a rather precarious position when viewed in the large. It had tottered again and again. But now its men thought it able to walk alone without help from any power—or they pretended to, anyway. In his spare time Ira Allen was drawing up a design for a coat of arms for the republic. There was even talk of minting a Vermont coinage. Its internal affairs were settling down out of the chaos of a no man's land. And the land was being tamed. As one poetic old Vermonter, Rowland Robinson, wrote of this period: "The wild streams were tamed to the turning of millstones, as well as to plying the saws that were incessantly gnawing at the woods. The wild forest had receded and given place to broad fields of tilth and meadows. The jangle of the sheep-bell was as frequent as the note of the thrush in the half-wild upland pastures." It began to look as if the Onion River Company's old advertisements were not so exaggerated after all. All might not be milk and honey, but things were as good here as anywhere and better than in most places.

Although a party in Vermont continued to work for admission to the Union, Ethan Allen gave the matter little thought. He knew well enough that the United States, which had snubbed his homemade republic, was burdened with debt. Its money was worthless. The Continental Army was unpaid and dissatisfied. Congress, so a contemporary wrote, was "daily sinking into a state of insignificance and contempt. . . . Weakness, disorder, and the want of wisdom and power" was on every hand.

Not so Vermont. She was not obliged to raise money to
pay the bills of a Congress that never had recognized her. The
state government had much valuable land to dispose of. Taxes
were still unknown, for the sale of public lands, as well as the
confiscation of Yorker estates, covered the expenses of a government that was careful how it spent money—except for lead
and powder. Yes, shaky as it was, and with no friends, Vermont was in much better condition than most of its neighbors.
Except for a handful of Yorkers its people were now coming
to be of one mind. Hatred of New York and of Congress
made them that way.

The Vermont republic even had two newspapers, the *Journal* of Windsor and the *Vermont Gazette* or *Freeman's De-
pository* of Bennington. The masthead of the *Gazette* carried
a bold legend:

> With generous freedom for our constant guide,
> We scorn control and print for every side.

Ethan Allen, the well known author, must have looked at
the motto of the new *Gazette* with considerable interest, and
wondered if it meant what it said. It reminded him that a
philosophical treatise he had written was gathering dust down
in Hartford, Connecticut, where printers had not feared to
print pamphlets against New York, New Hampshire, Massachusetts, and even against Congress, but were shy of locking
horns with the dominant Congregational church.

With his neck seemingly out of the noose and with Vermont quieter than for many years, Ethan turned back to Philosophy. He appears also to have had something else on his
mind.

> *"Hold on! Hold on!* Which *God* are you talking about?"

| CHAPTER XII |

The General Takes a Wife

———◆◆———

There lived in the town of Westminster, Vermont, during the winter of 1783–84, a beautiful young widow described as both daring and dashing. Her name was Fanny Montresor Buchanan, and she lived with her mother and second stepfather, Mr. and Mrs. Patrick Wall. Fanny's first stepfather had been the celebrated Crean Brush, Irish lawyer and adventurer, who once acquired some sixty thousand acres of Vermont land.* Mother and daughter, aided by mother's third husband, were in Westminster for the purpose of getting some cash out of their lands.

Westminster was perhaps the best town in Vermont for

---

* Crean Brush, long since forgotten, was one of the most notorious characters in America of the time. Born in Dublin, he came to New York in 1762 and became prominent in politics and land jobbing, eventually claiming sixty thousand acres in the New Hampshire Grants, most of it under New York title. He was naturally in the Yorker clique against Ethan Allen and the Vermonters. During the Revolution he sided with the British. Arrested in Boston for looting, he made a sensational escape from jail dressed in female clothing, smuggled in by his alleged wife, Fanny's mother. But in time even the British soured on him. On May 21, 1778, the *Independent Chronicle* of Boston reported with ill concealed joy that in New York City "the notorious CREAN BRUSH . . . retired to his chamber, where, with a Pistol, he besmeared the Room with his Brains."

such a purpose. The court met here. So, often, did the Assembly, which had a habit of meeting where it pleased in this highly individualistic republic. Thus men of parts and of vision flocked to Westminster for various purposes. Many were interested in Vermont lands.

General Allen was often in Westminster, too, and in January and February this year he was there in command of Vermont troops, to see that the term of court was not disturbed by any Yorkers who might still have sufficient temerity to became riotous.

General Allen became acquainted with Fanny Buchanan, twenty-four, handsome, pert, and full of what backwoodsmen then and now invariably refer to as perspicacity and vinegar. Fanny's real father had been a Frenchman, an officer in the British army. From him, it was said, she inherited her delicate features and boundless verve. Married at sixteen to a British officer named Buchanan, she was presently widowed when he was killed in an early engagement of the Revolution.

Just how or where Ethan and Fanny first met is not of record; but before January was out the middle-aged General and the young widow were seen together often enough to cause talk. Old John Norton who operated the village tavern and knew everything, or almost everything, that went on in town, went so far as to ask Fanny about it. "Fanny," said he one day, "if you marry General Allen, you will be queen of a new state." Quick as a wink Fanny had a comeback. "Yes," she replied, "and if I married the Devil I would be queen of hell." Norton, of course, retailed the snappy reply, and it caused considerable talk around Westminster. Ladies in Vermont of the time didn't use such words as "D--l" and "h--l."

The courtship, if there was any at all, must have been brief. All that history knows of it took place on the cold morning

of the 9th of February, 1784. Stephen Bradley, one of Westminster's *eminenti*, was entertaining judges of the superior
court in his house at breakfast. They heard sleigh bells, and
presently General Allen entered the room. "Morning, your
honors," he said. The host and the judges asked him to pull
up a chair, but he replied that he had broken fast at the
tavern. He walked on into the other side of the big house,
where Mrs. Wall and her daughter Fanny had lodgings.

Fanny Buchanan, dressed in a morning gown, was standing
on a chair arranging dishes in a china closet when the General entered. "Whereupon," says history, "Mrs. Buchanan
raised up a cracked decanter and calling General Allen's attention to it, accompanied the exhibition by a playful remark."

What did Fanny say that caused the General to "laugh
heartily at the sally"? History does not tell; and doubtless it
is history's great loss, for whatever she said, General Allen
came to the point at once. "Fanny," he boomed, "if we are
to be married, now is the time, for I am on my way to Sunderland."

Fanny Buchanan was far from surprised. "Very well," she
replied, descending from the chair, "but give me time to put
on my joseph." A joseph was some sort of coat.

And that, so far as the state of Vermont knows, was the
span of the second courtship of its most remarkable man. It is
possible, of course, that neither the state of Vermont nor even
Landlord John Norton knew everything that went on in
Westminster that winter.

While the courtship of General Allen was progressing so
famously, Colonel Bradley and the judges finished breakfast
and began smoking their long pipes. Ethan stalked into the
room leading Fanny by the hand.

"Judge Robinson," he roared, addressing the chief justice

of the republic of Vermont, "this young woman and myself have concluded to marry each other, and to have you perform the ceremony."

This sudden announcement nearly took old Robinson off his feet. "When?" was all he could think of.

"Now!" bellowed General Allen. And he continued: "As for myself, I have no great opinion of such formality; and, from what I can discover, she thinks as little of the formality as I do. But as a decent respect for the opinions of mankind seems to require it, you will proceed."

"But, General," warned the Judge, "this is an important matter. Have you given it serious consideration?"

"Certainly," replied the General, who had taken Fort Ticonderoga with little consideration and attempted to take the city of Montreal with even less. "Certainly," he said.

The ceremony then began and proceeded to that part of the business where the Judge turned to ask the groom the formal question usual at this point. "Do you, Ethan Allen," he said, "promise to live with Fanny Buchanan agreeable to the laws of God?"

"Hold on! Hold on!" thundered the groom. "*Which* God are you talking about? If you mean the laws of God as written in the great book of Nature, pray go on. My team is at the door."

This break in the ceremony stopped things only for a moment. Judge Robinson apparently referred specifically to the God of Nature, for he proceeded to tie the bonds.

Although the marriage had no political aspects at this time, spectators pointed out when the couple had left that it was an odd match. The late Crean Brush, Fanny's stepfather, had played the leading part in causing New York to post the reward of £100 for the capture dead or alive of Ethan Allen, the well known outlaw.

The wedding tour was brief. Bundling Mrs. Allen, her

guitar and clothes into his sleigh, the General drove the lady across the Green Mountains to Sunderland, where they took quarters in the house owned jointly by Ira and Ethan. With her fancy clothes, her big-city ways—she had lived in New York—and her guitar, Fanny made no little talk and tut-tutting among the more sober folk of the village; but she made an excellent wife for the General and became a mother, on November 13th, of a daughter who was named Fanny.

Once married, Ethan turned his attention to his unpublished book on philosophy. Down at Bennington, as related, Haswell & Russell were publishing the *Gazette*, with its bold masthead about "printing for every side," and were also printing all of Vermont's legal forms and state papers. Ethan made a bargain with them. They were to print fifteen hundred copies of his book; he was to pay them certain amounts as the work progressed.

Ethan owned plenty of land. Indeed, he was land-poor; and, for all of his buying and selling and trading, little actual cash changed hands. He sent a friend to try to raise a loan at Albany on Onion River land mortgages, but apparently this was not accomplished; and he finally sold his share of the Sunderland house to Ira. Then he packed up and moved Fanny, the children, and himself to Bennington, where they boarded at Timothy Follett's, handy to the printers.

The wars and riots were over, and the times must have seemed very quiet to the old Man on Horseback, who had laid Yorkers by the heels, defied Congress and three states, and hoss-traded the British out of Vermont. And the printers dawdled over the book, probably because insufficient money was forthcoming from the author.

The old soldier was beginning to consider retirement, a peaceful life in the midst of the Nature he so often spoke of. In August of 1784 he wrote to brother Ira, who was then on the Onion River, in charge of a sawmill, a gristmill, a store and trading post, a real estate office, and was also doing a big trade with the British in Canada:

"My positive determination is to move to my farm at Onion River as soon as possible and there fore send you the exact dimensions of the House I purpose early in the spring to build that you may without fail git the Bords Sawed accordingly that they may be Seasoned as much as possible. I have plan'd the House 24 by 24 two story High which plan I will not depart from. Early in the Spring I determine to be personally on the premises with the Workmen and provision suitable to Compleat the little Building with all Expedition and Desire you to procure me some provision and money if Possible. If you Look out and Lay in in Season you may effect something for me which on a Sudden you cannot. Do not think I will change my scheme for the Decree is gone fourth, therefore let the Boards and provisions be in readiness."

He signed this letter to Ira, "From the Philosopher."

Vermont was about to have an election of its principal officers. Governor Chittenden, Treasurer and Surveyor-General Ira Allen, and Ethan, who had no office and needed none, had been coming in for local criticism for their dealings with the British while the Revolution was still on. This criticism was to be expected from men who had done little or nothing for Vermont, who had never risked their lives in its cause. The little men of Vermont now talked big about throwing the "traitors" out of office. Just before election day Ethan wrote a letter that was printed in the *Gazette* of Bennington.

He said that it was sometimes injurious to the public good to expose the counsels of the Governor and his "Cabinet." Enemies might avail themselves of advantages thus given. He thought, he said, that all honest men would agree that the indiscriminate publication of Vermont's policy would often defeat itself and work toward "annihilation"—a word he liked—of the state. Then he turned on the tap of irony, which

Ethan was never much good as a trader,
but he managed to get in a few deals.

he knew how to pour. "I would by no means debar the populace from talking," he wrote, "and plotting in politics, for this would deprive them of a great share of their happiness and importance; but I would not have them complain of their benefactors nor alter the measures of their superiors." The next few lines he thought worthy of italics: "*The Foreign Policy of this Government* [Vermont] *has been demonstrated to be good in the final consequence of it, and the State is in good and respectable condition at present.*" He closed the epistle, which was to be his last public utterance in writing, with an admonition to all to support the "honor and dignity of our laws," and signed himself, "the Public's most obedient and humble servant, Ethan Allen."

A few days later Governor Chittenden and Treasurer Ira Allen were re-elected, and everything thereto was "conducted with the greatest parade, by discharging of cannon, small arms by about 100 Militia and a number of Light Horse." It was a great victory for all the old officers, and especially for Ira Allen, who had been the target of much of the opposition. It is not too much to believe that General Allen's public letter had some influence on the result.

Time hung very heavy with General Allen, waiting for proofs of his book, and waiting for money to pay the printers. It was doubtless at this period that Fanny felt obliged to do something about her husband's drinking. Tradition has it that Ethan was hitting the bottle pretty hard—which would have been tolerably hard—and Fanny chid him for his excesses. She drove a nail rather high in a wall of the kitchen. "When you return late at nights from the tavern," she said, "you are to hang your watch on this nail. If you manage it, we will agree that you returned home sober." Ethan agreed, and more than one evening, legend has it, he was obliged to use all his

vast powers of direction and concentration to accomplish the
feat. But never once did the watch miss the nail.

The printers stalled. Ethan apparently tried to raise a loan
in Albany again, without success. He now made a trip to
New York and Philadelphia, probably on the same errand.
In any case, in New York he met Hector St. John de Crèvecœur, the consul-general of France. The two hit it off at once
and began a lasting friendship which left its mark on Vermont.

The gallant, poetic, and curious Frenchman thought Ethan
Allen one of the most remarkable and certainly one of the
most interesting men in the United States, a wholly original
being like none other. A short time after their visit in New
York, he was writing Ethan for maps and facts and stories
about this pretty and rugged independent republic of Vermont. He offered to have a state seal made, "elegantly engraved on silver," and suggested that Vermont name some of
its new towns after notable Frenchmen.* He even asked that
he and his sons be made citizens of Vermont, which was
hardly diplomatic in view of what the United States, the
country to which Crèvecœur was accredited, thought of the
Green Mountain rebels.

Several letters were exchanged between the two men, some
of them touching on philosophy, immortality, and such matters. Among other things, Ethan wrote to the Frenchman
that if there was anything to the idea of transmigration of
souls, he himself hoped to return to earth in the form of a
fine, snorting white stallion, and to be allowed to roam the
hills of Vermont.

All this was a pleasant interlude, but it did not get the book
published. Ethan arranged with Stephen Bradley to sell some
of the Westminster land Fanny had inherited, and he was also

---

* It was done, too, as witness Vergennes, named for a French foreign
minister of the period. St. Johnsbury was named for Crèvecœur himself.

raising money on his own property. Tradition has it that the first thing he did on awakening, these mornings, was to damn the printers; and he damned them again when he took his nightcap. This quiet and deplorable state of affairs was interrupted on August 12, 1785, by a messenger from Hartford.

The message contained twelve proprietory rights in the Susquehanna Company, with the compliments of the management, and a letter which explained this handsome gift.

The company had been formed many years before by Connecticut men to settle the Wyoming Valley of Pennsylvania, which they considered from an old treaty to be merely an extension of Connecticut. Ethan's father, Joseph Allen, long since dead, had been one of the original proprietors.

Pennsylvanians thought otherwise about the Wyoming Valley. They claimed it, too. Double land grants had been made, much as in Vermont, and for some time the two groups had been fighting, forensically and even with guns, over the debated ground. Apparently, the Connecticut men had been getting the worst of it, and this had led them to call the leading riot-raiser in the United States to aid them. If anyone could make a doubtful title stick, they well knew, it was the man who had taken the lands claimed by New Hampshire, Massachusetts, and New York and made them into a sovereign republic, come hell and high water.

Well, printers were slow, the days were quiet—too quiet for a man of action. Ethan's blood stirred again. He accepted the twelve proprietory rights as a retainer and wrote to W. S. Johnson of the company: "I have agreed with the Committee of the Susquehanna Proprietors," he said, "to speedily repair to Wyoming with a small detachment of Green Mountain Boys to Vindicate (if appears to me practicable) the right of soil of those proprietors to that territory, whatever may be the legal decision relative to the jurisdiction."

In other words, the Wyoming Valley was to belong to

those who fought best and hardest for it, regardless of who owned it. Ethan was even ready with a line of policy which he described to Director Johnson. He termed the opposition to the Connecticut settlers "oppressive," and said his first move would be to make friends in the Pennsylvania Legislature with the idea of dividing its members on the subject.

This was gloriously fine fodder for an old warhorse to chew on while waiting for printers. A bit later Ethan wrote to Colonel Zebulon Butler, chief of the Susquehanna Company, who was on the ground in Pennsylvania. Colonel Butler was something of an old warhorse himself and, like General Allen, a Connecticut man. He had emigrated to the Wyoming Valley in 1769, settled there, and had fought bravely under the redoubtable General John Sullivan during the Revolution. Now, like many another Connecticut man in Pennsylvania, he was trying to hold the land he had reason to believe was his by right of Connecticut title.

In his letter to Butler, General Allen discussed the comparative legality of the double grants in the disputed region. The Connecticut grant, he said, was eighteen years older than that to William Penn. He pointed out that the Susquehanna Company had been in "possession" of the land for twenty-five years; but the justice of the claim, which already he termed "our" claim, would probably have no weight with "our haughty antagonists, who seek our lands and labors." On the other hand, such injustice should inspire the Nutmeggers to defend their rights with great zeal & fortitude, "even to blood." (He was smelling powder already.) Continuing, he promised to make "a tour of the Hostile Ground" early in the spring. "In the meantime," he counseled, "crowd your settlements, add to your numbers and strength; procure firearms and amunition, be united amongst yourselves. I hope to see you, face to face, next spring, nor will I give up my interest, to usurpers, without trying it out by force of arms."

He brought in the good old "Liberty & Property," and closed on a familiar note by calling Pennsylvanians a pack of "Penemitish land thieves."

All this was first-class rabble rousing, done by the hand of a master, and it put determination into the hearts of the Susquehanna Company.

In the meantime the philosophy book finally made its appearance, and its appearance created an uproar that will be treated presently; but even a battle of Literature and Divinity could not keep General Allen from defending the God-given rights of the oppressed Connecticut settlers in devilish Pennsylvania. Just as soon as the roads were passable, he put on the gold-laced regimentals he had worn briefly during the last of the Yorker troubles, took his sword, and rode a horse out of now comparatively quiet Vermont.

The Susquehanna proprietors had prepared the ground for General Allen's coming; but Ethan needed little introduction, even so far from home as Pennsylvania. His reputation as a soldier of the Revolution, as an outlaw, as the commander of the terrible Green Mountain Boys was known all over settled country and beyond the frontiers; and his appearance in the Wyoming Valley created a sensation. Loyal Pennsylvanians sent messages by express couriers to Philadelphia, warning state and Congress officials that all hell was likely to break loose immediately. Even serene Ben Franklin was alarmed.

General Allen looked the ground over. He casually proposed a new state, to be carved out of northern Pennsylvania and a part of his old enemy, New York, extended to 42° North Latitude. This was a notable insult to the Congress of the United States, and Ethan doubtless meant it as such. The "viperous skunks" of Congress had not recognized Vermont, had they? He would be damned if he would recognize Congress.

General Allen rode through the embattled ground, haranguing the Connecticut settlers, firing them with some of his own zeal & fortitude. His opponents were busy, too, "beating up for volunteers" for their side. After a rather grand tour of the terrain, the General, John Franklin, and other Susquehanna proprietors went to Hartford, Connecticut, for a meeting of the company. Ethan and three others were named to serve as a committee to locate townships and "settle" claims, whatever that might mean.

Although Ethan had planned to return at once to the Hostile Ground, he was unavoidably delayed. It was money trouble again. A Mr. Hudson had sued him on an overdue note. He went home and tarried on in Vermont for some weeks, probably attempting to raise cash, for he was hard up. "I am drove almost to death for money," he wrote brother Ira at this time. "I have not a copper to save me from the Devil. We are such poor cursed rascals by God, alter our measures or we shall be a hiss, a proverb, and a bye word and derision upon earth."

Mr. Hudson would not be denied his money any longer. Ethan appeared in court, with his attorney, Stephen Bradley, to ask a continuance. Bradley, an able lawyer, said nothing to Ethan about it, but he planned different tactics to delay settlement of the case.

Bradley stood up and told the judge that the signature on the note was a forgery. The attesting witness was not present to prove the signature genuine, and a continuance of the case would have been inevitable, or so Bradley planned. And so too it would, had it not been for the man most concerned. Ethan was amazed at the chicanery of his own lawyer. He jumped up at the back of the courtroom and came down the aisle as fast as he could. "Hold on! Hold on!" he cried. Turning to his startled attorney, he bellowed: "Mr. Bradley, I didn't hire you to come here and lie. That is a true note.

I signed it, I'll swear by it, and by God, I'll pay it. I want no shuffling. I want time."

The court granted a continuance.

Ethan seems to have had a pox of financial troubles at this period. On one occasion, of which there is record, Sheriff Elisha Bartlett of Charlotte, Vermont, was put to a deal of travel to serve a body writ on the General. A good while later, when no doubt the sheriff had forgotten the incident, he was awakened one morning by a horse pounding over the frozen ground to his door. He heard a thud on his doorstep, then receding hoofbeats. Putting on his pants, he went out to see what was up. He found a bundle which proved to be a length of fine broadcloth, sufficient for a Sunday suit. With it was a scribbled note: "The man who serves a body-writ on Ethan Allen does not go without his pay."

With the various money troubles in hand, General Allen put on military attire again and disappeared from Vermont. Presently Ben Franklin, down in Philadelphia, was writing to Governor Clinton of New York: "Ethan Allen of Vermont and one Solomon Strong of your state have lately been among the settlers in Wyoming, persuading them to join in erecting a new state to be composed of those settlements, those on the west branch of the Susquehanna, and a part of the State of New York. . . . Chimerical as it appears, and unlikely to succeed, we thought it nevertheless right to acquaint Your Excellency with it, that such inquiries may be made and measures taken as you may judge proper to prevent these restless spirits from exciting disturbances that may divert the people's attention from their industry, and be attended with mischievous consequences."

On this second tour of Wyoming, Ethan found the region still in ferment, and he stirred it a bit more. But Pennsylvania was far wiser than New York had been with Vermont. Its Assembly made the Wyoming townships into a county,

Luzerne, and sent a commissioner to organize it. Conciliatory measures were used. The Connecticut settlers were
promised the lands they lived on. Other claimants to the
property were given land elsewhere in the state. Such enlightened methods pacified both parties to the dispute and left
nothing for a man of General Allen's talents.

He did not remain to see the affair settled, although he
must have seen a peaceful end coming, for he rode out of the
valley after a few weeks and never returned.

On the way back to Vermont, late in 1786, the General
stopped at Lebanon Springs, New York, and was introduced
to an eminent visitor, President Ezra Stiles of Yale College.
Stiles already had seen author Allen's new book on philosophy, which was a treatise to shock more liberal men than
the head of divinity and learning at New Haven, and during
their brief visit, Ethan incensed him almost to the point of
apoplexy.

With the shocked countenance of Dr. Stiles in his mind,
the Great Infidel rode happily back to Vermont, there to face
and probably enjoy a flood of abuse that would have broken
a less resolute man.

> *"I am a hardy mounttaineer and scorn to be intimidated by threats. If they fright me, they must absolutely produce some of their tremendous fire, and give me a sensitive scorching."*

CHAPTER XIII

Horned Devil of Vermont

———◆·◆———

The title of Ethan Allen's philosophical work was of about average length for books of the time: "Reason the only Oracle of Man, or a Compenduous System of Natural Religion. Alternately Adorned with Confutations of a variety of Doctrines incompatable to it; Deduced from the most exalted Ideas which we are able to form of the Divine and Human Characters, and from the Universe in General." Freethinkers of the day immediately rechristened it "Ethan Allen's Bible."

In a Preface that is refreshingly brief for the period, the author says that it is impertinent in writers to offer an apology for the works they put before the public and he will dispense with such. If a book cannot stand on its two hind legs, it should have been stifled in the birth. He goes on to say that he has been called a Deist and although he has never read their writings, he is content to be denominated with them. But of one thing he is positive; he is no Christian, "except mere infant baptism make me one."

The desire for knowledge, begins the author, has engaged the attention of the wise and curious of all ages, much to the physical improvement of mankind. It has excited the contemplative to explore Nature's laws with the result that philosophy, astronomy, geography, and other sciences have arrived at a great degree of perfection. It is to be regretted, however, that the great bulk of mankind are still carried down the torrent of superstition and thus continue to entertain very unworthy ideas of God and of their duty to him.[*]

After positing a First Great Cause, the author admits that this Cause, no matter what it is called, is utterly incomprehensible to finite beings.

This romantic notion of a personal God, so prevalent these days, says the author, must have originated from a universal sense of dependence. In other words, weak Man must have something that is wiser, more powerful and beneficent than himself, to lean upon. The various sorts of Gods which Man has conjured up, and belief in which an artful clergy has fostered, are incredible wretches. "The Lord thy God is a jealous God." Well, jealousy is patently the offspring of finite minds. If God is infinite, as the parsons and priests say he is, then he can have no part of jealousy. The same goes for a revengeful God.

If we could comprehend God at all, he would cease to be what he is. The ignorant among mankind cannot even understand the wise of their own species, much less the perfection of a God.

Why, sirs, when we extend our thoughts, through our external sensations, to the vast regions of the starry heavens, we are lost in the immensity of God's works. It is laughable that a God who worked such creation as we see on all sides should be so small as to confine his goodness to one sect or communion of puny Man.

Prayer to God is no part of a rational religion. Worse, it is sheer impertinence. We ought, rather, to act up to the dignity of our nature and not attempt to dictate anything to the

[*] In this book Deity does not rate an upper-case pronoun.

governor of the universe, who rules not by our fervent pre-
scriptions, but by an eternal and infinite wisdom.

The various doctrines of fate, infant damnation, predestination, and such dreadful things are useful to armies in the field
as a policy to induce soldiers to face danger, perhaps, but
they should be no part of man's religion. God has put Man
on earth to go his own way without interference from on
high. We really ought to discharge the public teachers of
these doctrines, and expend their salaries in an economical
manner, which might better answer the purposes of our happiness. A feasible suggestion would be to lay out the money
paid to priests and preachers in good wine or old spirits to
make the heart glad, and then laugh at the stupidity or cun-
ning of those who would make us mere machines, incapable
of conducting our own destinies.

Revelation? If ever there was such a thing, which is to be
gravely doubted, it was long since twisted out of shape by
the vagaries of countless retellings and translations, as witness
the disagreement of Christians over versions of their Bible.
The only way Revelation could retain its purity and force
would be for the governor of the universe to endow a particular academy of the arts and sciences, with tutors rightly organized and intellectually qualified to carry on the business
of teaching. But this has never come to pass. God has never
given out a manuscript copy of his law. That which is super-
natural, or above the comprehension of humans, is contradictory and impossible.

Look at Nature, ye clodhoppers, and there you will see
God in action. Consider him well on all sides—the sun, the
moon, the stars, the forest, the mountain. It is as near to God
as we can hope to approach, and it should be enough. Some
persons, it is true, mistake their own reflections on Nature to
be God's inspiration, as witness the enthusiasts and fanatics
who seek to impose all sorts of different and contradictory

notions on us as God's veritable revelation. If God actually spoke to a human being, what he said would be so powerful that all would *know* it to be the truth, and believe. There simply could be no bickering about it. But as it is, the varied "revelations" of fanatics the world over make for chaos. The whole bustle of it is mere enthusiasm. If ever The Truth were dictated by God, who is the very spirit of truth and uniformity, it would influence all alike.

The idea of miracles is founded on an alteration of natural laws, hence it is not to be taken seriously by reflective men. To suppose that God should subvert his laws is to say that God is mutable, hence imperfect. A belief in miracles is directly opposed to a belief in a perfect, all-wise God. If God knows his business, miracles simply can't happen.

Comets, earthquakes, and northern lights, all of them to be ascribed to Nature, often intimidate weak minds. A Jack-with-a-lantern is a frightful appearance to some people, but not nearly so terrible as an imaginary specter. But, of all scarecrows which have made human nature tremble, the devil has been chief; his family is said to be very numerous, consisting of legions, with which he has kept our world in a constant uproar.

Men will face destructive cannon and mortars, they will engage one another in the clash of arms, they will meet with all sorts of natural horrors undaunted; yet the devil and his banditti of fiends and emissaries will unman them, scare them out of their wits, and plunge them into desolate superstition. Why, sirs, it is not fifty years since the Parliament of England became apprised of the natural impossibility of any magical intercouse between mankind and devils, witches, and other evil spirits. That was on March 24, 1735, when it repealed an act against witchcraft. Thus was another of the so-called laws of Moses abrogated.

He who waits for the aid of devils, prayers, or miracles to

help him in some enterprise had better spend his time by the application of his natural powers. Praying for this or that thing to happen, indeed, is simply a murmuring against God, a finding fault with his providence.

Beware of prophets. In this and all other ages they have ever been loose fellows, vague and indeterminate in their meaning; either that, or they have been translated improperly. Consider their prophecies well, and you will find that they equally answer to events of the period of Cicero as to those in the age of General George Washington. Given a liking for prophets, a man can prove anything he chooses.

Faith is governed by our reasonings. "He that believeth shall be saved, but he that believeth not shall be damned." This text is considered as crowding hard upon unbelievers in Christianity; but when it is critically examined, it will be found not to militate against them, but to be really a trick of theologians to overawe some and make others wonder. The Christian believes the gospel to be true and of divine authority. The Deist believes it is not true and not of divine authority. So, the Christian and Deist are both believers. A Deist may as well term a Christian an infidel as the reverse. Christ's whole being has been perverted in the interest of multitudes of sectaries. He was an honest man who never claimed to be God but specifically ranked himself with finite beings. He would be astonished to know what the prophets and scriveners have done to him.

Now we come to the imputation of sin. This is horrible to contemplate in an infinite God. So is the imputation of righteousness. Much better is the old proverb: "Every tub stands on its own bottom." There, sirs, is a proverb for a man to remember. It has no ghostly parentage. It is founded on plain reason and therefore makes mincemeat of the gloomy doctrine of predestination.

The author of the Oracle, Philosopher Allen, was ahead of

his time but not far. Punishment, says he, will finally terminate in the best good of the punished—which is a tenet of Universalism. The doctrine of the Trinity, he says, is destitute of foundation and tends manifestly to superstition and idolatry—which, although Ethan Allen couldn't know it, was the kind of preaching that was soon to sweep most of intellectual New England into Unitarianism.

When one considers that the Oracle was the very first work published in America in direct opposition to revealed religion, it is not difficult to understand the uproar it occasioned.

Forty of the books were bound and ready by mid-November of 1785. Ethan presented the first copy bound to wife Fanny, inscribing the title page with what perhaps was his only attempt at verse:

> Dear Fanny wise, the beautiful and young,
> The partner of my joys, my dearest self,
> My love, pride of my life, your sex's pride,
> And partner of Sincere politeness,
> To thee a welcome compliment I make
> Of treasures rich, the Oracles of Reason.

Like many authors, Ethan was far better in the text of his book than in his inscriptions.

The Philosopher sent copies to Jean de Crèvecœur, and one to his lawyer and old friend, Stephen Bradley. "I fancy, sir," he wrote Bradley, "you will be diverted when you read the 12th chapter. It rips up and overturns the whole notion of jockeying, alienating, transferring, or imputing to sin, or righteousness, from one person to another, and leaving all mankind accountable for their own moral agency. This is fatal to the Ministerial Damnation Salvation, and their merchandise thereof." He then estimated the income of the Church of Rome at twenty million pounds sterling annually, that of the Protestant sects at ten million. "To remedy the human Species from this Ghostly Tyranny," he concluded, was his object in writing the Oracle.

At Bennington on November 16, Ethan wrote to Benjamin Stiles, prominent citizen of Woodbury, Connecticut, who had apparently inquired about the book: "As to my Philosophy, that you mention, forty of the Books are bound and will be sent to New York tomorrow, 1500 are printed, and contain 487 pages, in large octavo. The curiosity of the public is much excited, and there is a great demand for the books, they will in all probability reach Woodbury in the course of the winter. In one of them you will read my very soul, for I have not concealed my opinion, nor disguised my sentiments in the least, and however you may, as a severe critic, censer my performance, I presume you will not impeach me with cowardice. I expect, that the clergy, and their devotees, will proclaim war with me, in the name of the Lord, his battles they affect to fight, having put on the armour of Faith, the sword of the Spirit and the Artillery of Hell Fire. But I am a hardy mounttaineer, and have been accustomed to the dangers and horrors of War, and captivity, and scorn to be intimidated by threats, if they fright me, they must absolutely produce some of their tremendous fire, and give me a sensitive scorching."

None of them, of course, were able to "fright" him in the least, although they rolled up their Artillery of Hell Fire at once. The attack was immediate and incredibly vicious and even hysterical. Clergy and laity left Christ to get along as best he could for a while, and devoted all their efforts to destroying this antichrist of Vermont. No holds were barred. The Hero of Ticonderoga was forgotten, and so, in large part, were the arguments put forth in his book. As usual on such occasions, the frightened godly folk sought to ruin the character of the writer.

In countless tracts and sermons it was said that Ethan Allen was a profane, blasphemous, and wicked man who drank rum, caroused on the Sabbath, and denied God at all times. The latter charge had no foundation whatever, but then, any means were good means to use against the unorthodox.

Illiterate parsons who had never seen the Oracle and could have made neither head nor tail of it anyway, shouted that this awful Infidel should be put down by law, or by force regardless of law. Prayers went up to God for a great wind to blow this Allen into Turkey, or some other heathen land. Jehovah was asked to smite him with a thunderbolt. The pious thought they smelled brimstone wherever the General walked or rode. Some nobody called him the Horned Devil of Vermont.

The Reverend Lemuel Hopkins inserted what he thought was a very telling sarcastic advertisement in the *Vermont Gazette* in which he referred to "the Genius of Vermont on the top of Mount Anthony in Bennington. . . . Deism Confessed and Good Manners Defended, with a Chapter in favor of Oracles and a section on the heat of good blood near the grand clymacterice, and the animation of youthful charms." The Reverend Mr. Hopkins also took a crack at Ira Allen in the same outburst, saying that a sequel to the Oracle would be a book on "The Pleasant Art of Money Catching Reduced to Practise, by I. A." This obviously referred to Ira's activity as surveyor-general of Vermont plus his real estate business and other affairs.

Another correspondent inserted in the *Gazette* a long-winded letter purporting to come from Lord George Gordon, England's own riot raiser, to Ethan Allen. According to this piece of heavy-handed satire and irony, Author Allen had sent copies of the Oracle to his lordship and proposed to dedicate a second edition to him. In this letter Gordon is made to say that he is unworthy the dedication of such a great work, that he has sent his copies on to the Grand Vizier, the Mufti, and the British ambassador to Turkey. Then:

"At a future day, when the sons of men will gloriously emerge from the ignorance and credulity in which they have been too long involved, through the pious frauds and artifices of the interpreters of the Scriptures, who, it is thought, have fashioned its texts to their own narrow, and no doubt, criminal purposes, as the potter moulds his clay; then I doubt not my venerable Vermonter Demi-God, but you will be admired as a miracle of holiness, and like a second Mahomet (your great antitype and patron) be worshipped on the Green Mountains with the veneration due to so much wisdom and pity."

And much, much more of the same.

The letter is patently a fraud. The writer speaks of "Vermont" and "Green Mountains" in a familiar manner, and it is doubtful that the English lord ever heard of either. Nor is it conceivable that, had Ethan Allen received such a letter, he would have given it to a newspaper for publication. He was backwoodsy enough in his manners, but he never lacked keen perception. The erudition displayed in the long communication, together with its easy familiarity with New England geography, points to someone nearer home, possibly one of the great divines of New Haven.

The freethinkers of the day—and they were numerous, although not all very bold—were overjoyed at a champion so able to lock horns with the dominant clergy. The heretics of Goshen, New York, were so pleased with one copy that they delegated Ephraim Starr, local storekeeper, to write to the author to send them several more copies in return for goods, as they had no ready cash.

Apparently, Thomas Jefferson, a freethinker of the first water, never saw a copy of the Oracle. And one wonders if Tom Paine read it. One historian has thought so. In his *Ac-*

count of Arnold's Campaign Against Quebec, J. E. Henry remarks that "long after the publication of Ethan Allen's book, which had fallen into oblivion . . . that vile reprobate, Thomas Paine . . . filched from Ethan Allen the great body of his deistical and atheistical opinions, which from the time of Celsus, down to the age of Chubb [and] Tindal, have been so often refuted by men of the utmost respectability of character."

It is true that "respectable" men have usually refuted writings like the Oracle. Otherwise they would cease to be respectable with the herd. But the Great Jehovah took a hand in the business soon after the books were off the press, but not all bound, and His criticism was the most telling of all. A fire broke out in the shop of Haswell & Russell, Bennington printers of the Oracle. One tradition has it that the fire came from lightning. Whatever its cause, the fire destroyed nearly all of the edition of fifteen hundred copies.* Legend also has it that Printer Haswell was so shaken by the Visitation that he presently committed a few remaining copies to his fireplace, and, to make the thing perfect, "joined the Methodist connection."

In later years scholars have discussed the Oracle as a collaboration of Ethan Allen and Dr. Thomas Young, the physician, who practiced in Salisbury, Connecticut, in Ethan's younger days. There can be no doubt it was a collaboration. Both Ethan and the doctor appear to have made notes of their long conversations in Salisbury taverns. It is plain they planned to do a book together, when time permitted. Young had begun the manuscript, then died. Ethan, as related, got it on one

---

* Walter J. Coates of North Montpelier, Vermont, who is well acquainted with the writings of Ethan Allen, says the record indicates but thirty copies survived the flames, and only seven are known to exist today. The work was reprinted, in part, several times. The last edition seems to be that of J. P. Mendum, Boston, 1854. A limited fac-simile edition, with the *Appendix*, is to be brought out in 1940, with a foreword and notes by John Pell.

of his many visits to Philadelphia, whither the doctor had moved.

Many of the thoughts expressed are doubtless those of the good doctor, and so, too, some of the writing. But the style of the book—fanciful, humorous, and barbarous by turns, with a homespun flavor that sounds little like the polished, educated doctor—is that of Ethan Allen. The long complicated sentences often get tangled. Some of the attempts to express an idea are at best hazy. Certain paragraphs are downright chaotic. But throughout there is a direct savage drive which belongs to Ethan alone. Mr. Dana Doten has summed up the collaboration.* Young without Allen, he says, might have been sterile; but Allen without Young would have remained a picturesque infidel, with no formulated theories.

Critics of Ethan Allen have delighted to point out that although Young had a part in the book, his name appears nowhere in title or text. Dr. Young had been dead seven years when the Oracle appeared. Ethan figured that dead men were dead men. He also knew that a book signed by General Allen would be assured of no little attention. He must also have known that a book like the Oracle would bring calumny and all sorts of abuse down on the author.

In recent years critics have been kinder to Ethan's book, giving it a rather prominent place in the early philosophical works of America. Isaac Woodbridge Riley says of the Oracle, in his *American Philosophy*, that "there is in this neglected volume much to remind one of the great system builders." He finds the book to have at least two points of originality: in its destructive side, it boldly voiced a protest against the prevalent high Calvinism—which took no little courage; in its constructive side, it essayed to be a homemade substitute for the prevalent cosmology.

* In *New England Quarterly*, Vol. XI, p. 361 et seq.

There can be no doubt that Ethan Allen with, a little later, Tom Paine delivered the hardest knocks to the structure of Calvinism. Ethan, indeed, seems to have been better than half-way down the road to Transcendentalism. He had set up two Absolutes: God, the efficient cause, eternal and infinite; and Nature, the eternal and infinite effect. It remained for Emerson to struggle with this apparent dualism between God and Nature and finally to come out for one Absolute.

The Oracle also did something else. It has exerted a powerful and sinister influence on the reputation of General Allen the soldier, the patriot, and founder of Vermont. Early biographers and historians felt it necessary to be horrified over his "infidelity" to the kind of God *they* professed to believe in. Old Jared Sparks was man enough, in his study of Allen in 1839, to say that biographers had not done justice to Ethan's writings. He calls the Oracle "much superior to his other works . . . and elaborated with great patience of thought and care in composition." Sparks even went so far as to indicate Ethan was not an atheist but described the Oracle as "a crude and worthless performance" except for the chapters "on natural religion, the being and attributes of God." He chid the author for passing over "historical facts," by which Sparks undoubtedly meant the Bible.

Other biographers and historians have referred to "certain blemishes" in General Allen's character, meaning his lack of formal religion, and his ribald blasts against orthodoxy in all its forms. And for the next one hundred years and more, many orators, while paying tribute to Ethan's courage and ability, announced themselves as pained at his "atheistic" opinions. Apparently they didn't know what an atheist was. Either that, or they had never troubled to read the Oracle.

Whatever his contemporaries said of him and his book, it was all the same to the Great Infidel of the Green Mountains. He had been abused by abler men. And if Yankees didn't like his Compenduous System of Natural Religion, they were coming to have a respect for the free and easy but tough little republic General Allen and his men were making, up there in the hills and along the shores of Lake Champlain.

> "*An awful Infidel, one of y^e wickedest men y^t ever walked this guilty globe.*"—THE REVEREND NATHAN PERKINS.

CHAPTER XIV

Old Soldier at Home

————◆•◆————

With the Wyoming Valley rebellion out of his mind and the echoes of the Oracle still in his ears, Ethan retired to his house at Sunderland to live quietly through the winter of 1786–1787. That the old soldier was mellowing, or failing in health, and was perhaps just a little tired, is made clear by his refusal to join in some fancy riot-rousing in Massachusetts.

Down there in the Bay State times were very hard following the end of the Revolution. The rich Tories had long since fled, and in their place a new aristocracy was rising, enriched by army graft, by smuggling and privateering. Farmers in the hill country around Worcester and in the Berkshires, many of them returned soldiers, were actually in want. Taxes had piled up, hard money was scarce; paper money, worthless. Children were dying from lack of food. The desperately poor talked and fumed and cried for a man to lead them against their oppressors, whom they saw in tax collectors, bankers, and mortgage holders.

A leader was soon found in the person of Daniel Shays, a man of action and almost a physical giant, who had fought bravely in the wars. Shays and a mob closed the courts at

Worcester and Springfield. In an attack on the Arsenal at the latter place, there was shooting and killing, and Shays with the remnants of his army fled into Vermont, which was a sort of foreign nation.

General Benjamin Lincoln and militia were engaged in putting down the rebellion. They chased the Shays mob to the Vermont border, and General Lincoln, who apparently recognized Vermont as a sovereign power, even if Congress did not, halted his troops. He sent spies into the Green Mountain country to learn what its leading men thought of Shays and his rebellion. They returned with bad news. One reported that in his presence General Ethan Allen had said of the Massachusetts government that it was manned by a pack of damned rascals. "Let Shays and his crew remain in Vermont," the spy quoted the General as saying. "They may cut down a few maple trees, but they will hurt nothing." Another spy reported that Governor Chittenden was sympathetic to the rebels.

General Lincoln, though, wasn't the man to be stopped by a little tough talk. Still holding his troops at the border, he sent Lieutenant Royall Tyler to ask officially for the apprehension and delivery of Shays and his men, or at least for a proclamation covering the situation and permitting Massachusetts troops to enter Vermont for the purpose.

The Assembly gravely considered the request for several days, with bitter debate, and finally approved a motion to issue the proclamation requested. Chittenden refused to sign it; he was affronted because General Lincoln had failed to address him as Governor of Vermont, an omission he might well have become used to long before this. In a few days, however, Chittenden did issue a public statement prohibiting Vermonters from harboring Shays or any of his mob.

Three months later, while Ethan was still at his home in Sunderland, two men appeared mysteriously at his house. They were Luke Day and Eli Parsons, two of Shays' trusted lieutenants, come with an invitation from their leader: if General Allen would proceed to Massachusetts and take command of Shays' army—which, it was said, would appear as if springing from the ground—a second rebellion would be staged which with the leadership of General Allen could be nothing but successful. When this was done, Ethan Allen would be crowned King of Massachusetts.

Now, there was a time when Ethan Allen would unquestionably have enjoyed being a King. Five years, even two years, previously it is possible he would have given the offer serious consideration. But Vermont was now a going republic. Fanny was a loving wife. And, anyway, he had long desired to return to the quiet of the woods. Even tiny Sunderland was too populous. He longed for the back country, which he had ranged alone way back in 1770.

He not only "rejected the Shays' proposal with disdain" and sent Day and Parsons packing, but he sent word to Massachusetts officials that Vermont was taking proper steps to prevent Shays' malcontents from getting aid up there in the hills.*

When Ethan Allen failed to mount his horse and ride in Daniel Shays' rebellion, it was the surest sign possible that the old soldier was mellowing, and tired. He hadn't missed a riot in nearly twenty years. The long years of exposure in the field, together with the interminable stretch in chains and dungeons and prison ships, were beginning to tell. His health was failing, and apparently the only medicine he took was the old remedy he had long considered sovereign for all ills.

This winter he was working on an Appendix to the Oracle, and planning life on the place he had selected for retirement with his family.

* Daniel Shays was presently captured, and along with several of his men, sentenced to be hanged. All the sentences were commuted. Shays was pardoned a year later and lived to a ripe old age.

On May 1, 1787, he and Ira entered into an agreement as to certain of their mutual interests in the Onion River Company. To supply Ira's sawmills with handy logs, Ethan relinquished his interest in four hundred acres of good timber surrounding each of the mills. In addition to other lands deeded to him in this trade, Ethan was to have a thousand-acre farm near Burlington, and Ira undertook to build him a house. An odd stipulation was that Ira also agreed to furnish Ethan with goods to the value of one hundred pounds annually, from the Onion River store and on the first day of each August, for seven years. The undivided lands, not in this trade, were to be assigned after a survey was made. Mary Ann, Ethan's daughter by his first wife, witnessed the signed agreement, the only time she appears in what might be called Vermont history.*

Leaving Fanny, who was on the way to becoming a mother a second time, Ethan rode to his site on the Onion. Ira had a house across the river, and was busily engaged in farming, in real estate, mines, mills, furs, and trading with Canada. The old quarrel with Levi Allen had long since been forgotten. Levi now spent most of his time at St. Johns, on the Sorel (Richelieu) in Quebec Province, looking after the rafts of lumber from Ira's mills, and selling the sheep and cattle shipped north from Onion River headquarters. He was also doing a business in masts with the British navy.

Ethan boarded with the Collins family while work on his own small house was going forward. Apparently he was doing something in the way of farming, for he wrote to Levi that "my farming business goes on very brisk but I tremble for bread and corn . . . it is a pinch with us and will be so till

* And this trade agreement certainly *belongs* in Vermont history. It was part of Ira Allen's highly successful plan to found a city on beautiful Burlington Bay, a scheme his brothers termed fanciful and poked ribald fun at. The city of Burlington, Vermont, is as fine a monument as any man could have.

harvest, pray help us. . . . You can send wheat or flour by Mr. McLean's boat."

This Onion River country at the time was the very backwoods of western Vermont, the country way back yonder where wolves still howled and hunted in packs, where catamounts padded through the forest, where a blazed trail was a first-class road. It was considered by the people of Bennington, Brattleboro, and other long-settled towns to be the end of the world. But even away up there one more echo of Daniel Shays' rebellion was heard.

Two of Shays' rebels, one Durham and one Baker, had managed to get out of Massachusetts, and they decided the backwoods was none too far to hide from General Lincoln. When they got to the Onion River, however, they made the mistake of stealing horses from a Mr. Starkweather, one of the settlers. Captured by some of Ira's hired men, they were turned over to Ethan, who took command of a party to escort the prisoners to Bennington and the Law. Here General Allen wrote to Lieutenant Royall Tyler of the Massachusetts militia that the outlaws were being returned with Vermont's compliments.

On the way north again, Ethan stopped at Sunderland for Fanny and the children,* and his household goods and ménage, which consisted of two Negro freemen, taking all to Burlington and to board at the Collins' home until the Allen house was ready. On November 24, 1787, Fanny gave birth to a boy who was named—but not christened—Hannibal.

There was a bit of excitement this month when word came to Ira that in October a band of Indians had suddenly appeared at the homes of settlers on his lands on Missisquoi Bay. They did no scalping but stole corn and burned the cedar fences. Although this was no business of Ethan's, it is indicative of

* Lucy, Pamela, and Mary Ann, by the first Mrs. Allen; baby Fanny by the second.

his failing health that he did not buckle on his sword and march.

Ethan was tending strictly to farming. In November he wrote to his old friend Stephen Bradley that "I have lately arrived at my new farm of 14 hundred acres in one body in which are three hundred and fifty acres of Swaley and rich upland meadow interspersed with the finest of wheat land and pasture land well watered and is by nature equal to any tract of land of the same number of acres that I ever saw. I have about forty acres under improvement. The country settles fast and I wish that you was well settled in it, little is said about Philosophy here our 'talk is of Bullocks and our glory is the gad' we mind earthly things."

There may have been little talk of philosophy in the backwoods of the Onion River, but the Allens had not forgotten the United States Congress and its refusal to dignify Vermont by admitting it as a state. The two brothers, Ira and Levi, were doing a rushing business in trade with Canada. The Constitution of the United States had been ratified. What would happen now? Would Congress step in and crush the independent republic? The Allens, no more than other men, could guess. Apparently they discussed the subject a great deal, for in the summer of 1788 all three went to Quebec and had several conferences with Sir Guy Carleton, now Lord Dorchester and Governor-General of Canada.

Ethan embodied his views on Vermont and Canada in a long letter to his lordship. Pointing out that the United States had adopted a Constitution, federating the thirteen former colonies, he said it was to be expected the Congress would attempt to subjugate Vermont, which was strictly on its own, and partition it among New Hampshire, Massachusetts, and New York.

But Vermonters, he said, were naturally inclined to the British on account of their state's situation, being contiguous to

Again and for the last time they asked for and heard Ethan repeat his terrible proclamation.

the province of Quebec and having Lake Champlain and the Sorel River for waterways of trade and intercourse. The leading men of Vermont, he continued, were not especially attached to a republican form of government. They were open-minded on things like that. He pointed out that during the last three years of the Revolutionary War "matters were so contrived between the General [Haldimand] and certain men of influence in Vermont" that it answered all the purposes of an alliance of neutrality.

He made it clear that Vermont would not be confederated with the United States. He did not believe, he said, that Vermont should accept a government under the British Crown, for that assuredly would bring on war. The status quo looked much better to him. Let Vermont and Canada continue their friendly trade and intercourse, as befitted two sovereign powers. If, in the future, it seemed best to either party to change its status, because of emergencies beyond their control, why, that could be taken up when occasion demanded.

It was the last of General Allen's state papers, rendered as unofficial minister-at-large for the Green Mountain Republic. It was forwarded by Dorchester to Lord Sydney. So far as Ethan was concerned, nothing came of it.

Ira and Levi sold a few rafts of lumber, and the three brothers returned to Onion River.

The year 1789 was a tough one in northern New England. There had been cold rains during the preceding growing season. There had been a partial and serious failure of crops, and the people of Vermont came to know something approaching real famine. Governor Chittenden was sufficiently alarmed to call a special meeting of the Council. He told of the distressed condition of the people. Many were in actual want, he said. He proposed and the Council voted an embargo on the exportation of wheat and corn.

Sheriffs and special agents were ordered to stop and inspect all wagons and sleds leaving the state. A vivid picture of Vermont that year was set down in the diary of a traveler through the region. "Visited 50 towns," he wrote, "was almost starved because I could not eat the coarse food provided for me—no candles—pine splinters used in lieu of them—bed poor and full of flees. No house for 4 miles—I was hungry, dry, night come on—I could travel no farther—I found a little log hut & put up there. Could get no supper—My horse no feed—Slept on a chaff-bed without Covering—a man, his wife & 3 children in the same nasty stinking room . . . People troubled with fever and ague. . . . The year 1789 will be remembered by Vermont as a day of Calamity and famine. . . . Several women I saw had lived four or five days without any food and had eight or ten children around them."

Things were not much better at the modest home of General Ethan Allen, first man of Vermont. His forty acres "under improvement" had yielded little hay. No one had any money, but the good-natured General acted as a sort of bank; neighbors passed drafts on him from hand to hand, like currency.

Over on South Hero Island in Lake Champlain the crops had been better. Hay had been heavy, and good, and Ebenezer Allen, a well-known cousin of Ethan, sent word to the General that he had hay to spare. Come on over and get a load, he said.

Taking one of his two Negro hired men—slaves were prohibited by Vermont's constitution—and an ox team, Ethan drove over to Ebenezer's across the thick ice of the lake. It was the 11th day of February, and was remarked a right coolish sort of day, even in that northern clime. Ethan, naturally enough, took a jug along. When he arrived late in the afternoon he was in fine condition, fit to wrestle with bears.

Ebenezer, who had been close at Ethan's side at Ticonderoga and was now called Colonel, had prepared for the coming of his distinguished relative; he invited all the old soldiers in the neighborhood to come and spend the evening at his place, with General Allen.

Milking was done early that night, and men on foot and in sleighs made their way to Ebenezer Allen's. There was a sizable crowd, for the backwoods. Many of the farmers and woodsmen had served in the original old Green Mountain Boys, against the Yorkers, while others had fought in the Revolution. A few had been with Ethan at Fort Ti. There was plenty to talk out. As the winds blustered across the icebound island, nearly a score of veterans bellied round the big fireplace in Ebenezer's and guzzled nobly of punch, of flip, and downed the inevitable stonewalls.

There was no fort to be taken this time, no riots to raise, no big wolf hunt afoot, but all these matters had to be discussed in detail; and, as is the manner of old soldiers of all time, the tales of alarums and excursions grew bigger, and more wondrous, with each round. It was good to have their old chief with them again, to hear his roar, his laughter, and to hear him tell, as none other could, of the wild doings that took place just as soon as the Boys had found the private rum cellar of Captain Delaplace at Ticonderoga, of the raids on the Yorker Scotch tenants at New Haven Falls, of the capture of Yorker Surveyor Cockburn, and of hanging Dr. Adams in a chair on the old Catamount Tavern's signpost.

Again, and for the last time, they asked for and heard General Allen repeat his "terrible proclamation," the one he delivered in the Tory-Yorker den of Guilford, with its resounding "Sodom and Gomorrah, by God!" And the older men tingled in every fiber as the Green Mountain Boy mounted the barrack stairs at Ti, a-swinging of his sword.

Along about midnight, several of the veterans who could still stagger returned to their homes, while others remained to drink the night through. Among them they put Ethan to bed. Put Ethan Allen to bed? Aye, and this in itself should have been fair warning that the ablest two-handed drinker in all Vermont was failing. Not a man present was able to recall the day, or night, when such had happened before. It was incredible.

But the sands were running out for General Allen.

The carouse was done before daylight. Bottlemen lay on the floor in front of the big fireplace. Others were draped on the table, on benches. Some actually found beds. And before daylight the house was aroused by a new roaring and thumping, loud enough to raise the deepest drinkers. It was old Ethan, calling for his Negro man, his coat, his oxen, and another snort. Cousin Ebenezer tried to restrain him, vainly. The team was made ready. The General's friends loaded him atop the hay, the Negro swished his goad stick, and off they started for Burlington and Onion River in the frosty quiet of a morning that was still night.

The oxbows creaked and wailed, and the sled runners crunched and sang clear and sharp over the white blanket that lay, unbroken by trees, to Burlington and beyond. A few late stars glittered faintly, and far to the north the sky glowed and faded. It was fitting enough that aurora borealis should see the Philosopher on his way.

At some point along the journey, the Negro thought to see how General Allen was doing. He found him in an alarming condition. He was "struggling violently," and his devoted man was obliged to use force to hold him in the hay and on top of the load. In half an hour or less, the General ceased his struggling, and lay back, exhausted and unconscious, but still breathing.

The poor Negro covered the dying man, and hurried the animals as fast as they would go, which was not very fast. It was afternoon before the oxen lurched into the Allen yard and the General, still unconscious, was carried into the house.

History is silent on what happened during the next twelve hours or so, and legend, as always it must, takes up the thread of events. One story has it that the General died in the afternoon of February 12, after a bloodletting, and without regaining consciousness. The other story, which is quite in keeping with the subject and thus gains strength year after year, is that Mrs. Allen, thinking there was no hope for her husband, called in a parson to comfort the dying man.

The parson, knowing something of the General's opinions on his ghostly office, approached the death bed with caution; but he was safe: the old warhorse was paralyzed almost from head to foot. But the eagle eye was open, sharp, clear, and terrible to look upon. "General Allen," said the parson soothingly, "General Allen, the angels are waiting for you."

The eyes in the great shaggy head seemed to shoot a beam of fire at the parson. The lined, wind-tanned face twitched, and General Allen spoke his last words. "Waiting, are they?" he rumbled like thunder on the other side of the mountain. "Waiting, are they? Well, God damn 'em, let 'em wait."

Then he turned his face to the unpapered wall and died very comfortably, at approximately a quarter to six o'clock in the evening.

Recorded history now picks up the thread again.

Mrs. Allen appears to have set the funeral for the next day, and a number of neighbors assembled at the General's home. But Ira Allen, who had just returned to Onion River from a trip, asked that the ceremonies be delayed. His brother, he said, had often expressed a hope that he would be "buried with arms," that is, a military funeral, and Ira needed a little time to make arrangements.

Accordingly, messengers were sent to notify all in the sparsely settled region around Burlington; and one seems to have got as far south as Vergennes, for Major Goodrich, an old soldier of that place, dropped everything and snowshoed to Burlington—the only way he could get there.

Ethan's body was taken to Ira's home, about a mile away, which was much larger than the General's. Here people came from every direction. Every old Green Mountain Boy, every old soldier, every hunter and trapper and farmer who got the word in time rallied to follow their chief to what he had often termed a sod jacket. Somebody turned up with a small cannon.

Major Goodrich marshaled the procession, which was surprisingly large and included at least sixteen squads of men in close order. Muffled drums beat the way, and crossed swords were laid on the coffin lid. Old Governor Chittenden was there and marched every step of the way, acting as one of the pallbearers.

In fresh snow the column moved across the ice above the mill dam at Onion River Falls. Every little way a halt was made and the cannon fired.

On the brow of a hill overlooking the river the procession came to its last halt. The grave had been dug through ground frozen hard as marble, in a small clearing in the forest. Stumps stood all about. The coffin was opened, and little Henry Collins, who had known the General at home, recalled years later that he looked "very natural" in the pine box.

The coffin was closed and lowered into the ground, while three volleys of musketry were fired. There were no religious exercises. Snow was still falling while Major Goodrich spoke briefly, referring to what General Allen had accomplished for his country and his state, and what he had suffered for them, too.

That was how they laid the old Green Mountain Boy away in the ground, and snow came down that night so thick it covered the grave a foot deep.

A few days later (February 23), or as soon as the news got

to Bennington, the editor of the *Vermont Gazette* prepared and published a brief notice:

It is with much regret we announce the death of General ETHAN ALLEN, who expired in an epileptic fit, on Tuefday laft; the patriotifm and ftrong attachment which ever appeared uniform in the breaft of this *Great Man,* was worthy of his exalted character; the public have to lament the lofs of a man who has rendered them great fervice, both in council and in arms; and his family an indulgent friend and tender parent; he has left a moft amiable young widow and three [*sic*] fmall children—and three amiable young daughters by his firft wife. While they are deluged in tears for the lofs of their beft friend, they have the confolation of being left wth a handfome fortune.

Almost a month later, the same paper printed what might be described as a delayed dispatch. It was dated at Burlington on February 18 and described the "order of the procession" to the grave, saying that

"the whole was attended with greateft decorum. And every one prefent manifeft a wifh to render his burial honourable as his character had ever been refpectable."

It was little enough for ye ed to say of the ring-tailed old peeler who had made Vermont a name and a fact.

And a few weeks later the Reverend Nathan Perkins, in Vermont on tour to note with horror "all ye men of learning deists in this state," went out of his way to gloat. "Arrived at Onion-river falls," he wrote with suppressed joy, "& passed by Ethan Allyn's grave. An awful Infidel, one of ye wickedest men y^t ever walked this guilty globe. I stopped & looked at his grave with a pious horror."

That would have pleased the late and profane General Allen a great deal.

> "... the said State, by the name and stile of 'the State of Vermont' shall be received and admitted into this Union."
> —Congress, Third Session.

CHAPTER XV

Footnotes for a Hero

The late General Allen did not enter the shades without a benediction. Down in New Haven, two hundred and ten miles as the gray goose flies, President Ezra Stiles of Yale presently learned of the Visitation in the green hills. Wrote he in his famous diary: "Died in Vermont the profane and impious Deist, Gen. Ethan Allen, Author of the Oracles of Reason, a Book replete with scurrilious Reflexions on Revelation. *'And in Hell he lift up his Eyes being in torment.'*"

A benediction of greater moment came a little later from the Congress of the United States, when on March 4, 1791, Vermont became the fourteenth state. The tormented General had done his work well.

A posthumous son, Ethan Alphonso, was born October 24, 1789. Both he and the other son, Hannibal, entered the United States Military Academy at West Point, from which Hannibal was graduated as a second lieutenant of artillery in 1804, and Ethan with the same rank in 1809. Both attained the rank of captain. Hannibal died in Norfolk, Virginia, in 1813. Ethan died at Lebanon, the family residence of his wife, near Norfolk, in 1855.

Ethan's children by Mary, his first wife—Lucy, Pamela, and Mary Ann—shared the General's estate with their stepmother and stepbrothers and sister. The estate, virtually all of it in lands, was not settled until December of 1802. It sugared off, as Vermonters say, at $69,823.36—which was pretty fair for a man whose last act was to borrow a load of hay.

The Widow Allen soon married Dr. Jabez Penniman of Westminster, and appears no more in history. It was Fanny, oldest child by the second Mrs. Allen, whose name is best remembered of all the Allen children. Aged five at the time of her father's death, Fanny was an odd child, much given to brooding. One day in her twelfth year she ran screaming into the house, calling for her mother. She had seen a monstrous serpent come writhing out of the water near which she was playing, she said. It had started after her when suddenly an old man appeared out of nowhere and stood by her side, a staff in his hand. "What are you doing here, little girl?" he asked, and commanded, "Run!" Then he pushed her toward the house and disappeared.

A bit later Fanny asked to go to Montreal to study French. In the convent an apparition of St. Joseph came to her, and she recognized it at once as the old man with the staff who had saved her from the big snake. She became a nun and was so noted for bringing heretics into the Catholic fold that the order of the Sisters of Hôtel-Dieu established a hospital in her name, the Fanny Allen Hospital at Winooski, Vermont.

Whether, as certain infidels have claimed, the apostasy of his daughter caused a great restlessness in the dead General's bones, or not, it is certain that patriotic Vermonters were soon to have bone trouble that grew into a local rumpus of note.

Some time after Ethan's burial the Allen family marked the grave with a plain marble slab that rested on a granite foundation. The slab was most appropriately inscribed, and said: "The Corporeal Part of General Ethan Allen Rests Beneath This Stone, the 12th day of Feb. 1789, Aged 50 Years, His spirit Tried the Mercies of His God, in Whom Alone He Believed and Strongly Trusted." This legend would doubtless have pleased the General, even if the age given was incorrect. He was fifty-two.

The marble slab was still in place and the inscription still legible at late as 1849, for in that year Benson Lossing visited the spot and made a sketch which appears in his *Pictorial Field-Book of the Revolution*. During the next decade, however, the marble slab all but disappeared. Rumor has it that Jehovah, not content with His destruction of most of the first printing of the Oracle of Reason, heaved a bolt of lightning at the slab, crumbling it into small pieces. And souvenir ghouls finished the job by carrying off the bits.

Then, in the 1850's, the Vermont Legislature appropriated $2000 to erect a monument, taller even than the General, on his grave. The resolution setting aside the money indicates that Vermonters of the time well knew the identity of the man chiefly responsible for their state.

The monument committee selected a handsome Tuscan column of native granite, forty-two feet high, with a capstone engraved, "Ticonderoga."

Vermonters are usually careful people, and the committee thought it best to do a bit of digging in order to find the exact spot for the monument. They turned up a good deal of earth in what had become Green Mountain Cemetery, but the remains of the restless General were not to be found. When this news got out, all the meddlers and homemade historians in the state put in a public appearance. They wrote to the *Burlington Free Press* and other papers to say many different things. One old codger said his father, who had been present, had told him that General Allen had been buried out behind Ira Allen's barn. Another letter gave "proof" that he had been laid away in Bennington, one hundred and twenty miles distant. Somebody said he was buried under the Ethan Allen house. Still another claimed Westminster, and bids were made from Windsor, Sunderland, Arlington.

Best of all the stories that came to light was the one that deserves, because of its incredible persistence, to be known as Ethan Allen's Bones and the Jolly Medical Students. It simply will not down, but turns up, stronger and better than ever, every few years.

The story ran that two or three medical students of Burlington dug up Ethan's body one dark night, while owls hooted protest from the firs, and used it for dissection. General Allen wouldn't have minded this in the least, for he always held that Science was to be Man's salvation; but the story couldn't be true. At the time of the General's death there was no medical college in Burlington, nor elsewhere in Vermont, and in Burlington only one doctor was in practice. This state of affairs continued until long after a corpse of 1789 would have had any value to medical students. But the story had that something about it that took the public's fancy. It also added to the uproar about a spot for the monument. The committee was bombarded from all sides with suggestions, even commands, to erect the shaft here, there, and the other place.

The dismayed but still determined committee finally discovered two old people, living in near-by Essex, who had been present at General Allen's funeral. They were Henry Collins, eighty-five, and Huldah Lawrence, seventy-seven, both in evident possession of their faculties. These two elderly folk did not pretend to know the exact spot of the grave, but they agreed it was in the general vicinity of the place selected for the monument.

So, the committee went ahead and had the handsome column placed in Green Mountain Cemetery, in 1858, with an inscription carefully calculated to preclude arguments as to the specific spot of burial. Says the legend across the west face of the monument's pedestal: "Vermont to ETHAN ALLEN, born in Litchfield Ct 10th Jan A D 1737 Died in Burlington Vt 12th Feb 1789 and buried near the site of this monument."

The inscription thus tended to foster speculation on exactly *where* the General might be buried and resulted in perpetuating Mystery Number One concerning him. In times when local news is scarce, Vermont editors often haul out the affair of Ethan Allen's Bones and the Jolly Medical Students.*

At the time the shaft was set in place the plan was to have a statue made to surmount it; but the Civil War intervened, and not until 1871 were sufficient funds raised by popular subscription. Two years later a heroic figure, representing the General with his left arm on high, was set in place, accompanied by proper oratory and exercises. The total effect is very simple and pleasing, and the spot could not be better, with many trees and a good view of what once was known as Onion River Falls.

Mystery Number Two surrounding the General really has something of mystery about it and concerns the portrait, or portraits, that are thought to have been painted of Ethan while he lived. A portrait of brother Ira, painted from the life, hangs in the Wilbur Room at the University of Vermont. The Museum at Bennington has a miniature of Ethan's daughter Lucy, and another of his grandson, General Ethan Allen Hitchcock, U.S.A. A portrait of Ethan's second wife, Fanny, is at Fort Ticonderoga. Ever since the middle of last century curious Vermonters have been trying vainly to find one of the two pictures that tradition says were painted of the General.

* The story was going strong as late as 1938, when both the *Banner* of Bennington and the *Free Press* of Burlington dusted it off and gave it light.

John Spargo, the writer, probably knows more than anyone else about the long search for an Ethan Allen portrait. Mr. Spargo's home is on the Bennington hillside, a few rods from the site of the old Catamount Tavern. He was president of the Vermont Historical Society for twelve years and is president of the Bennington Battle Monument and Historical Association, which he founded. For more than twenty years he has continued a personal search for an Ethan Allen portrait, which he has no doubt exists somewhere.

Mr. Spargo thinks that a true portrait of Ethan was in New York City as late as 1893. In that year a letter was received by the postmaster at Bennington, describing certain relics and a portrait. The relics consisted of a number of pieces of Lowestoft china, some of them bearing the General's initials. Both the portrait and the china had then lately been in possession of a grandnephew of Ethan, John Allen of New York, and the picture was said to be that of the General, painted from life. The person describing these items asked that his letter be turned over to the local Historical Society. This was done, and thirty years later the letter came into Mr. Spargo's hands. On it was a notation that it had not been answered.

Well, it proved a hopeless task to trace the writer of that letter. Spargo tried, and so did the late James B. Wilbur, biographer of Ira Allen, and John Pell, who would have liked to use a genuine likeness in his biography of the General. The American Antiquarian Society also took a hand in the search. All failed. This lost portrait, Mr. Spargo thinks, may have been done by Ralph Earle, who painted a number of Revolutionary worthies and spent some time in Bennington and other places in Vermont toward the end of Ethan's life. It is doubtless now in the hands of someone who has no idea of the identity of the subject—just a picture of an unknown man of the eighteenth century.

In 1935 Mr. Spargo's search was given new impetus by a

letter from a woman friend of sound and trained artistic knowledge and of unquestioned integrity. She wrote that in a prominent art gallery was an undoubted portrait of Ethan Allen, done in Philadelphia in 1783 by the French painter Du Simitière. With the painting was an engraving of the portrait, indubitably engraved from the painting and bearing the name of a master engraver of London of the period, as well as the name of Ethan Allen. Noted art dealers had pronounced both painting and engraving authentic.

Mr. Spargo was elated. He got into touch with the head of the art gallery, securing a ten-day option to buy the portrait and engraving for $1,800, should they prove genuine, for the Vermont Historical Society. Then he delegated his good neighbor, Hall Park McCullough, the artist, to examine the goods. In the course of his inquiries, Mr. McCullough got wind of a band of picture forgers who had victimized a number of museums and galleries. He did a little detective work and pronounced the engraving a fraud, and the portrait not of Ethan Allen.

The forgers figured they had a foolproof racket, and their method was simple. An old portrait of the period, showing a man of about the right age, its identity unknown, was the starting point. Such a picture can be picked up for a few dollars. Then, competent engravers were employed to make an engraving from the portrait, and to engrave on the plate the name of Ethan Allen and the name and address of a well known English engraver and print-seller. They used genuine old handmade paper, which can still be picked up, and made an engraving that would fool almost anybody and did fool a number of admitted experts. It did not fool Mr. McCullough. Through ways and means best known to himself, he proved beyond doubt that the engraving was a fraud, hence destroying the claims of the painting.

Another attempted fraud which Mr. Spargo tracked down

was that of a silhouette, purporting to be the work of "the distinguished French miniaturist, Millette." This picture bore on its back an inscription represented as in the handwriting of the artist, stating it was a profile of Ethan Allen done in Philadelphia in 1782. A long investigation proved it a forgery.

Attempts at forgery go back at least as far as 1873. In that year Lucius E. Chittenden, Vermont historian, found in the library of an exclusive club in New York a steel engraving, allegedly of Ethan Allen, "made from a portrait in the life by Trumbull." Chittenden was exultant, but not for long. Investigation proved the engraving a fake, and the original of it a sketch by Trumbull of General Henry Dearborn.

There is a tradition that Fanny Allen took with her to Montreal a miniature of her father. And there is that portrait, quite possibly of Ethan, which was in New York in 1893. Mr. Spargo is inclined to believe that both are genuine and doubtless in possession of persons who have no idea of the subject. He thinks that he might be able to identify them. Lucy Allen Hitchcock, Ethan's daughter, always said tha' her son, Ethan Allen Hitchcock, was "the living image" of her father. Several portraits of this man exist, one of the best being in the Museum at Bennington. Spargo believes that should a late eighteenth century portrait turn up, bearing an unmistakably close resemblance to those of General Hitchcock, his long search would be ended.

The face of Fort Ticonderoga, happily, has been preserved through the interest of the Pell family. Before and at the time of the Revolution the Pells owned much property at Pelham Manor, New York, where they made their home. The war split the family, and the Loyalists hit for Canada, not returning until many years later.

Following the Revolution, all Crown lands reverted, not to the Federal government, but to the states in which they were.

The government bought from the states such forts and sites as it considered useful. Ticonderoga no longer had any military significance. In 1796 the state of New York granted to Columbia and Union colleges, jointly, a parcel of the former Crown lands which included Ticonderoga.

The fort fell into decay, and was forgotten except for history books and as a spot of pilgrimage for a few hardy souls with an interest in American history. For many years its only resident was an ancient of the Revolution, Isaac Rice, who had been deprived of his pension rights, he said, because of missing documents, and made a precarious living by guiding visitors who came to see where the Great Jehovah and Colonel Allen had collaborated.*

Early in the nineteenth century William Ferris Pell, one of the Tory branch, returned to New York and entered business. He leased the land at Ticonderoga and in 1820 bought it. It has been in the Pell family ever since. Restoration was begun years ago and has continued down to the present day. It has been carefully and lovingly done, with strict attention paid to the original structures, even to their materials and measurements. Many of the cannon General Knox did not take to Boston are there, and a museum contains perhaps the finest collection of eighteenth century arms in this country. The Ethan Allen collection is large.

Bullets, balls, pieces of firearms, tools, money, and many other things are constantly being found in ground around the fort. This isn't strange, for the fort, known first as Carillon, dates from 1755 and saw much battle long before the Green Mountain Boys arrived.†

* For his *Pictorial Field-Book of the Revolution,* previously mentioned, Lossing did a sketch of old soldier Rice, sitting on the crumbling ruins. He presented a grim old face adorned with a sort of Horace Greeley whiskers.

† Milo King, superintendent of the Fort Ticonderoga Museum, reports in 1939 that most of the thousands who visit the place annually want to "see the place where Ethan Allen shouted about the Great Jehovah and the Continental Congress." It would please the General to know that.

Ethan Allen was a legendary character long before his death, and the legends about him multiplied for the next half-century or so; then production dropped. All the legends now current have probably seen service for more than a century, and many of them go back to the times of the man himself.

Some legends, unquestionably, are historically true, and many others are elaborations on historical fact. And a few no doubt are pure invention, concocted for sheer amusement or for some reason in the mind of the inventor. In the latter category doubtless belongs the hardy old story of Ethan at the bedside of his dying daughter, one of those by his first wife. It goes that the child *knew* that she was going to die, and further that she knew her profane father to be a gross Infidel. During her last gasps this precocious infant said to Ethan, "Father, now that I am going to leave you, in what should I put my faith—mamma's religion, or your Nature?" The Great Infidel is supposed to have cried gently a moment, then to have told daughter to die in the faith of her mother.

Better authenticated is another child story, told to Zadock Thompson, the Vermont historian, in 1841 by T. Bradley of Williston, Vermont, who had it direct from Dr. Baker, first president of the Vermont Medical Society. Dr. Baker had been called to a home where a child was suffering from worms. General Allen and two parsons were present. Ethan walked up and down the room. "I wish," he said, "all the worms which were ever permitted to torment an innocent being were in my body all at once."

"What would you do with so many?" inquired one of the parsons.

"Do?" cried Ethan. "Do? I'd take a dose of hellfire and destroy them."

Then, there is the famous white-horse story. In a discussion with St. John de Crèvecœur, Ethan once said that if the transmigration of souls were a fact, he hoped to return to his

Vermont hills in the form of a great white stallion, when he would snort, whinny, and range all over the claim. A Colonel Graham, who came to live in Rutland, Vermont, in 1785, has been quoted as saying, "I have often heard General Allen affirm that he should live again under the form of a large white horse." Just such an animal has been seen a number of times since 1789.

That Ethan could and did bite nails into bits and spit them out with the force of buckshot has never been doubted by any true Vermonter.

A signal used at night by the Green Mountain Boys was three mournful hoots of an owl. Ethan was so good at this call that on one or more occasions he was attacked by large male owls, jealous of some lady owl in the neighborhood. Another time when Ethan was hurrying through the woods a huge catamount leaped onto his back. It was the last time that catamount leaped anywhere. Reaching up and behind his head, Ethan grabbed the big animal around the neck, heaved it forward and to the ground, then strangled it where it lay, without once removing his hands. When he arrived at Cephas Kent's tavern in Dorset that night, he excused his delay. "The goddam Yorkers," he said, "have trained and set varmints against me, God damn their miserable Tory souls."

Not a legend but simply a favorite Big Story often told of Ethan Allen and Seth Warner, to illustrate their differences in character, is revealing. The two were fishing from a boat on Lake Champlain, when Seth's powderhorn fell into the water.

"What'll I do?" complained Seth.

Ethan didn't reply but dived overboard at once. The cautious Warner waited some minutes, then he too dived in. Down deep on the bottom he found Ethan. He was trying to pour Seth's powder into his own horn.

The straight hunting stories told on the man would make a

sizable monograph. A favorite has him shooting the horns off a buck deer at one hundred yards, with a smoothbore. Another has him killing a mean and wounded bear by ramming his powderhorn down the animal's throat.

The best of the real estate stories brings in Ira. The property at Charlotte, Vermont, of an exiled Yorker was to be sold for Vermont by the sheriff to the highest bidder. The speculating Allens had tried to keep the coming sale secret, but news leaked out and a number of speculators showed up. The Allen boys didn't like the look of so much potential competition, and the sheriff, at Ethan's order, and on some pretext, announced that the sale would be put off "until one o'clock tomorrow." The crowd went away, planning to return at one the next afternoon. But promptly at one o'clock next morning the sheriff and the two Allens were back on the ground. The sheriff asked for bids. Out of the dark came Ethan's bid—one dollar for house, barn, and a hundred acres. Ira bid two dollars. "Sold," said the sheriff, "to the short man in the coonskin cap."

It seems strange, or possibly it is significant, that no legendary tales concerning extramarital adventures have been told of Ethan Allen. Certainly it was not respect for the Seventh Commandment that kept him "moral" in the generally accepted sense; nor was it a case of inability, as witness eight children, the last of them posthumous. His contemporary enemies called him almost every name conceivable except that fine old English compound word used to describe a man of vast adulteries. He must have been essentially a monogamist.

But the stories of his drinking prowess are without end and, except for the rattlesnake incident, will not be repeated here. Ethan did not like rattlers, which in old times were found in certain regions of southern Vermont. On a hot day in August he was making a long trip afoot with Remember

Baker. Up late the night before, the men became sleepy and lay down for a nap in a rocky glen. Sometime later Baker was roused by a noise and woke to gaze horrified at the spectacle of Colonel Allen asleep, while on his broad chest was coiled a huge rattler, all of five feet long. It struck Ethan again and again, on the neck, the arm, the hand, but did not rouse him. Baker jumped up, grabbed his gun and advanced to poke the snake away.

At his approach Baker was startled to see the snake glide off the man and onto the ground, its head weaving from side to side and its body making contortions strange even in a reptile. Baker held his blow, watching fascinated, while the snake stopped and turned to gaze at him, cross-eyed. The snake then gave forth a mighty "Burrp!" and collapsed into sound sleep. "Drunk, by Jesus!" exclaimed Remember Baker, who was an acute if not a pious man.

When Colonel Allen awoke he complained bitterly to Baker about "these eternal, damnable, bloodsucking mosquitoes" which had bitten him while he slept.

Long a favorite story, and dignified in print for more than a century, is the one about Ethan and the dentist of Sunderland. A woman, suffering terribly from toothache, had approached the dentist, then became frightened at his devilish gear used for extraction. Colonel Allen urged her to submit to the grim business. "I'll show you, madam," he said, "that losing a tooth is nothing." Thereupon he sat in a chair and had the dentist extract a perfectly sound tooth, by way of demonstration. "I didn't feel it," he lied gallantly, and the lady took courage.

Rough and tough, Ethan Allen most certainly was. In a rough and tough region during a rough and tough period, he could hold his own, and more, in any feat that required quick strength, lasting endurance, or simply courage. He was a product of the backwoods, wild and never once tamed, for not even the chains, the dungeons and the abuse he had suffered were enough to break one of the staunchest spirits this or any other country has produced. Even his worst enemies granted his courage. And his courage, even when it approached rashness, as it often did, was calm and deliberate —which is the finest kind of courage.

It has been the fashion these later years to sneer ever so slightly at his military ability. Writers have pointed out that Fort Ticonderoga was in decay, was improperly manned, and that taking it, while bold enough, required little ability. Those writers have overlooked a number of things. Colonel Allen had little time to plan a campaign, but he planned most ably. He had a spy inside the fort the day before he attacked. He knew the number of its garrison, and he also knew of the break in the outer wall. He sent two parties to secure boats for transportation.

In 1775 there was probably not another man in America who could have led eighty hunters, trappers, and farmers across a lake at night, kept them in some form of military order, and successfully attacked a fort that was Crown property. Many of those men must have trembled inwardly at the thought of assaulting the King's own bastion, and it must be remembered that this was the first attack made by Colonists on the Crown. Both Lexington and Concord were defensive measures, and both failed to defend. Those eighty men with Ethan knew they would face a firing squad or a gallows, if they failed. It took something of a military genius to make them do what they did.

Writers have pointed to the election of Seth Warner to lead the Green Mountain Regiment as an indication that Colonel Allen was thought lacking as a leader. They do not consider that the brave, though safe, pious, and uninspired Warner was elected not by the men whom he was to lead, but by the safe, pious, and uninspired older men, the so-called solid citizens of the Grants.

Yet, Colonel Allen took his licking like a gentleman. He did all he could to aid recruiting for Warner's regiment. Then came Ethan's disastrous attack on Montreal. This affair was cooked up by Major Brown and Colonel Warner, both of whom had commissions, while Ethan was nothing but a scout. And Brown and Warner, or at least Brown, failed him most miserably. The failure to capture Montreal is not to be laid to Ethan Allen.

In his war with the Yorkers General Allen conducted a long and dangerous guerrilla campaign and won every move. The odds against him were tremendous, but he never once failed to outsmart the city slickers from the other side of the lake. In the war of words he outgeneraled the various governors of New York and their henchmen. And it must be granted that his entire conduct in forming the New Hampshire Grants into a republic and holding it against Congress, against adjacent states, as well as against the British, was nothing short of brilliant. I think it was magnificent.

In making Vermont, Ethan Allen was of course counseled and aided by Ira Allen, by Chittenden, by the Fays and a number of others, all more or less able men; but it is historically of record that whenever dash or courage or propaganda was required, or all three together, it was Ethan who did the job.

In spite of his noise, his quick temper, and his violent talk, Ethan Allen was a kindly man. Driving out the Yorkers was his business and pleasure, and many good men and families had to suffer, as they always do, in civil or foreign wars; but the fact remains that not one Yorker was killed in action, and only one hanged. General Allen threatened them all with their lives, which was a part of his policy to keep them out of his domain.

Ethan's lack of piety has been held against him, held terribly hard in some quarters; and I am told by other Vermonters who ought to know, that that is the reason why no highway, no mountain, no lake, no river, no town has been named for the man most responsible for the state itself. But I doubt that the General would care. He was fond of good horses, and right near his last home just outside Burlington is an army post, Fort Ethan Allen, which serves the United States Cavalry. It is enough.

No one, I think, in the past hundred years has taken seriously the old charge of "traitor" hurled at the General and other leaders in Vermont by small-minded politicians who for various reasons wished to impeach him and thus trim his wings. His horse-trading with the British during the Revolution and afterward was exactly the tack, it seems to me, that any really bright leader would have taken, given the same complicated conditions. And I have no doubt, had Congress attempted to dissect Vermont, General Allen would promptly have made it into a British province, and it would now be a part of Canada. He might well have been able to do it, too. What he and his men wanted was a separate state, and they got it.

Lastly, there's the old sneer about real estate: that Ethan and his Boys were fighting to make their doubtful land titles stick, and not wholly because of "patriotism." I have no doubt that this charge is true. If it is, then what of it? At the time of the Revolution General George Washington was one of the largest owners of land in the country. Mr. Jefferson was another. Nor were the Hancocks, the Adamses, and scores more of hot patriots without possessions. None of them, so far as I am aware, were forced to borrow a load of hay. If a man must own nothing, if he can have no personal stake in his country to be a patriot, then we need a new definition of the word.

As to Vermont, one is forced, against all inclination to the contrary, to agree with Mr. Matt B. Jones, one of New England's outstanding legal minds, and a Vermonter to boot, that the New York title to the New Hampshire Grants was doubtless the legal title; that the grants of land made west of the Connecticut River by Governor Benning Wentworth of New Hampshire were worthless—until Ethan Allen read *his* chapter in backwoods law—and that Vermont of the time legally belonged to the Province of New York.

Yet, Yorkers today should be chary of tossing charges about "squatters." Their right to much of New York was nothing to be bragging about. A considerable portion of that province was taken from the red men by force and skullduggery beside which the measures of the Vermonters appear mild and honest. It is best, perhaps, not to go into either matter very deeply at this late date.

The statute of limitations voided New York's claims to Vermont many years ago, and I, for one, am happy that it did. A Union without Vermont in it would lack something, something both rugged and fiercely independent, which Green Mountain men and women have contributed to the Republic these past one hundred and fifty years. Nor does the native independence of Vermonters yet show serious signs of petering out, even in these latter days when it is so much the fashion to lean on government and to run with the herd in all things. The United States can well stand this hardy Green Mountain seasoning.

And I like to think that the staunch spirit of the original old Green Mountain Boy has had something to do with it.

Acknowledgments and Bibliography

Up to some twenty years ago, all the many books and pamphlets and essays about Ethan Allen were pretty much confined to the same few high lights of his career and a number of generalities, things that had been more or less of public knowledge. Then, and all within a decade or so, a considerable amount of new material came to light. The important Canadian Archives were made available, and American historians mined them to good effect; the British account of the capture of Ticonderoga was found; Vermonters and others like Henry Steele Wardner, Allen French, J. B. Wilbur, John Clement, John Spargo, and Hall Park McCullough delved into long dusty letters and documents and made known their contents; Matt B. Jones spent years in gathering the material for his book on Vermont; and John Pell, with a staff of able researchers, combed collections of materials in many states and found doubtless about all that ever will be known of Ethan Allen's early and obscure years, which appeared in Mr. Pell's exhaustive biography.

To all of these the present author is indebted, just as both they and he are indebted to earlier writers—Zadock Thompson, Benjamin Hall, Hiland Hall, Jared Sparks, and Benson Lossing among many others.

In addition to those named, I have to thank others for aiding and abetting me: the men and women of the Boston Public Library, Harvard College Library, Massachusetts Historical Society, Connecticut Historical Society, Vermont State Library, Vermont Historical Society, Bennington Historical Museum, the libraries of the University of Vermont, and S. H. P. Pell and the Fort Ticonderoga Museum.

275

Books

Adams, James Truslow, *Revolutionary New England*. Boston, 1923.

Aldrich, Lewis Cass, and Holmes, Frank R., *History of Windsor, Vermont*. Syracuse, N.Y., 1891.

Allen, Ethan, *A Brief Narrative of the Proceedings of the Government of New-York*. Hartford, 1774.

——*An Animadversory Address to the Inhabitants of the State of Vermont*. Hartford, 1778.

——*A Narrative of Colonel Ethan Allen's Captivity*. Boston, 1779.

——*A Concise Refutation of the Claims of New-Hampshire and Massachusetts Bay*. Bennington, 1780.

——*Reason the Only Oracle of Man*. Bennington, 1784.

Allen, Ira, *The Natural and Political History of the State of Vermont*. London, 1798. (Reprinted by Vermont Historical Society.)

Allen, O. P., *The Allen Memorial*. Palmer, Mass., 1907.

Arnold, Benedict, *Regimental Memorandum Book*. Reprinted by the *Pennsylvania Magazine of History and Biography*, 1884.

Beckley, Hosea, *The History of Vermont*. Brattleboro, 1846.

Brown, Charles Walter, *Ethan Allen*. Chicago, 1902.

Chittenden, L. E., *The Capture of Ticonderoga*. Rutland, 1872.

Cothren, William, *History of Ancient Woodbury*. Waterbury, 1854.

De Crèvecœur, Robert, *Saint Jean de Crèvecœur, Sa Vie et Ses Ouvrages*. Paris, 1883.

French, Allen, *The Taking of Ticonderoga in 1775: The British Story*. Cambridge, Mass., 1928.

Goodhue, Josiah F., *History of the Town of Shoreham, Vermont*. Middlebury, 1861.

Hall, Benjamin H., *History of Eastern Vermont*. New York, 1858.

Hall, Henry, *Ethan Allen*. New York, 1892.

Hall, Hiland, *A History of Vermont*. Albany, 1868.

Henry, J. E., *Account of Arnold's Campaign Against Quebec.* 1877.

Hemmenway, Abbie Maria, *Vermont Historical Gazetteer*, 1867–1891.

Jones, Matt Bushnell, *Vermont in the Making.* Cambridge, 1939.

Lossing, Benson J., *Pictorial Field-Book of the Revolution.* New York, 1860.

Macdonald, George E. H., *Fifty Years of Freethought.* New York, 1929.

Moore, Hugh, *Memoir of Ethan Allen.* Plattsburgh, 1834.

O'Callaghan, E. B., ed., *Documentary History of New York.* Albany, 1850–51.

Pell, John, *Ethan Allen.* Boston, 1929.

Perkins, Nathan, *A Narrative of a Tour Through the State of Vermont in 1789.* Woodstock, Vt., 1920.

Riley, Isaac Woodbridge, *American Philosophy.* New York, 1907.

Robinson, Rowland E., *Vermont: A Study in Independence.* Boston, 1892.

Smith, J. E. A., *History of Pittsfield* (Mass.). Boston, 1869.

Smith, Justin H., *Our Struggle for the Fourteenth Colony.* New York, 1907.

Sparks, Jared, *Life of Ethan Allen.* Boston, 1839.
——*Memoir of Colonel Ethan Allen.* Middlebury, 1848.

Thompson, Zadock, *History of Vermont.* Burlington, 1842.

Van Doren, Carl, *Benjamin Franklin.* New York, 1938.

Wardner, Henry Steele, *The Birthplace of Vermont.* New York, 1927.

Wilbur, J. B., *Ira Allen.* Boston, 1928.

Williams, Samuel, *The Natural and Civil History of Vermont.* Burlington, 1809.

NEWSPAPERS, MANUSCRIPTS, DOCUMENTS, MONOGRAPHS, AND PAMPHLETS

Baker, C. Alice, "Ethan Allen and His Daughter," in *Pocumtuck Valley Memorial Assoc. Proceedings*, Deerfield, Mass., 1905.

Bascom, Robert O., "The Ticonderoga Expedition of 1775" (pamphlet of New York State Historical Society).

Benedict (George W.) Collection of MSS. and depositions relating to Ethan Allen, University of Vermont.

Coates, Walter J., "Ethan Allen's Religion," in *Driftwind* (magazine), North Montpelier, Vt.

Connecticut Courant, files in the Connecticut Historical Society.

Doten, Dana, "Ethan Allen's Philosophy," *New England Quarterly*.

Kent, Dorman B. E., unpublished MSS., Vermont Historical Society.

Rife, Clarence W., "Ethan Allen: An Interpretation," *New England Quarterly*.

Spargo, John, *Address to Bennington Battle Memorial and Historical Association*, Bennington, 1937.

Trumbull Papers, in the Connecticut State Library.

Vermont Historical Society, collection of MSS. relating to Ethan Allen.

Vermont, *State Papers*, Middlebury, 1823.

Vermont, *Records of the Council of Safety and Governor and Council*, Montpelier, 1873.

Vermont Gazette, files in Vermont Historical Society.

University of Vermont, collection of documents relating to Ethan Allen.

Wing, Colonel Leonard F., "Ethan Allen, the Soldier," in *Vermont Historical Society Proceedings*, 1937.

Index

Adams, Dr. Sam, 48
Albany, N.Y., 43, 53, 79, 216
Allen, Ebenezer, 46, 248 ff.
Allen, Ethan, plans and heads Fort
Ticonderoga expedition, 3 ff.; birth,
23; brothers and sisters, 24; father's
death, 26; with Col. Marsh's regiment, 26; iron furnace, 26; first
marriage, 27; learns about Philosophy, 28 ff.; inoculation experiment, 30; hauled into court, 30;
charged with fighting, 31-32; mining venture, 31 ff.; ordered to leave
Northampton, 32; cruises the
Grants, 33; buys land, 42; at Albany hearing, 43; makes famous reply, 44; forms Green Mountain
Boys, 45; catches Yorker surveyor,
48; chastises Dr. Adams, 48; beats
sheriff, 49; damns governor, 50;
burns squatters' cabins, 50; is out-
lawed, 50; makes awful pun, 51;
writes atrocity stories, 51-52; in
Onion River Co., 64 ff.; destroys
Yorker settlement, 68 ff.; builds
forts, 69; threatens Durham settlers,
70; acts as judge, 71; reward for, is
increased, 72; defies Governor
Tryon, 73 ff.; has Hough whipped,
80; discusses coming war, 82; at
St. Johns, 90; urges Congress to action, 92; interrupts sermon, 98; ad-
dresses Congress, 98; fails to head
regiment, 100; becomes scout, 101;
is captured, 106; his captivity,
113 ff.; visits General Washington,
132; returns home, 133; celebration
for, 137; prevents lynching, 138;

confiscates Tory estates, 140 ff.;
writes *Animadversory Address*,
141; lobbies in Congress, 149; refuses to take test creed, 150; row
with Levi Allen, 153; writes his
best seller, 157; marches on Putney,
160; disturbs trial, 163; writes the
Vindication, 172; writes the *Concise Refutation*, 174; buys powder
and lead, 175; intrigues with British,
177 ff.; resigns commission, 180;
warns Congress of action, 180;
raises riots in York State, 182;
writes the *Oracle of Reason*, 194;
marches on Guilford, 196 ff.; his
"terrible proclamation," 199; first
wife dies, 203; meets Fanny
Buchanan, 209; his second marriage,
212; plans to retire, 213; meets St.
Jean de Crèvecœur, 216; goes to
Wyoming Valley, 217 ff.; the
Oracle appears, 225; refuses to aid
Daniel Shays, 243; trades land with
Ira, 244; has home built at Burlington, 245; goes to Quebec, 246; at-
tends party at Cousin Ebenezer's,
248 ff.; his death, 251; funeral, 252;
his children, 257-258
Allen, Ethan, Jr., 257
Allen, Fanny, wife, 209 ff., 258
Allen, Fanny, daughter, 213, 258
Allen, Hannibal, 245, 258
Allen, Heber, 24
Allen, Heman, 5, 24, 27, 46, 64, 100,
133
Allen, Ira, 24, 46, 54, 62 ff., 100, 135,
169, 183, 197, 202-203, 214, 246, 251
Allen, Joseph, 23 ff.